THE

MAN

WHO

COULDN'T

EAT

THE MAN WHO COULDN'T EAT

A MEMOIR

JON REINER

GALLERY BOOKS

New York   London   Toronto   Sydney   New Delhi

Gallery Books
A Division of Simon & Schuster, Inc.
1230 Avenue of the Americas
New York, NY 10020

Certain names and identifying characteristics have been changed and certain events have been compressed, consolidated, or reordered.

First Gallery Books hardcover edition September 2011

GALLERY BOOKS and colophon are registered trademarks of Simon & Schuster, Inc.

For information about special discounts for bulk purchases, please contact Simon & Schuster Special Sales at 1-866-506-1949 or business@simonandschuster.com.

The Simon & Schuster Speakers Bureau can bring authors to your live event. For more information or to book an event contact the Simon & Schuster Speakers Bureau at 1-866-248-3049 or visit our website at www.simonspeakers.com.

Designed by Jaime Putorti

Manufactured in the United States of America

10   9   8   7   6   5   4   3   2   1

Library of Congress Cataloging-in-Publication Data
Reiner, Jon.
   The man who couldn't eat : a memoir / by Jon Reiner.—1st Gallery books hardcover ed.
      p. cm.
   Summary: "Based on his Esquire magazine article, The Man Who Couldn't Eat is the very personal journey of Jon Reiner's struggle with chronic illness"—Provided by publisher.
   1. Reiner, Jon—Health.   2. Crohn's disease—Patients—New York (State)—New York—Biography.   3. Crohn's disease—Surgery.   I. Title.
   RC862.E52R45 2011
   616.3'440092—dc22
   [B]   2011005441

ISBN 978-1-4391-9246-7
ISBN 978-1-4391-9254-2 (ebook)

For Susan,
in sickness and in health.

PART
ONE

the mess I'm in. But they're not talking. They're silent in the bag
I left in the kitchen after dinner last night.

I did not give in to temptation; I didn't even eat one, yet
I'm in bad shape, with my body in full storm, so I've got my
eyes on them. Yes, I did *breathe* the apricots, hiding from Susan,
Teddy, and Finn behind a swung-open cabinet door. I did inhale,
fighter pilot–style, pressing the bag's hole over my nose, sucking up the deliciously trapped fragrance. However, that was all.
No wrinkly apricot chew passed my lips. It can't have been the
apricots' aroma, can it? Unless the air is dusted with poison,
breathing is not supposed to kill you; only giving in to cravings can do that, and I deny the most dangerous of them like
a recovering junkie, supposedly, for my own good. *Just a taste,
man, that's all I need. Just a little taste.* My diet demands self-
imposed exile, and I complied: I didn't eat a single apricot. At
dinner, I dutifully weeded the chopped orange cubes from their
couscous bed and pushed them to the rim of my plate, banished
like the broccoli our boys won't eat, doing my best to kill the
thing I love. What else could it be that's hammered me to the
floor? Answer me! Christ, I'm talking to apricots.

This food fight between desire and regulation is a strange
condition. In my case, the fruit is forbidden. That's where the
walking contradiction begins.

I once worked for a notorious ex-drunk, a famous film director, who said the only thing he missed about drinking was the
alcohol. I used to think I knew how he felt—my history with
food is complicated—but whatever has got me now feels more
perilous than falling off the wagon. This depth of torture can't
be the penalty for sniffing the apricot cork. And even if I did

CHAPTER 1

I'm a glutton in a greyhound's body. To look at me, you wouldn't know I have the appetite of a gastric bypass candidate. I'm a walking contradiction, not what I appear to be, in the grip of the thing I want most and can't have—food.

Some time ago, I'm not sure how long it's been, my guts exploded. It was that long hour before the clock sanctions lunch, when the hunger is so deep you could eat paper. I was planning to make tuna fish—my grandmother's recipe of tuna, chopped celery, onions, olives, ground pepper, and a lemon—and, in a moment, became surprised to find myself here suddenly dying. "Here" is my living room floor, where I'm alone at the dusty feet of our cracked leather love seat. My wife is at work, my two sons are at school, and I spent my last cogent minutes figuring out who could pick them up. Since then (whenever "then" was), the explosion has shot me to delirium, and I'm seeing visions through lenses of pain and panic.

I want an answer from the apricots. The dried ones in the paper bag on the counter. I need to know if they're to blame for down a bite or two of mouthwatering, heavenly flesh, is that really all it would take to finish me off? Death by dried fruit.

The pain is killing me.

I don't know how long I've been down. What time is it? One o'clock? Three? Saturday? Real time is shattered into a fever dream. My flashing thoughts run on and lose their train like baggage pushed from passenger windows. They tumble end over end down a slope off the track, and nothing makes sense. I am at their mercy, searching for meaning in a story I don't understand, to explain why I am here and figure out how to survive. The apricot images spring from the part of my brain that has yet to bury the dead.

Collapsed on the busy Persian rug, I wait for the ambulance, trailed by the chaos of a surprise attack. The apartment's rooms are ransacked: vomit sprays in the bathroom, hand towels pulled to the floor, pills spilled in the sink, three layers of blankets strangled on our bed, tea bags bleeding their last into water gone cold on the stove. It's a brilliant February day— absurdly, Friday the thirteenth—a reprieve of midwinter sparkle that motivated me out of the house, until this spear started goring my insides. Bright sun is smoking overhead through the living room's two dirty windows. The steam radiator behind the love seat hisses and heats like a sauna, but I'm freezing beyond reason. A fever spike soaked my fleece-lined jeans and wool turtleneck, they're swamping me and stink like a shipwreck, and I let go of the digital thermometer when it hit 106°F. It lies near the cordless phone I used for three 911 calls and to wail to my gastroenterologist, Dr. Abrams, "It feels like a blockage but worse! Like something has ruptured!" I know this because I've been sick with Crohn's disease for more than half of my forty-six years.

Crohn's is a gastrointestinal condition that exacts a nasty kind of food revenge and currently has me hemorrhaging on my living room floor. It's the Bernie Madoff of medical conditions: outsider, unglamorous, crooked, devious, hounding, determined, destructive, unaccountable, its motives hidden, stealing from the body with the larceny of a petty thief. It eats its own, the way Madoff swallowed other rich Jews. The disease causes essential good bacteria to be mistakenly attacked by the body along with the bad, a blunder that destroys the gut's ability to properly absorb vitamins, minerals, and fat. Without those basics, good health is impossible. Diet may help, hurt, or even trigger the disease in people, but it's an inexact food science. The contradicting scientific views aren't limited to what I can't eat—they include what I can. Food, too, is not what it appears to be.

Crohn's is a relatively new disease, first described in 1932 by the eponymous Dr. Burrill Crohn. Anyone can be afflicted, but there's a higher rate of disease among people of Ashkenazi Jewish ancestry, like me. This misfortune is also evidence of a larger cosmic joke—leave it to the Jews to make pot roast lethal. *Eat! Don't eat!* Life and death in a single bite. It's a bizarre strain of steerage-class masochism that couldn't have been concocted by anyone with a flair for the exotic. Crohn's doesn't have the status or glamour of other serious diseases, like certain cancers, whose survivors inspire glossy magazine covers, celebrity appeals, and public rallies, or even Lyme disease, with its evocation of country houses and weekend retreats. At the core,

Crohn's disease is a failure of bowel function, hardly the stuff of which Julia Roberts movies are made.

This disease and all autoimmune diseases are treaty-breakers. You hold up your end of the agreement—eat right, swallow a fishbowl of pills and potions, shun what you crave, adhere to the regimen, change your life—and they attack you anyway. Or, in language my grandma Jennie knew, *"Mentsch tracht, Gott lacht."* Man plans, God laughs. Resolving the opposing forces of eating and illness is my chronic burden. Uncertainty is my state.

Generally, the condition is merely debilitating, but today it's trying to murder me. Ten years ago, devouring half a bag of green pistachios sent me to the hospital with a blockage at three A.M. This is different.

Rotten timing for an emergency, too. I tried calling Susan, but she's in her windowless bunker teaching reading to immigrant high schoolers, supporting the four of us by herself while I'm out of work. Finn and Teddy, ages six and nine, are closing out a normal day in their public school, not knowing. Mercifully, I reached my friend Jodi. She'll pick up the boys when she gets her own kids.

"Whatever I have, I'm sure it will pass," I reassured her, clenching my teeth to bite through the shakes. "But if, for some reason, I can't make it to school, I'd really appreciate you getting the boys. Thanks, Jodi. I owe you." *If, for some reason,* like the fact that I'm coming apart. I'm relieved that pickup is settled. Even if I spontaneously combust and they find pieces of me on the ceiling, the kids have to get picked up at 2:40 P.M. Two-forty—when is that? How much longer? This, whatever it is, *must* pass; like all stay-at-home parents, I don't have the luxury of getting sick. Susan and I don't live in a sitcom where the kids disappear quietly for the season like tulips. And we can't pay the going rate for child care. Hoping that time would heal me, I waited before calling the doctor.

Everything changed in an instant. It wasn't supposed to happen this way—without warning, without a chance—and I've got to slow things down, or I won't last until the ambulance gets here. Fortunately, I have just the salve: Denial is the strongest medicine, a tonic I've drunk over two decades of episodes. A shot of coping juice should see me through.

Here we go, a diversion. I see that Finn left his map project on the coffee table. I've got to get it to school before Ms. Jordan goes home. Today is the last day of class before winter break, and she's leaving at the bell for the Caribbean with her husband. They're so young, free to escape. I wonder if people still eat *callaloo* where they're going. Finny did a nice job on the project. From here, it actually looks like a map.

This has to pass. Our ski trip is planned; the car is rented. I confirmed this morning with Ellen and Matt that we'll get to their house for lunch tomorrow. I can buy the wine on the way home from school. I'm thinking about Shiraz and Riesling. Gotham Wines still has the sale going on, so it should be under twenty dollars for both.

This will pass. The boys will bitch about detouring to Gotham, but I don't want to leave it for the morning. I should wash their long johns tonight; the house in Millbrook is cold. The weather forecast is good, sunny and in the high thirties. We'll have fun and it's free. Aspen on the cheap. The boys will fly over the hills, racing like they're Bode Miller. Howling. Susan and I will watch them from the plate glass of the lodge and drink hot chocolate. We're flatlanders in the rich man's sport. They'll knock on the window at the bottom of their runs. It will be a great time.

The pain is excruciating.

I scream louder than the boys on the slopes, but no one hears me. The plaster walls of our prewar Manhattan building are three feet thick, so not even the nanny in the apartment next door can hear. In more than ten years of living here, this is the first downside there's been to residing in a fortress of silence. My cries expire inside this sealed room, and I flood the rank air with aching moans. In my state of isolation, it makes no difference that I'm in New York City. What I would give to have gotten sick in a cab.

I look to the front door, hoping for EMS to surprise me. Nothing but white door. I crane my neck to see through the window overhead. The passing slant of sunlight has cleared the water tower on the neighboring roof and freckles the walls of our combination living-dining space. It's after two o'clock. I hope the boys won't be scared when I don't show. In three years, I've never missed a pickup. The oblique light yellows the jag of plaster cracks above the couch and the food stains next to the table. A mosaic of a thousand meals. Peanut butter, plum jelly, red pasta sauce, chocolate ice cream, orange juice, milk, olive oil, Thanksgiving sweet potatoes, apricots flung from the couscous last night. Food as art. Crusted smears of candle wax and silver model-airplane paint. What a shit hole we're living in. The walls are vividly decrepit in this light. Highway rest stops look cleaner. Is that what everyone sees? All this time I've been focused on nutrition and portions and the rituals of eating together; I wasn't aware what a mess we'd made. I'll have to paint one day next week when we get back from the trip. There's still a half-gallon can behind the ice skates on the floor of the coat closet. Apple Crunch.

Where's the damn ambulance?

My neck is wrenched from the shaking, and I can't move out of this fetal position. The pain seized me right before noon. I'd finished unpacking the groceries, eight bags to last us the week. Damn, I forgot to buy eggs. I was going to hard-boil them for the drive to the country tomorrow. I can get eggs when I'm out. Overall, it was a productive morning. While I unpack the food, I have a phone interview with an employment recruiter, vaguely about a job:

"I'm a senior-level blah, blah, blah really interested in blah, blah, blah. That's so interesting. I'll look forward to blah, blah, blah. Yes, I was laid off in 2007. Yes, and in 2004. And yes, in 2001. No, I don't have a drinking problem. Perhaps I should. The serial jobbing? I needed to eat, I have four mouths to feed, and I served the wrong master."

Every time I'd begun to put away a few bones in savings and imagine the prospect of stability, the bottom dropped out, and I had to start over. Now I have the liability of too much experience, or too much time unemployed, or I'm too tall, or the jobs just don't exist. All the regulars I know at the school playground are out of work, and the same goes for my friends in other places. And if I *have* hit the trifecta of unemployment, bankruptcy, and debilitating illness, there may be a limit to my bounce this time. Losing my purpose and income was one set of troubles, my confidence ground to dust; losing my ability to function and provide would be quite another. I better send the recruiter a follow-up. A cut-and-paste should do it.

After the phantom job call, I go to the toilet. Ordinary start to business, but then it feels like a mass gets stuck in my plumbing. Shitus interruptus. A kind of alien stomach cramp squeezes my lower right gut, weird but nothing alarming. That feels odd. Maybe I'm forcing things too hard, trying to get unstuck, or maybe it's something else. This is strange.

In a matter of seconds, the cramp clenches and punches inside at my beltline. Right away it feels severe, and I try lying my way to recovery. *Whatever it is, it will pass. Nothing to worry about. I'll make tuna for lunch. The celery's still okay, and I'll make enough to pack for the trip. Teddy won't eat it.* If I ran to the hospital every time some pain, or nausea, or fever, or the shakes hit, I'd have an emergency room named after me by now.

I burrow under the bedcovers for refuge to pass the misery, rubbing my limbs like a mad cricket, trying to generate heat. Already, I'm freezing. Thirty minutes in, vomit wrenches out of me in the bathroom with the other eruptions. I keep waiting to feel better. I know that when these attacks pass, they're soon forgotten, the way the clearing sky makes you forget the rainstorm. This pain is like nothing I've ever experienced. More intense than obstructions, kidney stones, and blood clots combined.

When will it end?

Thank God I finished the food shopping this morning. I'm living the old joke about the babysitting Jewish grandmother: The parents return to their home and discover in its place a pile of charred rubble. The grandmother tells them, "There was a little fire, and the house burned down. But the children ate beautifully."

I forgot to buy Teddy more Lactaid. Our food issues aren't entirely funny. My typically bad childhood eating habits have come full circle, and I police the boys' intake, worrying about Crohn's disease from me, diabetes from Susan's side of the family, and the contribution of the wrong diet to both. Call me Sergeant Sadie. Given everything healthy I wouldn't eat as a kid, I should be more understanding, but worry has zapped my empathy.

My own adult food issues, servant girls to disease, carry the unfunny stigma of making me something less than a normal man: Counting calories up instead of down, restricting the good stuff, standing outside the midlife fraternity of paunch, love handles, beer gut, indulgence, gluttony, and the collective unconscious of spiritual tailgating. Skin and bones don't make for the same crowd pleaser as grabbing your flab for show. Without these weighty traditions, I'm an outlier as a man, a husband, a father, a joke teller. It's a sham when I laugh at the flabby punch lines.

"Dis-moi ce que tu manges, je te dirai ce que tu es," or "Tell me what you eat, and I will tell you what you are," Anthelme Brillat-Savarin wrote in 1826. Carnivore, pescatarian, vegetarian, fruitarian, vegan, ascetic, health nut, junk food junkie, overeater, weight watcher, binger, dieter, faster, drinker, teetotaler, alcoholic, coffee drinker, tea drinker, latte sipper, Kosher, nosher, meat-and-potatoes, cheesehead, chowderhead, chocoholic, gum chewer, macrobiotic, crunchy granola, organic, connoisseur, gourmand, omnivore—you are what you eat. The relationship between food and identity, food and health, philos-

ophy, spirituality, religion, politics, geography, heritage, status, and being goes back eons before Brillat-Savarin coined it, at least to Adam and Eve's fruit habit and, later, to the first Holy Communion. The bread and wine of transubstantiation literally connect eating and drinking to the soul. Forget about the eyes being the window to the soul; it's the mouth that opens the gate. I'm not a Catholic, but the Eucharist is the tastiest tenet of belief I can imagine. For this, I'd convert.

What you eat is your Food ID, your Food DNA, your Food Self.

But to truly understand a person's food identity, "You are what you eat" doesn't go deep enough. Any empty vessel can fill up on what's put in front of him. As the code for your Food Self, "You are what you eat" is too general and random. What really says food identity to me is "You are what you *choose* to eat" or "You are what you *crave*." Cravings are the sharp hook on to your personality, the expression of your essential self. You show me someone who says "I love it, but I shouldn't," and I'll show you someone at war with himself. Worse yet, show me someone who says he doesn't have cravings, and I'll show you someone without a soul.

Dis-moi ce dont tu as envie, je te dirai ce que tu es. Tell me what you crave, and I will tell you what you are.

Food is our common experience from birth to death. Food has the power both to give life and to take it, to nourish the body and mind or to infect them. What we do with food determines the quality of our heath and defines our humanity.

Who are you, though, if you can't eat or drink? What is your Food Self? How do you live—with people, with community, with culture, with history, with yourself—without the food and drink as fundamental as breathing and as essential as joy? Who are you if you're reduced to smelling the apricots? *Tell me what you crave, and I will tell you what you are.*

Time to get up off the floor, Grandma. Two blueberry muffins and cashews for the boys' after-school snack. We'll stay too long at the playground, and they'll be starving. Salmon and French beans and brown rice for dinner. Teddy can have the hard-boiled eggs. I'll get a bottle for dinner with the others at Gotham. I hope the sale is still going on. The apricots. I need to put them in Tupperware. They'll get stale in that paper bag. Or eat them before they go bad. Are there any left? The bag on the kitchen counter is blurring. Forgive me they were delicious.

It's Friday, the last day of school. We're driving to Matt and Ellen's tomorrow. We'll get there for lunch, and all the boys will ski together. I'd been feeling so well the past months; I can't believe this is happening. Susan doesn't know I'm dying. I'm confused. The past and present are melting. The living room's light is closing orange and dark. The ancient images flicker and fill the frames. Is this what it is to have your life flash before you?

Apricots. Yes, of course, the apricots.

■

I'm six years old and sitting in the school nurse's small, cluttered office, on the hard chair by the scale. My mother is on her way to pick me up. Nurse Mauer called her when I finished in the bathroom.

"Mrs. Reiner, this is Nurse Mauer." She speaks in a distracted monotone that sounds like a table saw passing through her nose. I've seen her in the parking lot at recess, blowing forks of smoke out her nostrils, and that's how the words come out. She has a circle of orange cotton-candy hair around a floury face, and a suspicious nature, but it helps your case if she knows your parents.

"I'm okay, how 'bout you? Good. Jon is here with me. He's not feeling well. He has diarrhea. A few times. How many times, Jon? Three times. I was surprised, too. I'm not aware of anything going around—it's too early in the school year for that—but he's not one of my complainers, so I'm going to send him home. Very good. He'll be in the main office when you get here."

It's my first time coming home early from school, and my stomach bubbles and turns loops as my mother parks the station wagon in our driveway. She's a jumpy two-footed driver, and I can feel why it took her three shots to get her license. Unbuckled, I lurch against the dashboard when we stop, and tear out of the car for a toilet run in the house. My mother lays out stretchy pajamas, the pair with the dartboard on the chest and blue-banded cuffs at the wrists and ankles. Depleted from the diarrhea, I dress and unfold flat on my narrow bed. My ass is sore on the mattress, bullied by all the activity on that end.

Down the carpeted hall of our ranch house, I hear my mother making noise in the kitchen. She doesn't do things quietly. It sounds like she's talking to herself, and her Keds are squealing loud on the vinyl tiles. My head pulses with hurt, like on those television commercials for aspirin. I'm so empty in my gut, but the thought of food is nauseating, even the sunflower-shaped chocolate-fudge Keeblers that I mow through by the stack.

There's a bottle sloshing in the kitchen, making that gross shaking sound. She's going to make me drink the pink stuff. It pours like Elmer's glue, and I gag into my pillow. I hope the pooping has stopped. I really don't want that pink glue. The kitchen cabinet door under the toaster opens and slams, and my mother shrieks. A moment later, she stands in the narrow rectangle of my doorway, holding a paper lunch bag.

"Jon, what happened to the dried apricots that were in this bag?" She rattles the crumpled bag like she's shaking down a thermometer.

"I ate them."

"All of them? How many?"

"However many were left. Maybe fourteen?"

Her brows lift and crease her forehead under the plank of dark bangs. "Fourteen? When did you eat fourteen?"

It's becoming clear I've done something wrong. I roll over off my sore bottom and face the wall, picking at its mustard-colored paint pimples with my fingernails. White drywall dots show through like stars where I pluck.

"I don't know. Maybe before school." This is a feeble mashing of the truth. My mother is short under the doorjamb, but she fills the room with her presence, and I'm caught. There's no point in fudging. The shit doesn't lie.

"You ate them before school? All of them? Why?"

I don't answer her straightaway. The dried apricots were supposed to be a special treat, partner to a second bag of mixed dried apples, figs, prunes, and bananas. We left for school before I could get to the prune bag. Both were take-home mementos from a family trip Sunday to the Lower East Side.

My parents took my sister, Lisa, and me for lunch to a place
called Katz's, an old deli that is noisier than my school cafeteria
and smells like the garlicked salami chandeliers hanging from
its crummy ceiling. We travel to the city from New Jersey in the
red VW Bug my dad drives, and he palms the knobby stick shift
back and forth twenty times to squeeze into a parking space
near Katz's. He's talked about this place a lot, in a throaty voice
he uses to exaggerate and get me interested in something, and
I'm excited.

I smell it first. Leaning hard to unseal the deli's front door
from its air lock, I am knocked back into the glass as an explosion of aroma bursts over me. It overpowers my nostrils; it's like
nothing I've smelled before. Then sounds blast: dishes, silverware, glasses yammering on tabletops; oven doors hinging open
and shut; the metal tumblers of the front cash register. And
shouting, people shouting to be heard over the tableware symphony: "Pastrami, lean on club," "Two corned beef with mustard
on rye," "Four Dr. Brown's—three cream, one Cel-Ray," "Where's
my French?" I push through a turnstile like at Yankee Stadium
and an unshaven guy curved on a stool presses a carnival-ticket
stub in my hand. He's a scary-looking sentry.

My mother takes off with my sister, weaving through the
packed dining room's chaos to a table barely bigger than a
TV tray, where four eaters are just getting up. She hangs her
bag over the back of one of the chairs and plants Lisa and her
frayed Raggedy Ann in another. The bag draws a laugh from a
tubby leaving the table. It's made of white plastic squares we cut
from Clorox bottles, hole-punched at the corners, and stitched
together with coarse blue yarn. We all made it over the summer

in Maine when the old swimming-area buoys were pulled in and replaced with new bottles.

I stand close by my father on one of the pushy lines fingering out from a counter that runs the entire long side of the dining hall. Behind us, a couple with wild hair tumbling over their denim collars dares each other to eat "a whole side of Hebrew cow." The buttons pinned to their jacket pockets are the same peace signs I helped stick on the trunk of the Volks above its slotted exhaust. The hippies have a funny, engaging way, but I'm too shy for eye contact. They catch me staring a little dreamily, in awe of their style, as I am with the college students who come home with my father after class and play Phil Ochs records on my grandparents' hand-me-down "Victrola" and write papers against the war and trouble my mother for more servings of vegetarian food that she frets over in the casserole dish with the blue flowers stenciled on its sides.

"What brings you to the People's Temple of Smoked Meats, little man?" the man hippie asks. He sways as if he's listening to music. I want to say something clever, like "A red VW with a gray front fender," but I go wobbly in my striped bell-bottoms. I'm mute, and the briny aroma of cooked pastrami is beginning to dizzy me.

My father rescues me and collars me up to the tall counter. He lifts a steaming slice of just-out-of-the-cooker meat from the small plate the counterman slides to us, and feeds it to my dumb tilted mouth. My first hot pastrami. I have a crooked front tooth from where I smashed into the dashboard in a car accident, and I bite the slice on a slant. The flavor is a revelation—salty, spicy, tender, hot—each chew melts on my awakened tongue. Cap'n

Crunch never tasted like this. This must be Jewish Communion, I think. The pastrami passes my mouth like something sacred, and I'm converted on the spot into the faith of Jewish soul food. Holy, holy, holy. Yes, Lord, I know the power, and the kingdom, and the glory; it's right here in Katz's. In rapture with the meat, I shed my shyness and get mouthy about my half of the sandwich the counterman is stacking like blocks. "I want a whole one," I blurt. I don't know what I'm talking about; it just comes out. My father laughs in the yellow deli light.

The counterman scoops a bready trench down the middle of the club roll like a dugout canoe and folds in the sliced hunks of meat. They're dark and notched at the edges and look like varnished woodcuts. Pastrami fills the whole boat. Dad asks me for the carnival ticket, and the pasty counterman pulls a grease pencil from the pleat of his paper hat. He crosses a black line through the numbered side of the ticket and scrawls another number on the blank backside.

"Next!"

We trickle through long lines at other counter stops, loading two damp trays with plates of fat french fries, potato knishes, chopped liver mounds, half-sour pickles that glisten bottle-green, and cans of Dr. Brown's cream and Cel-Ray sodas. At the small table, we devour the piles of heart-attack-on-a-plate, while my sister busies herself with a bunless salty frank and trips to the twenty-armed shiny silver fountain to refill our scratched water glasses.

Quickly, our paper napkins are blotted with grease and Katz's own brown-flecked mustard, which they spoon into used yogurt containers. My problem pickiness is back in New Jersey, and I polish off my share of the pastrami on club in rapid bites. Evidently, despite my featherweight frame, I have inherited the gluttony gene of my bloviating ancestors, the ones who measure their vacations by the inches padded on their waistlines: "What a time I had. I gained twelve pounds in two weeks!"

My relatives crow about food in weird ways, like when my uncle Richard lies on Grandma Marly's scratchy living room carpet after Thanksgiving dinner, unbuckles his belt, opens his trousers, and moans like a cow. It looks funny. But here, under the gastronomic spell of chopped liver, I'm beginning to see the light.

I see the people jamming Katz's tables and counter lines, digging into the food like pirates into treasure: the families with teenagers and strollers clogging the aisles, the old-timers sitting against the wall beside pictures of grinning big shots, the swaying hippies, us. For the first time, food makes sense. Food is fun. Food is a party I'm part of. It's our cultural identity. It's our bond.

The lunch at Katz's is my initiation into the pleasure of indulgence, and incredibly, the day gets better.

We hand in the greased tickets to another stern codger at the checkout, then roll a block west on Houston Street to the next Old World outpost, Russ and Daughters' appetizer store. Apparently, on the Lower East Side, "appetizer" doesn't mean Cheez Whiz and Ritz crackers. If the smell at Katz's was like being doused with smoked perfume, opening the belled door at Russ and Daughters makes me feel like I'm inhaling from a magic pipe. In the crowded store, I ask if my bedroom can be sprayed with "appetizer air." I think of the punky older kids on their bikes trailing the insecticide clouds out of the bug truck that sprays our mosquito-infested development. They always seem to be having more fun than I am, standing on a chair looking out the parted living room curtains. Now, I know, the DDT clouds on our block can't compare to Russ and Daughters' draft.

The store is a pantheon to the opposing forces of salty and sweet, jammed to the ceiling with dried and cured riches — smoked whitefish, carp, sturgeon, lox, and herring on one side, facing off against dried apricots, prunes, pears, figs, apples, and bananas in counters and bins across a linoleum floor two steps wide. I'm becoming convinced there isn't enough room in the place to hold all the good this new world has to offer. A tide rolls in my mouth. My eyes leak. My heart races. I'm overwhelmed, even more than when I went to the Yankee game on my birthday in June and saw Mickey Mantle. (He struck out.)

This place is perfect. It makes you feel things, and I want it all, even the food I can't pronounce, like the halvah with its guttural throat-clearing H. Saying the name is a natural palate cleanser preparing for the food itself: "kkchchchchalavah." My parents buy it, and the lox, the chopped liver, the whitefish. They buy yard-long ropes of waxy, dense cherry-red licorice that my sister and I go crazy over. They buy the paper bag of mixed dried fruit and the one of just the apricots. I already have designs on it.

The four of us leave Russ's and walk through crowded sidewalks on blocks called Ludlow and Delancey. We have to run through a paddle wheel of elbows and legs to keep up with Dad; he's walking fast, springing on the bumpy rubber of his desert boots, pumping his hairy arms. He stops us at the building where he was born during the Depression, where his family lived when they immigrated from a part of Europe called Galicia. He says the houses had dirt floors there, but I don't know. He points out the corniced rooftop where his mother, Jennie, pulled feathers out of the chickens she cooked for the family, and the single men for whom she made fifty-cent meals after Grandpa Jake died and they were broke. I didn't know her, she died when I was two, but I found in a shoe box a small black-and-white picture of her sitting on a barrel on a roof, raisin-skinned, holding a dead plucked chicken by the neck. I guess my dad is telling the truth.

My mom swings us around to where Marly—her mom, who's still alive—grew up. Her name should be Molly, but she spells it Marly after a perfume bottle she says she saw in a store as a girl. I don't believe that one, either. The buildings are dirty, run-down tilters of broken bricks and rusty fire escapes like leg braces. My parents say they're worse on the inside. But the people live so close to the amazing food. It's no wonder my relatives are so fat.

On Delancey, we come to a restaurant called Ratner's that Dad says makes the best blintzes. I look in the big front window around the script writing on the glass and see plates of cheese and blueberry and strawberry blintzes served by slumped old men wearing gold jackets. The waiters are short and round, like Grandpa Sid, who's also still alive and married to Marly. My mother says Sid once had his hand slapped here by a man in a gold jacket for eating too much split-pea soup. I believe it; these guys look nasty. The afternoon sun floods the dining room and sparkles on a blintz plate that travels past my eyes.

"Those blintzes are as good as your aunt Sylvia's," Dad says, and he stands at the window like he's still hungry. He strokes the back of his dark hair and looks like he remembers something, seeing all the old stores in this neighborhood, all the old food. My father talks a lot. He tells my sister and me stories, and they're funny, but they don't always make sense. They're just made-up stories, I figure, like about Baron Münchausen. But now the stories turn in my head, connecting the people and the food—Jennie's plucked chickens, Sid's soup, Sylvia's blintzes— they fit together in these grimy, busy blocks. It's so different from where we live in New Jersey, where everything's far apart, and the food is flavorless, and people don't get their hands slapped over split-pea soup.

"How can they be as good as Aunt Sylvia's?" I ask. "She says hers are the best."

I ate the blintzes last Saturday when we visited Sylvia and Uncle Nat in Coney Island. My parents called it the "Grand Tour." Sylvia and Nat live on a street near the beach called Mermaid Avenue in an apartment above Nat's fruit and vegetable store. After Jennie plucked all the chickens on the Lower East Side, the Reiners moved to Coney. Nat and Sylvia are the last ones there.

Aunt Sylvia's blintzes press together in my mouth as a mash of crunchy shells and cream and berries, and they don't draw blood like the Cap'n Crunch sometimes does. I eat four of them before my mother tells me to stop. Everyone howls, especially Nat, who's reclining on a curvy upholstered lounge chair in the small living room next to the kitchen. The russet-colored chair looks like a potato chip, and it vibrates when you turn on an electrical switch. My sister and I got thrown off the moving chair so Nat could lie down, but I'm shoving more blintzes in my mouth, so everything is beautiful. Nat fell out of our back-yard hammock the one time they visited New Jersey. I guess that's why he wants the potato-chip chair so much, as it's low to the floor.

Nat and Sylvia both talk in a funny way, as if they're about to burp, and Nat yells in a scratchy voice like a worn-out record. He turns off the chair vibrator and walks me down a dark stairwell. We emerge in the daylight of his cramped store, where he teaches me how to tell if fruit is ripe. He grips canta-loupe and honeydew melons with hairy, rawboned hands. He's short, even shorter than Grandpa Sid, and bald, with elephant ears and huge hands and feet that belong on a bigger body. My father says Nat's feet are so big that he can bend straight all the way over like Charlie Chaplin. This I want to see, and I knock a lemon off its pyramid to try to make him go flat, but he picks it up off the floor like a normal person.

Nat and Sylvia live over the store, even closer to the special food than the old folks did on Ludlow Street. Nat's market is open to the street in the front. There are cardboard stalls of produce parked in a row on the sidewalk, and I can smell the salt air of the Atlantic and hear chimes from the boardwalk, where my father worked calling games as a teenager in the summers:

"Play Fascination. What a sensation. World's greatest cre-ation. Thrill of a nation. Across the street from the BMT station."

It's another one of his stories, but I hear the voices echoing from the beach. The musk of the ocean and the melons fills my nose, and I don't want to leave Nat's store, unlike the cold and dreary supermarket in our town, but we have a home delivery to make. We drive in an aircraft carrier that Nat handles like a maniac, a blue Chevy wagon. He sits on a wood apple crate to see over the steering wheel and doesn't look before he turns. I'm loose in the back well, holding on to the brown bags of melons and rock fruit and lettuce and cucumbers and squash, and we drive through Coney Island to a neighborhood called Sea Gate. We pass Nathan's, where my father says he used to get a whole meal—dog, french fries, orange drink—for fifteen cents.

Nat climbs down from the car to unlatch a splintering wooden fence, and we roar up to a house attached to another one just like it. Lawn statues of mermaids and tridents stand on a strip of grass bordering the front steps. A woman with gold hair piled on top of her head like a chef's hat, Cleopatra-painted eyes, and a sea horse pinned on the shoulder strap of her shimmery dress opens the door. She talks in a loud voice. She's been waiting for the delivery and gives Nat a hard time, but he makes a joke, blaming the delay on the new kid instead of on him shaking too long in the potato-chip chair. She digs in a sea-green purse and hands me a stick of Wrigley's. I tear through the paper and foil that shines in my hand like her beaded metal dress. "You like it?" she asks, and laughs.

Nat and I drive back to Mermaid Avenue in the boat car, and my sister is vibrating in the chair. Aunt Sylvia pushes a cellophane package of blueberry blintzes into my mother's hands to take home to our town where we don't have this kind of food.

Clank, clank, pow!

A hammer pounds by my head, and I come to from the fever dream. What's the noise? Yes, the heat is cycling on the living room radiator behind the love seat. I'm still here on the floor. The building's heat cycles on every hour. I wonder how many I've missed since passing out. I call out in a garbled caveman voice, but the kids aren't home. Either it's early or they're at Jodi's. Why isn't the ambulance here?

I try to push myself up; however, my limbs have gone lifeless and the gut pain has me nailed down. I can't get to the phone, but 911 has had it with me, anyway. The radiator pipes bang like a metal rainstorm. I throw one more cry for help into the ether, and a vise turns on my head. "Where are you?" The yell rushes the blood out of my brain, and I'm blacking out again, falling back into this scene from the past as if I'm living it.

Play Fascination. What a sensation. World's greatest creation. Play Fascination. Play Fascina . . .

October 1968. We're leaving the Lower East Side, cradling the Russ and Daughters apricots and the other parcels of Old World exotica like new toys. Provisions for a year in the hinterlands. They stuff the VW's rear well up to the window. My sister and I pull braids of licorice from the stash, loop them around like necklaces, and eat down the length of the candy jewels with our heads bowed.

It's a warm Indian-summer day, and we park by Washington Square Park. Just inside the green, some hippies, a few barechested and in fringed vests, unroll army-surplus sleeping bags. Dad opens the car door and darts across the street past the shirtless guys. Between them, they're passing apples and dark nuts and raisins from paper bags that are spread on the patchy grass. Compared to the smoked meat I've discovered, their vegetarian food looks pretty bad. I wouldn't want to have to eat that.

They're sitting cross-legged holding guitars like ripe pears in their laps, strumming and singing. It sounds like a Rolling Stones song I've heard at night on WABC, listening to the small transistor radio through the earpiece under the bedcovers. I know the melody, but the words are hard to understand.

Dad runs back to the car with flyers screaming about a march on Washington. My sister and I fold them into paper airplanes and fling them from the cramped backseat as the Volks' engine revs like a bomber, and we drive away. The paper planes dive on the brown spots where I spilled a chocolate milk shake that's stained the waffled white upholstery. I hear nothing more from the singers; we all agree to keep the windows shut, luxuriating in the appetizer bouquet sealed inside the bubble cabin.

There must be something special happening. My parents spent so much money on the food, and they *both* shopped, excited, calling for whitefish and lox like song requests. This doesn't happen in the aisles of our grim town market. There, my mom holds clipped coupons up to the food on the shelves like she's inspecting for head lice. She buys soggy green beans and corn in metal cans, and you can see blood sloshing under the plastic when the meat tips in the shopping cart. It tastes tough like it has pits in it. I hate eating that food and wait for lunch when I bite off the ends of my beloved Hostess Twinkies and snare the sugary vanilla crème center inside, curling my tongue like a bullfrog's. At least I get a Twinkie every day.

Where we live, nothing tastes like the hot pastrami in Katz's, nothing smells like the appetizer store, no one looks like the guitar players in Washington Square Park. We ride in the Volks for barely more than half an hour to the yellow house in the floodplain, but the distance might as well be around the world. No one has ever heard of our flyspeck town except that the guy who invented Pop Rocks lives here, but I've never seen him, and anyway, I'm not allowed to eat Pop Rocks because if you mix them with soda your stomach will explode and you will be killed.

There are no restaurants in our town that have plates of blintzes circling twenty-four hours a day like the flying saucers inside Ratner's. The only restaurant is a dump called Sam's that serves gummy spaghetti and has a yardstick of water marks on the walls from all the floods. We never even go to Sam's, like my friends' families do. The families are all Italian and Irish and German with a lot of kids, and they eat big meals with their relatives, who live with them in the garage rooms or in the houses next door. My best friend's family has potato chips delivered in metal cans and jugs of Coca-Cola syrup in his house. You push down on a pump, and the gooey syrup swirls into the seltzer water in the paper cups his mom gives us. His father gets the syrup near where he works as a security guard for the Port Authority. He stands around all night outside a trailer, where the giant twin towers are being built. That's where he gets the pumps, too. He says he'll take us on the roof of the towers when they're finished.

My parents sure knew about the food at the appetizer store, so all this stuff must be good for me to eat—the salty fish, the oily brick of halvah, the apricots. They're always nagging me to eat more. I'm tall and skinny, "a stick with a face," as Sid says about me in my new class picture, standing high in the back row like a radio antenna. The VW turns in to the driveway, and my mother hands me a bag while she opens the house's screen door. Helpless, I pull another yard of licorice into my mouth.

"Save room for dinner. We're having tuna casserole," she scolds. Her breath smells like pastrami. She gets close and yanks the red rope from my salivated mouth. She's in my face, still tan from the Caribbean.

We were living in St. Thomas, where my father taught in the college, and just came back to New Jersey four months ago, the day before Bobby Kennedy was killed and I woke up to see my mother on the living room floor, crying in front of the Zenith. In the West Indies, I went to kindergarten at a school called Tu Tu Elementary, in a sloped hangar of a building beside a dirt parking lot. I was the only white kid out of six hundred. In that class picture I look like a ghost. I ask my parents when I will be as dark as the other kids.

Everyone wants me to eat more in St. Thomas, too, but the food is weird. I don't eat the school lunch of soup and funny meat that I tried once on the outdoor cafeteria tables and left on the plate. My father picks me up at noon in a white VW, like all the cars on the island, and takes me home for more familiar plain macaroni. I know he's arrived when my classmate Dale Braithwaite announces, "John, you fadda come" in his brisk island accent.

The Volks strains up the twisty road with no side rails to the top of Rapoon Hill, where we live in an apartment house with screens for windows and Siamese twin square bathtubs. The

road is scary fun, like a roller coaster. Once I saw some workers'
white pickup truck turn out of our driveway and sail right off
the road over the cliff. The two men jumped from the truck and
hung on to an elastic saman tree. From the apartment's screened
front hallway, I also see the cruise ships docking in the harbor when I wake up, some days three at a time. I look for the
enormous black S.S. *United States* and its red smokestacks. The
liner holds the Atlantic-crossing speed record.

My parents call St. Thomas "the Rock," I guess because we
live on one. They're meeting all these new people—teachers, artists, sailors, doctors—and they say that "everyone has a story
to tell," everyone is escaping from something that happened to
them in the States. The Rock is a funny place to hide, consider-
ing that the sunshine is endless and the house doors have no
locks.

When we first move in to the apartment, Roger Cook and
Viola Nesbit and Avaricia Todman and my father's other new
students come over and cook us a welcome-to-the-island feast
in the skinny galley kitchen. They make something called *callaloo* by boiling down floppy green taro leaves and coconut milk
in a black pot. The students jam the counter and pull crabmeat
to toss in the pot and scoop a dark, slimy, squirmy conch from
the pink and yellow shell that they say you can put your ear to
and hear the ocean. I want to hear the ocean, but I'm afraid an
angry conch will bite me.

Roger Cook unwraps wet newspaper and lays fat silver fish
on the counter and chops off their heads with a long knife. It's
a bloody mess. He bones the fish and throws the meat, including the heads, onto a sizzling oiled pan. He cooks the heads

and slaps them on the bed of *callaloo* when it's finished, with their glassy fish eyes looking right at me. The kitchen is hot and smoky and smelly, and I can't stand the sight of the fish heads with the dead eyes, so I escape to the living room, where Herbert Broadman is serenading my parents, singing along to a Mighty Sparrow record playing on the portable turntable we shipped here. He's got a brash tenor voice that calls in time with the Sparrow:

"Good morning, Mr. Walker, I come to see your daughter. Sweet Rosemarie, she promise she gone marry me." The students move to the music and sing calypso, and everybody drinks the bottles of duty-free wine and rum we bought in Charlotte Amalie and looks at the twinkling boat lights in the harbor and eats the fish-headed *callaloo,* even my parents.

I hate it.

I'm so hungry in this strange place and nag my mother for plain wagon wheels. In the morning, my mom takes my sister and me to the Red Rooster café after she gets her hair freed for the heat in a pixie style at Jacques's salon. The Rooster rises on a steep street behind the pink salon. We sit on the Rooster's dark benches, and I stir spoonfuls of sugar in tall glasses of iced tea. This I like. It's delicious, smoother than the powdered tea my mother mixes in the plastic jug at home. I drink two and try to forget about the *callaloo*—dead fish eyes quivering like frightened jelly—but the sugar and caffeine give me the jolts. My father meets us in blinding sunlight outside the shuttered café and takes us to a sagging wooden dock in the harbor. We stand in line for a boat that delivers boxes of packaged goods and food, like Yodels and Devil Dogs from the States. He pays a lot of money for them. I eat three Yodels on the drive back up the Rock.

The sky over the brimming harbor is orange. The sea is orange.

"Why?" my mother asks again. "Why did you eat the entire bag of apricots?" She's at the side of my bed. Her expression has broken from heat to confusion.

I have the answer. The apricots are like magic leather. Imagine if your shoes were made of apricots and you could just eat them when you wanted, like Chaplin does in the old movie my father took me to see at his school. I ate a toe and then a tongue and a heel and the rest of the shoes in the bag.

"They tasted so good," I tell my mother. "I didn't know they could be bad for me."

Her mouth opens a slit, but she doesn't speak. I can't tell if she's going to yell or do something else, but she turns and leaves, silent on the olive wall-to-wall. I press my fingers again to the paint pebbles next to the bed, feeling around for the familiar points. I feel nothing. The pebbles are gone. I look and the drywall stars are gone. The mustard room is gone. My hand flails in open space.

Play Fascination. What a sensation. World's greatest creation. Play Fascination. Play Fascina . . .

"Where am I? Are you here?" I scream.

Is it all over? I don't hear anything from the radiator. Sid and Marly and Nat and Sylvia are dead. The produce store on Mermaid Avenue is closed. Ratner's is gone, along with the waiters in gold jackets. A hurricane blew our apartment house on the Rock over the cliff, smashed into that gorgeous turquoise sea.

The S.S. *United States* is gutted and dry-docked. That's ancient history. And I cut out eating apricots ages ago. I cut out Cap'n Crunch and Twinkies and Devil Dogs and caffeine and refined white sugar and flour and high-fructose corn syrup, and I never even ate a Pop Rock, so why is my stomach blasted apart? I cut out any food or spice or spirit that brings pleasure and irritates the gut. What is there left to cut out?

Echoes outside the room wake me back to the present. I'm on my back on the living room rug in our apartment. I don't know how long I've been out. The sun has gone from the window. The pain has spread across my middle. In the dim light, the ceiling's two shadowed crossbeams look like they're dropping down to crush me.

I plead in conflicting screams to an ambivalent God: "Get me to the hospital now and heal what's gone wrong. If the damage will destroy me, then I'm ready to die now."

I wait, but no voice answers the call, no direction, no sign other than the searing pain. Salvation is not coming to end this crisis. I am erupting, spewing, leaking—the shakes have beaten me. I've lost control of my body, and now I am losing my mind, "burning up on this red coal carpet." The Stones! That's the song the hippies playing the pear guitars sang in the park.

I waited too long. The situation was clear, but I didn't want to face reality and took too long to act. A deathbed confession. If it's too late, take me.

The room is rattling, rolling like an oil drum, and I'm in the way of an avalanche. Thumps, slams, the walls quake, and noise in the hallway erupts in yells. The door crashes open. Voices get closer, shouting down at me, barking orders, but I don't respond.

I can't. I can't talk of apricots. I am rolled, flattened. The pain shatters me; it shoots my gut with every move. I am raised from the floor and taken from the room. I am gone.

The air is cold. Drawing breath is a knife to my lungs. I am outside by the building's service entrance. The wrought-iron doors are propped open like when furniture is moved out. I'm strapped flat on an accordion stretcher, headed for the back of an ambulance. It's not from the hospital Dr. Abrams called. The lettering on the cab and the crew's jackets is from some other place. Where am I going?

Around the building's corner, Susan appears. She's carrying book bags, and the straps section the puffy shoulders of her down coat like bread loaves. She's getting in from school; it's nearly five o'clock. I've been dreaming all afternoon. Her pretty face is rounded under a wool hat and earmuffs. A gust strikes, and the stretcher lists against the ambulance. This is the windiest corner in New York, on a bluff above the Hudson. Violent river wind rattles the corner trash can, scattering wrappers and blowing loose strands of hair across Susan's mouth. The trouble in her blue eyes tells me how I must look. She squeezes a white paper bag in her gloved hands.

I recognize the bag and know what's in it. Éclairs from the bakery. A treat to start the holiday.

CHAPTER 2

NPO is an abbreviation for the Latin phrase *nil per os*, which translates roughly as "nothing by mouth." For a hospital patient, an NPO order is a condemnation. It translates more personally to: "starving on an intravenous drip while your roommate groans over the vulcanized chicken, limp penne, and lumpy custard on his tray."

"Reiner" is handwritten across the top of an NPO circle-slash paper sign taped to my hospital door. Indeed, tonight my roommate's French-accented gripes are coupling with his lousy dinner's aroma, infusing the air between our mechanical beds. Parisian-born and laid up with a bum tibia broken in what sketchily sounds like a restaurant fight, I'm sure he knows what he's talking about. J.P. is a charmingly well-mannered guy, gently introducing conversation through the flimsy pretense of privacy hung on the room's dreary center shroud. However, I am agitated by his Continental grousing. Three times today an avocado-shaped orderly has delivered a loaded tray of miserable, flavorless—and for me, prohibited—institutional food to J.P.'s windowed half of the room. Three times I have been subjected to his complaints, unable to respond in kind. Not only is NPO restricting me from eating a meager cup of Jell-O, it's also excluding me from the shared experience of a meal—in this case, bitching.

"Oh, shit. This is worse than yesterday. I think they find this food in the trash with the used bandages. Jon, you don't know how lucky you are," J.P. humors me from the other side.

I have been NPO for nearly three days since a five-hour emergency intestinal surgery that began midnight Friday. I'm keeping count. Like an expectant mother, I'm guided by a common established timetable, in my case to regain digestive function and open my mouth to the salvation of garbage hospital food. These sixty-plus hours are like pre-labor, and based on the previous gastrointestinal operation I had the year Teddy was born, I calculate as imminent the arrival of awakening gurgles of beloved motility that delight both colorectal surgeons and their starved patients. The excitement is that of baby's first gas. Passing puffs of precious gas through my gut will license the doctor to unthread me from the catheters and tubes that probe from end to end and introduce the first infant swallows of an initially liquid diet. Apple juice never tasted so good. From there it should be a short GI walk to the Holy Grail of peristalsis: smooth muscle contractions that propel foodstuffs distally through the esophagus and intestines. Man, that's poetry! Ay, gastro motility, I am thy hungry servant. Deliver me to thy involuntary state of grace.

I'm stalled through the evening hours, though, in the clogged room J.P. and I share, where even the single visitor's chair facing the bed prohibits passage. I have no flatulence to celebrate; my proverbial water has not broken. My gut, after the trauma of rupture, lies silent and fallow and remote, like plowed farmland sunk in a valley. I recalculate the hours of the crucial motility equation when the young surgeon who, I'm told, saved me from a permanent state of lying silent and fallow, enters wearing an OR shower cap that bunches her long honey blond hair. Despite her youth, pouches bag the doctor's saucer-size brown eyes, puffier under the room's cruel fluorescents, and signify another marathon day wielding the knife. She operated on me during the graveyard shift, and I doubt she sleeps much. As a surgical fellow, she's assigned the grueling schedule of a baker's apprentice.

"Dr. Paz, hello, I have nothing new to report," I begin hurriedly, pushing up in my folded bed, as if I've been home all day waiting to share the dinner menu with Susan. "No noise, no movement, no gas. Nothing. With the prior operation, it was about two days before the gut started working again."

The doctor purses her lips and approaches the side of the bed. I peel off the pilled cotton blanket for her to press a flattened hand on the dressing that covers my insides from groin to rib cage. Nothing, not even an alien life-form stowing away in my surgically parted stomach, could be felt through the thick padding holding my guts in place, but hers is a humane gesture— side-of-the-bed behavior. I'm encouraged to see her so close.

Having logged too many hours in hospital beds, I've observed two kinds of physicians: side-of-the-bed (SOB) and foot-of-the-bed (FOB) doctors. The consequences can be enormous; the difference between recovering with dignity or suffering in silence.

In this case, being called an SOB is a compliment. SOBs approach and touch the patient. They try to form a human bond and be better clinicians by paying attention to the whole patient.

They practice an old-fashioned bedside manner, resisting the nagging stopwatches of insurance companies.

FOBs don't touch the patient. They stand away, arms crossed, read the chart, look at the MRI, and, by their remove, dull the doctor's sharpest skill—his power of observation. MRIs and the like provide good information, but they can't get to know the patient, they can't make the ultimate decision. I often know my body's health intuitively and more insightfully than a dye scan. FOBs miss hearing that critical reading and sacrifice a crucial dimension of healthcare. People talk about how a restaurant meal is about more than simply the food. You can't appreciate the chef's work if the service is cold. Likewise, FOBs have us eating linguine and clam sauce with a plastic spork. It's a mess of bad medicine.

I can quickly distinguish between SOBs and FOBs and, when in the presence of medical residents, often resist the urge to call out, "You, the SOB making eye contact, you should be a doctor. You, the robot FOB buried in the chart, you should be a researcher—you should not see patients. The lab is waiting for you."

"You look like something's on your mind," Doctor SOB says, tapping my split gut. We met each other for the first time as I was being rushed into the operating room. We're strangers. All she has to go on today are my post-op numbers, and the history I've begun to share.

"I should feel something by now."

Dr. Paz scans my medical chart, unconcerned about my dormant furnace, then cautions against comparing the two surgeries and the anticipated digestive scenario I'm clocking. "Your earlier operation was scheduled surgery," she says, clarifying events. "I don't mean to minimize a terminal ileum resection and fistula closure, but compared to this, that was a fender bender. This was an emergency situation. It's completely different. You had a head-on collision, with all the corresponding damage. You're still in a critical period. It would be unrealistic to expect the same timetable."

It's not what I want to hear, but the crash analogy is dead-on. Post-surgery, despite the analgesia of a self-administered morphine drip, I do feel like I've been crushed by a semi. Stubbornly, I'm clinging to the schedule I know, the one experience I have to compare this to. But if it is a false comparison, as the doctor says, I'm starting to wonder what I'm in for. The previous surgery kept me in the hospital for a week and then home for another three before I pushed myself back to work a little sooner than ideal. That wasn't entirely my choice. A phone call from my boss, bracketed by the silence of his dwindling patience, forced my early return. This was the same overseer who once questioned why I didn't call in from my honeymoon.

Susan and the kids are home from school on winter break, so this is actually good timing on my part. However, next week, somehow, I've got to get back on duty. Staying in the hospital through the weekend is not an option; I can't even begin to think of how the kids' schedules and our home life will be managed if I'm not on my feet. I already missed taco night. And who knows what's become of my refrigerator? Susan suffers from top-shelf syndrome—everything gets put back on one shelf and jammed like the unmatched socks in her dresser drawer. I was supposed to help my sister find a restaurant for our parents' fiftieth wedding anniversary this week, too. Farting is the first movement to getting home.

"Doctor, do you think I can expect to be discharged by this Sunday? That would make it nine days since the surgery."

The doctor turns to acknowledge the team of residents congregating at the door and addresses me quickly. Her flat midwestern vowels are squeezed in the rush. "I wouldn't think of this in terms of hours or days. Your body went through significant trauma, and the healing may take a while."

She exits, and I roll my hips like a car axle in the divots of the mattress, enduring the sting of the incision, determined to stimulate the gas loops hibernating in my idle intestines.

J.P. stifles a low growl over his cup of uninspired pudding. Perhaps he feels awkward about eating in my presence, even if the dessert is stirred from a sandy mix. But NPO is nothing new to me. I've had food and drink stricken on many hospitalizations, sometimes for as long as a week. It's a monotonously intractable period, days strung together with the sameness of insomnia, until finally, gratefully, it's party time and a meal is served to celebrate the erasure of those three alphabetically dyslexic letters—a meal that has been imagined during NPO as a tango on the tongue, a mouth dance seasoned by the allure of an anticipated seduction.

During previous NPOs, my acute medical problems receded as the first washes of dumb pleading hunger took the shape of specific food cravings. When visions of Entenmann's airy Rich Frosted Donuts, or Totonno's crisped brick-oven thin-crust pizza, or tart glasses of Newman's lemonade filled my sensual obsession, I knew my head and gut were operating in sync, crooning to each other in the song of reunited lovers, and I was hungry for discharge. Desire—for food, for sex, for breathing unfettered air—is the patient's most vital sign. Yet the desire index is the one that is paradoxically missing from medical tests.

As a therapeutic prescription, NPO is barbaric and counter-intuitive. When you get sick, you turn to food for healing: Give me chicken soup, hot tea, a shot of Glenfiddich. Give me pepper-mint, fresh root ginger, my buddy Geoffrey's penetrating mulled cider, any remedy with the natural properties to cure what ails. Recovery without food is inhuman. It starves the essential impulse that makes us both live to eat and eat to live. In my hunger for a prosaic chocolate donut, desire is a life force more potent than the most powerful prescribed infusion. Desire, as it has been said, is the opposite of death. Nurse, forget the iron drip, just bring me a burger.

For the famished convalescent, tearing off the NPO tag like an ice-cream wrapper is victory over sickness, triumph over medicine. It's a welcome-home to the food rites and normalcy of human experience, my human experience: the Friday-night tacos and cold Coronas and all the excited talk over dinner about the ski trip to Matt and Ellen's.

In the hospital bed, though, inexplicably, hunger and crav-ing don't press on my nerves. My brain isn't incubating donut pictures. Even the burnt-rubber aroma of J.P.'s reheated din-ner plate doesn't stir me. Something's wrong with my drained pipes, and I'm worried. Impatiently, I strain again to roll in bed, urging the intestinal movement that will usher me back.

My half of the room has no view. It's a cell without a win-dow to offer the humanizing distraction of city sights. Presum-ably, it is night, judging by the shift-change commotion at the nurses' station outside the door. I haven't seen daylight since my ambulance joyride. The dayless, hourless hospital corners are a disorienting confinement, like being trapped in a casino after losing everything fast—down and out in Caesar's Palace, that was my inaugural trip to Las Vegas. Inside the dark hall, nothing ever changed, no one ever moved, and the world outside seemed to disappear. I sat on a stool and stared at the slots without a coin to change my luck.

This afternoon Susan brought the book I was reading, but my arms are too weak and encumbered to lift it. With Entenmann's fantasies unformed, I shut my eyes and try to visualize something to soothe me out of worry, maybe the early sun casting on the lake beside my parents' house in Maine. Susan summoned it as her special place during Teddy's birth, though she said the image did nothing to ease the agony. Frustratingly, I know what the picture should look like, but I can't see it. No lake.

Instead, in the void, I hear Dr. Paz's voice speaking to me in the pre-operating room on the path to surgery.

"A stool blockage formed in your small intestine and tore a perforation in the intestinal wall. The rupture in the ileum occurred where stricturing had formed in an area of acute active disease at the site of resection. Since the moment the perforation opened the small bowel, bacteria has been pooling in your abdomen, causing peritonitis. It's an unusual scenario. We'll have to operate immediately."

She presents this concise clinical diagnosis in a large square of a room where my gurney rests alone, having been wheeled from the combustion of the ER. *A stool blockage?* Undone by my own shit. A fitting epitaph.

Of the various possibilities I considered in the previous

hours, perforation is the worst, and I hinge up on my elbows to look directly at the doctor. She stands with her back to me, studying X-rays. Equipped for medical proofs and consultation, the room's perimeter is lined with light boxes above a ring of computer stations. The layout suggests a command center, the kind of data-driven chamber that makes the television news during coverage of natural disasters, or the interior of a B-movie spaceship. Maybe there really is an alien life-form inhabiting my stomach. "People of Earth, this shit looks bad."

CT scans of my ruptured gut—the exploded perforation, the accreted strictures—shade one wall of light boxes. Clouds of photopositive loops define the murky images. The surgeon's lead hand addresses my personal gallery of gut-wrenched crosscuts, gesturing deliberately to identify the agents of emergency trauma exposed in milky backlit swirls, either for my benefit or for hers, I'm not sure. As with the other body blows that hit me today, the news comes startlingly fast and with devastating impact. I'd been hoping for a mere false alarm, but this worst-case diagnosis kills a desperate hope—now emphatically a delusion—I have clung to like an airplane seat cushion since the trouble began.

Presently, it is approaching midnight, about twelve hours since the "unusual scenario," as characterized by the doctor, flattened me and led me to the spacey abyss of this room, plunging me from relatively good health to the business end of a shit joke. Compounding the trauma of the perforation and the spilling of my guts is the "active disease" she referred to, the knots of narrow channels in the CT scan leaking radioactive contrast into a mottled intestinal sea. The combination of perforation and disease intensifies the degree of the emergency.

While "operate immediately" still registers with shock, I am floating on the draft of blessed sedation, lulled to listen and watch, processing only pieces of my new reality. I'm outside myself again, the way I was on the living room rug, watching the old home movies of flying-saucer blintzes. The catastrophic consequences of the emergency—for eating, drinking, working, parenting, marriage, sex; in short, living—are sidelined somewhere outside this room, and I observe the medical picture show above me, detached from the main act like a spectator. The X-ray mural appears to me as if captured from an otherworldly body. Instead of my guts, I see in its figures galaxy formations, like the planetarium ceiling projections that the boys and I gaped at, tilted in our cinema chairs during the Christmas holiday. My insides are the Milky Way, foreign matter suspended in the hole of deep space. Situated between ER and OR, I'm in a way station where the familiar continuum of time that grounds my thinking—*Why did this happen? What will be next?*—has vaporized. Aside from the doctor's measured voice, the room is silent, its smell neutralized, a vacuum of open space. The agonizing pain of my breached gut has been numbed, and I drift passively across a temporal wasteland between the known past and an inconceivable future.

Play Fascination. What a sensation. World's greatest creation. Thrill of a nation. Across the street from the BMT station.

The doctor's flagging hands return to my field of vision, and I see how small they are and how tiny she is in the room's warehouse dimensions. The sight unsettles me. Reflexively, I measure her against my regular surgeon, Dr. Eberhardt, who operated on me ten years prior. Eberhardt is Paz's complete physical

opposite. He's a man of prodigious appetite and inflated proportions who would eclipse her at the light box. His hands are
outrageously enormous mitts, slabs of fists like Sonny Liston's
revered hams—meaty and inexplicably laced with the scabs of
what appear to be fresh cuts. The disparity between the pair
of whopping, punished, sausage-fingered hands and the delicate cutting his profession demands always mystified me but
somehow also inspired belief in his stature and skill. As far as
I'm concerned, tonight is no occasion for subbing the headliner
with the understudy. However, regrettably, alarmingly, Dr. Meat
Hands will not be the slicer in the operating theater tonight.
This is not where I wanted to be.

My usual hospital—the one where Eberhardt reigns, where my
gastroenterologist, internist, urologist, hematologist, and radiologist practice, where my medical history fills a database, where Dr.
Crohn endowed the disease, the world's leading research facility for my particular dose of trouble—declined my ambulance
driver's request, and my pleading, to deliver me to the ER. Apparently, hospitals can do this, even though Dr. Abrams, the gastroenterologist, called ahead to have me admitted. It seems that the
ER was glutted with other sickies, and they have the right to turn
away patients who've decided to spin by in an ambulance. As I
learned, if I had just walked in on my own, they would have been
required to admit me. But if I could have walked in, I wouldn't
have needed the ambulance to take me to the ER, now would I?

The hospital's ill-timed pulling of their velvet rope complicates George W. Bush's assertion that Americans can just go to
emergency rooms for medical treatment. Technically, he would
have been more correct to say Americans can go to *some* emer-

gency rooms. W.'s claim also, conveniently, ignored the patient
experience that all ERs and the hospitals to which they are
attached are not created equal. I first experienced this unnerv-
ing truth during W.'s father's presidency, when I was living in
Washington and was taken to an ER about a mile from the Oval
Office due to an attack of uncontrollable fever, diarrhea, vomiting, and the shakes. The attending physician worked diligently
to have me acknowledge that I was HIV-positive, a condition
with some symptoms common to the ones wracking me. After
contending with him for several hours, I checked myself out and
took a taxi to another hospital.

Now, having been denied admittance by my medical home away
from home, there's no choice but to cast my lot in this untested
hospital with the tiny young surgeon. I have nowhere else to go.

Or do I? Scared patients can rationalize away any incident or
symptom no matter the severity. Why, just this morning I waited
for two hours after my guts exploded to call my doctor. From the
gurney in pre-op, I speak by cell phone with Dr. Abrams, who is
awake at home, aware of the bureaucratic barrier at his hospital and trying to help. Since he's not affiliated with this neighborhood joint, he can't set foot in the place or treat me, but
we can speak. I have him confer with the surgeon, then Susan,
who's allowed in the room and hands me the phone. Quickly, he
disabuses me of my concocted scenario to wait out this ordeal,
unclamp myself, get in a cab, and crawl through the ER doors
of capricious Mount Save Me. He corroborates that immediate
surgery is imperative, building his case on the strength of some
startling news: "You're on the verge of developing sepsis. You're
at a dangerously high risk. There's no other way to stop the bac-

teria flooding your abdomen. If you don't have surgery now, it could spread to the bloodstream and kill you."

He speaks faster than in our routine office conversations and concludes with the dead pause of certainty. His urgency stops the escape fantasy cold. "I see. Thank you, Dr. Abrams. Sorry to trouble you so late."

In this state, I turn my desperate body over to the stranger standing beside me, a medical lifeline of appealing eyes consuming an unlined oval face, and the encouraging surname Paz.

Susan and I say our good-byes in the tiled OR that's empty except for the core staff roused to assist a surgery we're told will last well into the morning. Having made it this far from my panic on the living room floor, I'm hoping for the best and refrain from introducing farewell drama. Neither of us wants to think that this could be the end. The critical nature of my situation goes unspoken, and we pretend to ignore the present danger. I am aware that we have never made out a will, despite discussing it many times. It always seems like a good idea, the kind of thing responsible people do, such as regrouting the kitchen sink every couple of years, but then one of us has to get Teddy out of the shower or work on Finn's penmanship or wash the dinner dishes. Talking about death in the abstract can wait.

Now is not the time to die. Susan buffers me, presenting the face of faith in her way. It's a strength of hers, an expression more outwardly hopeful than my own, and she steers our good-bye to mundane details. The emotions are implicit. We could be having this conversation as the subway doors close.

"Good luck. I'll come by in the morning," she says, resting

her ring hand on the operating table's edge. "I'm so tired. I hope I don't have to wait too long for the bus."

"Honey, forget about the bus. It's too late. Just take a cab, and don't worry about it. By the way, Teddy has pitching tryouts for West Side Little League at nine thirty, so you'll have to take him. It's at the school on West End and Eighty-second."

Susan is a tall woman, but I'm not used to her towering over me. I see that the tears she's swept during the day's ordeal have striped her girlie cheeks like finger paint. She's laboring to keep her eyelids open. Her eyes are bloodshot, veined red to the dark fleck in her left iris, the scar from a childhood accident. Sitting on a boat dock, she was whacked by the flying handle of a waterskiing tow. The impact left her with a severe blind spot. It's an impairment she never complains about.

She still carries the schoolbooks and paper bag from this afternoon. "Don't forget to eat the éclairs," I say. "It's cold. They should still be good."

"They are good," she updates me, coy and familiar. "I ate one when they took you for the CT scan."

"O most pernicious woman." A nurse lifts my head to roll on the bathing-beauty cap and prong an air hose into my nostrils. She's silent and must be tired, too. This is it. "Is it after midnight?" I ask Susan.

"I don't know. Why? You've got someplace to go?"

"It's Valentine's Day," I realize. "Your present is in my top dresser drawer."

Lying on the operating table, stabilized by our ordinary conversation, I'm comfortable. I have no sensation of pain or even the expected aches of exertion or hunger, given how many hours

I've been in free fall. I am adrift on a life raft, receiving the pleasure of peace, before losing myself to the anesthesia filtering in.

———

"Jon, are you awake?" J.P. has pulled open the bed curtain and sits on the office-surplus vinyl chair with his leg cast elevated on the bed. He pushes away the dinner tray like bad news. I get the feeling he's in the mood to talk.

"I am," I stumble. "I was hallucinating. It must be the morphine. I heard my surgeon's voice, and I was remembering the operation. I guess I survived, unless this is hell. Do you know what time it is?"

"It is night, about eight thirty. It's early. Maybe we should go out?"

"I like the way you think." I elevate the bed to eye level. I'd like to see the black sky, but there's no clear shot to J.P.'s window. "Sure, that sounds like fun. Just let me get my kids to sleep." I've got cotton mouth, and the words draw out like pulled teeth. The room light is sharp.

"Your wife, Susan, she said you have two boys. Will I get to meet them?"

"I think so. Susan said she might bring them tomorrow. I know she's afraid of them getting scared by the sight of me."

"They are young, yes?"

"Yes, six and nine years old. They've never seen anything like this. We do a pretty effective job of sheltering them from my health problems and the other issues. They're kids; they shouldn't have to worry."

J.P. gives that an approving nod. "My girlfriend, she wants to have a baby, she says, but I can't imagine what that will do."

"It will change everything." I grin, and my dry lips crack at the stretch. Vaseline must cost extra in this place. "You'll start to think that eight thirty is someone's bedtime. Every expecting parent says he won't change, but the kids have other plans. There is an upside, though—you also won't be out late at a restaurant getting your leg broken."

"Ah, this is a plus." J.P. mugs like a hammy actor and flashes a good-looking smile. His face is angularly handsome, a classic Gaul profile creased deep beneath the cheeks, long nose, his hair dark and wavy, thrown back from a flat forehead like he's riding without a helmet. His expressions dart from high to low like a boy's, maybe a liability in his job as a blue-jeans wholesaler. At sixty, he'll still be debating with a girlfriend whether or not to have a child. "No more bad times at Capri."

"Your accident happened at Capri? I ate there once, many years ago, before Teddy was born." I perk up at the memory.

"The food was good?"

"Superb. We took my in-laws for dinner, or rather, they took us. Susan's parents, they live in Indiana and were visiting. It was a Saturday night. We sat upstairs."

"By the fireplace?"

"Yes. It was February, and the fire was blazing. We were seated at the table closest to the fireplace, and my poor father-in-law sat with his back to it. He wore a wool blazer that got so hot it almost melted on him. By the end of dinner, he was stripped to his shirtsleeves. When the chef came to our table to tell us the night's menu, Bernie, Susan's father, asked if he stuffed the sausages himself. The chef—what's his name? Paul something—looked so insulted I thought he was going to throw Bernie into the fire."

J.P.'s face sours in disgust. "These restaurant people. Who do they think they are, treating customers like firewood?" His accent grants the indignation a worthy-sounding pedigree.

"It was okay. Bernie lived to tell the tale of the night he crossed a celebrity chef. He still talks about it. It's the perfect country-mouse story for his clients. I remember the sausages were so good and smoky. Sad to say, we've never been back."

"Grilled sausage and lentils, I think. Yes, that is not bad. You are hungry, talking about the food?" J.P. curls his toes sticking out of the cast.

"I should be. But I can't taste what I'm saying."

An object drops from J.P.'s lap to the floor, but he leaves it. No one moves to pick things up in this room.

"Tell me, what do you see out the window?" I ask. "I can't picture where we are."

"Lots of lights. Some of the city. The cathedral is close, but it is dark."

"We must be facing south."

"Yes. We get the morning sun. So much brighter in New York. I don't even want shades in my apartment. That's what keeps me here, you know, the light. It's certainly not the cathedrals. We have enough of them in France."

Picked-over dinner trays stacked on carts roll and clatter in the hall. Chinging metal in the trapped air. I'm still in Caesar's Palace.

"I used to work with Brits, and they always said the same thing about the light. But that Greek Revival cathedral out the window? You must admit, it's a worthy replica of what you have at home."

"If you like that kind of thing, a copy. Like Cameron Diaz, maybe." J.P. laughs at his joke, and I hear what could be a smoker's rasp. I've noticed he sometimes touches his right hand to his mouth, as if he's lost a cigarette.

"It's a less oppressive building now that the scaffold is gone," I appeal. I can't look outside, so I talk up a substitute, lying prone in the therapy position. "They gave up, you know. The scaffold was kept up in the hope that the stonecutting could be finished someday on the tower. I guess a hundred years ago that made sense, but the stonecutters all died before the carving was complete. For a while, the cathedral was trying to train new stonecutters. I talked to a guy in the bishop's office once about doing the training."

"This would be job security, yes? Why didn't you do it?"

"There weren't enough interested cutters, so the diocese finally accepted that the stone would stand uncut, forever unfinished. The scaffold just came down a few months ago. It's my favorite thing that happens in New York, when scaffolding comes down. The light comes out, and it's like the buildings are reborn." J.P. seems unmoved by my rapture. His hand searches his mouth for the cigarette, and I think of Jean-Paul Belmondo invoking Bogie. Our conversation is waking me up. "You see everything again that you forgot existed."

"The scaffolding is everywhere. I think New York would fall down without it."

I'm still touring what I can't see. "They keep peacocks on the cathedral grounds strutting around. When the boys were little I would take them to see the birds on Thursdays, after the farmers' market on Broadway. The white ones and the others with that amazing iridescent blue on the plumage. They make terrifying noises when they spread their tails, though, like they're possessed. It scared the shit out of the kids."

J.P. strains to reach under his chair and grabs the fallen object. He raises a book by its paper cover for me to see. "I heard that you did not sleep last night. I am finished with this book, if you would like to read it. Do you like mysteries?"

"That's so thoughtful of you. I wish I could. I can't fall asleep without reading, but I don't even have the strength to hold the book. Maybe tomorrow night."

Again, night comes and I can't sleep. I'm uncomfortable. My lower back hurts from too much time in the same position; my arms are sore from the IVs; the urinary catheter pricks me where I live; edema has swelled my joints to marshmallows; and I ache from terrible distention in my gut. I'm hopeful the stomach bloating is the prelude to the long-awaited first movement of the Motility Symphony.

J.P. is snoring, and I hear a party coming from the hall, amped by the hammer thumps of rap music. Somebody's having a good time. I buzz the nurse and ask for a sleeping pill, but she refuses the request. It's past the window for sleeping meds, and she's short with me. "The doctor left no instructions for sleep. You can talk to her in the morning."

She goes back to the party, and I am soon surprised by neither prelude nor symphony but an unexpected blast of gastro dissonance: diarrhea. Though I have consumed nothing but memories of food over the past seventy-two hours, I evacuate an explosive flow, then ten more episodes through the night, of scary-colored sand sifting out of my ass in the room's toilet. On the first four runs I race to unplug the snaked IV-pump cord from the wall outlet and schlep the pole and bags to the bathroom, clumsily navigating the chair and tables clotting the narrow space. Eventually, I spend the rest of the night on the seat. Nurse Lee, the attending supervisor with the sweet pudding face, lights the room at five o'clock to check vitals and finds me there. She takes my temperature, then takes it again to be sure. The thermometer registers 104°F. My dirty hospital gown is soaked. I am nauseated, and, though empty as a ruin, I vomit. "What is wrong with you?" she asks and leads me back to the bed.

Seven o'clock brings the surgical team on their rounds, and I share the good news, provoking an internal discussion short on the optimism that fed the previous days' visits.

Avocado Gal crashes the conference, rolling J.P.'s breakfast tray past the doctors, and the team takes its business to the hall. J.P. is undone by the first taste of charred coffee. "Oh, shit. It can't be. Swamp mud tastes better. This one is trying to kill me." The orderly shuffles out of the room without looking at me. "Man, you don't know how lucky you are."

A junior team doctor comes back in the room. He must have drawn the short straw. At the time of the surgery, due to the presence of peritonitis, Dr. Paz decided to leave the incision area as an open wound in case further infection necessitated medical access. I've been told it will take several months for new skin to grow and close the hole. Now my suddenly percolating bowel symptoms warrant a look at my insides.

Dr. Patel, a young guy with large features on a kind face, strips away the saturated dressing, and I see my opened self for the first time. I have an enormous hole, a wide trench an inch deep carved from a point north of my circumvented belly button south to the edge of my groin, like the club-roll work of a Katz's counterman. Horror-movie carnage. Again, foolishly, I compare this to what I know. Unlike Dr. Meat Hands' relatively modest, stapled, closed cut of ten years ago, this gash is a beast, and the impact strikes hard. It seems the surgery is unfinished, and I've awakened before the end. I should look away, but I navel-gaze further at the cratered mess of raw flesh and discharge as the resident flushes and fills the gory cavity with fresh gauze. He goes about the gruesome business in bracing silence, and I mirror his stony quiet through the anatomy lesson. Presumably, he's concentrating on the delicate maneuver of packing the exposed substrata of dermis, or he's staying composed to stanch my freak-out at seeing the disconnected tissue. Poor guy. Yesterday after rounds, we had an eaters' chat about the sloppy pizza in the joint next to the residents' dorm. His voice is pitched like a teakettle whistle, but he's not talking now.

The wound is repulsive. I'm repulsive. This is a new degree of brutality, a new exposure.

Strangely, though, I believe I've seen the jagged contour of this gulf inside me before. The scalpel's outline reveals the topographical form of our lake in Maine, as charted on the map hanging on the wall by the boys' bunk beds—oblong, asymmetrical, narrowed at the ends, with a small pond orphaned in the north by a causeway of skin, a pool bulging the middle. That ten-mile body of water was glacier-formed twenty-five thousand years ago and has yet to close. The chiseled shape is familiar, and I'm shaken by the incongruous sight grafted onto the plain of my stomach. "Jesus Christ, why is Thompson Lake carved into me?" I mutter.

I think it's the shock of morphed recognition that's most disturbing, like seeing a fist in an inkblot, or looking closer at the clump of rubbish moving on the subway tracks and discovering a crawling rat, or when I'm sitting on the dock in Maine gazing up at swaying birch-tree leaves pressed against the dusk only to jump when they emerge as a rustling swarm of bats.

Dr. Patel examines the red mass with his gloved hands and shows no outward sign of alarm or suspicion. Whatever is causing my body to skip motility and go straight to the runs must be hiding elsewhere. Methodically, he stretches white tape over the shaved spot of skin where our house would stand on the shore of my empty lake. Jerking my head for another view dislodges the breathing tube pronging my nostrils. I retreat back into a clammy pillow.

Over the next few days, my health gets worse. Motility and peristalsis never blow their gassy horn, and the diarrhea, fever, and nausea continue rampaging like blood sport, gutting my strength and slimming me to a reed. I have a sore on my right hand from repeatedly unplugging the IV motor for anxious toilet sprints. It would make more sense to move my bed into the john.

"Dr. Paz, what's wrong?" I ask during morning rounds after another sleepless, spewing night.

"I suppose we always have to worry about infection," she says somewhat breezily through a small smile. Her teeth are a brilliant white. "However, I would be very surprised if that were the case. I have a feeling this will pass, but you'll have a CT scan today. If that comes out clean, we can think about sending you home."

Sending me home?

I know how terrible I feel, so discharge sounds like patent nonsense, though I can't help but be encouraged by the prospect of getting out of this place while I'm still breathing.

It proves to be wishful thinking. The CT scan shows a large pool of infection as the high fever's cause. A bacterial abscess has collected at the area of the anastomosis—the joint where the surgeon connected the small intestine's two surviving ends in a kiss—and a catheter is inserted in my gut to drain the dirty pond into a gallon-size bag hung from a spigot poking out my right side. Due to the bag's dodgy siting, the tape used to form a seal around the spigot can't be fully secured, and this faulty drainage tube is added to the plumber's list of pieces of me that are defiantly leaking. I'm a river dammed with sealing wax. The bed and I have to be changed every hour, which really endears me to the nursing staff.

I call Dr. Abrams about my metastasizing problems. He doesn't know of any gastro specialist on staff who can intervene with the surgical team. It's clear to me that this bunch is stumped, and there's a more serious mystery inside my gut than what they've considered. The longer I'm in this hospital, the more my health becomes a losing game of pickup sticks; with every move, another stick in the pile is disturbed and falls. I'm slipping away, a position that troubles my sleepless nights with doom, and I prevail upon Susan to take on the arduous job of persuading our insurance company to approve my transfer to Mount Save Me. It's next to impossible for her to make phone calls from school, but there's no one else who can do this. My health is at the mercy of a cubicle death panel. I've got to move.

Five, six, pickup sticks.

The weekend comes, and the doctors and nurses who've been supervising my decline leave. I hate weekends in the hospital. The wards empty into desolation, and you know that nothing is going to be done for your problems. Only the barest, most cursory maintenance medical attention will be provided. In my current state, I'm looking at forty-eight hours of untreated suffering. Just holding on is the best hope.

True to form, the sole doctor who shows is a hawk-faced Russian with chilling black eyes and the suspicion of a jailer. He has me take a drug I stopped using years ago, and I continue coming unsewn, draining like a spaghetti strainer. It's another blind try that doesn't stop the slide, and the doctor disappears on Sunday night. What's worse, J.P. has been discharged and replaced by a guy who's driving me crazy, a shut-in with a shiny head like a soaked lima bean, a twenty-four-hour-a-day TV habit, and a cell-phone itch. He repeats the same stories and mossy jokes incessantly to an indulgent calling list. "So I say, 'But, Doc, my *left* knee is the one that's busted.'" I've heard that ripsnorter ten times since dinner. *CSI* and reality shows about obese weepers competing to lose weight blare from the set.

I should find this funny, at least in a perverse way—the freak roommate and the fatties who eat half a meat locker by lunchtime and then cry on the scale. I remember one Christmas I spent in a hospital bed, the year that "Feed the World" was on MTV round the clock over the holiday. The British pop stars were singing their lungs out, I watched the whole world marshaling to send food to the starving Africans, and I was NPO, ready to kill for the forbidden chocolate donut. The joke was lost on me. My sense of humor is gone again.

The Oscars are on, and I try to watch. The diversion will probably do me good. A friend is nominated for Original Screenplay, and Susan and I had party plans, but the teary podium platitudes are no match for the drug-dealer mayhem blasting from my roomie's TV. New York is getting blown to smithereens. Appeals get me nowhere, and *CSI* rules the room. I shut off the Oscars and, absurdly, attempt to sleep. Under the best circumstances, I'm not a great sleeper. Now, diarrhea spills out of me, the abscess bag leaks, and the stalled distention has my belly pipes stretched tighter than a Capri sausage. And I'm freezing. The cold took hold of me a few days ago. A vented ceiling tile blows air-conditioned drafts down on my head. I'm wrapped tight in the thin cotton blankets Susan found in linen supply, and the fleece comforter she brought from home, and my down jacket, which she added to the pile this afternoon. Still, I can't get warm.

I'm miserable in this leaky limbo and decide to force the situation, ignoring the foolish risk I'm about to undertake. I bring my arms up from the IV tangle, peel away the bedcovers, and attack my gut, pressing my fingers on the bandages, massaging the raw tissue of the open wound, trying to get my stomach to remember its duty, to pass the basketball in me before I explode like George the Pig. I address my entire middle, gently at first, as if I'm kneading biscuit dough. The big hole under the dressing is both tender and numb, like the nerve endings have been cut, so it's hard to gauge how much pressure is right. I knead the area more, still cautiously, and scissor my hips and legs in a vain attempt to siphon a blast out of the full tank of gas. The tubes running out of me swing at the bedside like jump ropes. I press harder. I'm working myself over with both hands, now angrier, a deep-tissue massage going hysterical. I'm in a fight, hammering at my useless gut like a punching bag, and then it becomes something more. Suddenly, I'm tearing at my insides. I'm a crazed animal with broken glass in its chewed meat. "Come on, come on, you sick piece of shit. Do something. Are you dead already?" I'm storming in the bed; my down coat's zipper bangs against the IV pole. Nothing changes. The glass is still in me. I stop my hands. I'm shaking. I'm cold. I'm ashamed. Pain sears my gut. Christ, I hope I didn't pull the stitches loose. My roommate tells the wrong-knee joke again.

Sometime Sunday night I actually doze off. I fall quickly into a scorched-earth nightmare. There is an apocalypse that I alone survive in a destroyed city. X-shaped towers burn in the skyline of my subconscious like crossed hands, quaking and colliding. As I walk empty streets, there's no sign of life, no people, no cars, no food in the torched storefronts. Lost among the strange ruins, I stand at the center of a decimated intersection wondering where I am and what has happened. The crumbled pavement collapses beneath me, and I'm pulled waist-deep into a sinkhole. Everywhere, the landscape is a charred mountain range of rubble, like in the newsreels of firebombed Dresden. Curtain walls of ash. A street grave. Then movement. From the corner of a burned-out shell, a figure appears. I'm trapped in the crushed pavement, unable to free myself, when the figure nears, blank-faced. I'm unsure. It closes in fast and strikes me, strikes me again, pounding with bare fists, the blows get harder, violent, the blood is everywhere . . .

I awake screaming like a siren. A light shaft splits the dark hospital room. The TV angled down from my roommate's raised shelf glows with the gruesome images of an autopsy in process, a dead body pulled open like a duffel bag. *CSI.* Sweet dreams. I've been nightmaring on my back, passing air through an empty mouth hung open in a rictus like a corpse's. I've got to cut myself off from the morphine. My mouth is parched like a wasteland. I'm so thirsty. But I'm NPO and know the rules. I roll my tongue against the peaked roof of my mouth and work up a gulp of saliva.

In the morning I'm visited by a staff psychiatrist. My midnight siren screams reached the nurses' station, and when I copped to my massage mania it put me in a new class of illness. On first impression, Dr. Singh is a suave and disarming provocateur, an elegant man of about forty, I'd guess, wearing an impeccable goatee that brackets a professionally inscrutable mouth. He faces me and sits with dignified formality in the crummy chair wedged at the foot of the bed, maintaining the decorum of concentration despite the rattle of gunshots firing from the neighboring TV.

"Are you a threat to yourself?" he asks, getting quickly to the mandatory safety question. I don't know how to answer. Even if I wanted to kill myself, I don't have the strength, freedom of movement, or tools to do it.

"Physically, no," I say.

The doctor writes on his pad with a black Mont Blanc in a fluid hand and looks up expectantly when he reaches the end of his note.

"Things have gotten harder from year to year. My health, my career, my family's finances. I try. I want things to be better, but they only get worse. I mean, look at me. Like death on a soda cracker. Nothing I've done to change things has worked, and here I am."

I'm silent in the bed while he writes. It's a grim confession and a frightening opener. For the first time, I see the prospect of the family without me and begin to believe that they would be better off. Susan is young, beautiful, charming, and accomplished. The kids have the world ahead of them. I've been failing for years, and this current situation is a severe plunge down the slope. Appendage to the misery of a permanent patient is not the life anyone wished for, and it's certainly not what I want for my family.

"Have you seen your family while you've been in the hospital?"

"Yes. My wife's been in every day. My parents and sister have come. My children were here yesterday for the first time."

"You must have been happy to see them." Singh strikes me as a cagey guy, in a clever way. It's been nearly twenty years since I faced off with a therapist, and his cool cadence is having the effect of surprising my thoughts, like I'm a step behind the beat. He crosses one creased pant leg over the other. Cuffed gabardine.

"I was. I miss them. My wife and I thought it was the right time to demystify my being in the hospital. They've been sheltered from it and shuttled around since I got sick, and they know something's wrong."

"And what happened?"

"It didn't go well." A fusillade of bullets fires over chilling screams. A commercial for foot-long subs. The TV is so loud.

Of course it spooked them, seeing me here, tied down in tubes, bandaged, monitored by beeping machines, not eating when the food tray passed by the room. No kid wants to see his parent sick, and I worry about the feelings of susceptibility and abandonment my situation is forcing on them, no matter how hard Susan tries to orchestrate a new routine. I worry about what my problems are doing to them. They're old enough to see and feel things and young enough to be damaged.

Teddy was just six months old the last time I was in the hospital for surgery, so they're not prepared for this—though I don't suppose anyone ever is. My last operation happened during Halloween week. I remember because Susan brought Teddy dressed in a bumblebee costume, striped black and yellow with fluttering antennae and wings. He was an adorable, slobbering joy, a living prop delighting me, the nurses, and anyone who came to the room. Susan told me that Teddy was entranced by the hospital's revolving-glass door; its motion wound him like a giant jack-in-the-box. He clamored to be raised up to watch the different people spin in from the door. Every turn of the glass produced a surprise entrance and a corresponding shriek from the midget bee, his fabric wings bobbing at each new face. At that age, the hospital was an adventure. He visited every day.

Yesterday, however, the boys were confused. Finny tried to jump in bed and hug me when he first saw me, and Susan had to pull him back. Teddy bugged Susan to give him change for a vitaminwater. I asked how he did at the pitching tryouts, but he acted spacey and distracted, familiar signs when he doesn't want to talk. He mostly looked away, his soulful eyes aimed toward the door. There's no place for the boys to run around, and they had to keep their voices down. They're kids; they got bored. I never found out about the baseball.

After they left, Teddy told Susan that I talked in a weak voice, and he asked if I was in a coma. I'm upset that he's pulling away. Already, he's been too-soon pre-adolescent this year, and my being sick isn't going to bring us any closer—the father who's in a coma, the father who can't do anything. I've seen this with a buddy of mine, Carmine, who's in bad shape. I keep him company on a bench while our boys play.

Teddy and Finn kept their coats on the whole time, obviously wanting to leave, and looked a little messy. Finn had a rash on his chin from chewing his coat collar.

"I don't think they'll be coming back," I tell the doctor.

Rubber soles squeak on the floor, and the conversation halts. I have a visitor.

"Mom, hi. What time is it? I thought you were coming in the afternoon."

"Hello, dear. I'm picking the boys up after school today, and I won't be able to visit then. I need to leave before I hit traffic at the bridge. Besides," she says breathlessly, "I found a great parking space by your apartment and walked over." She takes off cabled wool gloves and a barn coat and folds them in her arms over her purse, ready to settle in. My mother's cheer is a break from the tone of the session, but Dr. Singh doesn't move from his perch. He's got more questions.

"This is Dr. Singh, Mom. He's a psychiatrist."

"Oh. Hello, Doctor." He barely acknowledges her, and I suggest that she might want to sit in the lounge. "All right. Why don't I go for a walk and come back in a few minutes?"

My mother leaves with her things, and the doctor asks if I've ever been treated for depression. He asks about my medical history. He asks about my medications. He asks about my family history.

I tell him I'm the product of my parents' yin and yang; that the present situation has exaggerated their poles of light and dark; that the three of us revert to our ancient roles when they're sitting by my hospital bed, to the point of caricature; that they're too old to be still dealing with my shit; that being sick is infantilizing. He asks about being NPO. He asks about food. He asks about sex. His voice never changes volume. An ambassador of mental diplomacy.

Perhaps too soon for him, there's scurried movement in the doorway, and my mother is back in the room. She waves an item bought in the sad hospital gift shop on her quick trip. It's a large yellow smiley-face Mylar balloon, bobbing like an apple atop a long plastic neck. Dr. Singh sits unmoved, his dark hands on the notebook, but this feel-good product of my mother's shopping spree can't be lost on him. If he doubted my cartoonish family-profile sketch, this surely corroborates half of it.

My mother plants the balloon by the stem into the floral foam of an empty flower vase on the bedside table and regards both of us with determined optimism. "Just look at this," she says.

CHAPTER 3

The air snaps cold and smells like a garage, but it's liberating to be outside, if only for the short moments I'm wheeled from the hospital's sliding exit doors to the gypsy ambulance. My belongings are bagged in my lap. I wish the grouch pushing my chair would roll me to the park and leave me there in the night air where the sky is blackberry dark. I bet you can even see stars. On a clear night I can make out the Big Dipper from our kitchen window when I can't sleep and I'm up noshing on marble pound cake and fruit. One of the seemingly inconsequential but disabling things you lose in the hospital is the ability to talk about the weather—it's more than just an icebreaker. I give it a shot: "This is the first time I've seen the sky in more than two weeks. The air is so cold I can see my breath—look at that. It feels great. You know, I'd be just as happy if you dropped me in the park."

My nature babble draws nothing but the exhaust rattailing from my mouth, and I'm strapped down in the well of the van. Grouchy steps on the gas. We pull away from the hospital's concrete awning into the dark. I'm moving.

By the end of my stay, Dr. Paz and the others were clearly resigned that something was inexplicably, drastically wrong, something beyond their capacity to fix, though they were peeved by my effort to get the hell out of their care. Doctors don't necessarily remember the patients they've saved, but they never forget the ones they've lost, and I was bringing down the team's win-loss percentage.

Susan succeeded in getting me transferred to Mount Save Me. Our insurer placed me in the "catastrophic" category and approved my request for transfer as "medically necessary," so it shouldn't have been a difficult case to make. Yet for eleven days, Susan called, documented, faxed, re-called, redocumented, and refaxed before, finally, I am riding at two in the morning on a seven-hundred-and-forty-dollar drive across the park. Another shining example of the world's finest healthcare system working efficiently and in the patient's best interest. After years of battling insurance companies and hemorrhaging money, I've concluded that the only people who don't see the need for health insurance reform in this country have either never been sick, never been hospitalized, never lost their job, work for private insurers, or are just bastards. Don't underestimate the prick factor when it comes to changing social policy.

I'm grateful to Susan for handling this monster that came to dominate our days. On her recent visits, I obsessed about the stymied hospital transfer and heaped more pressure on her, which was particularly helpful the day she misplaced the file holding all the insurance phone numbers. The ordeal has been great for our marriage. I thanked her on the phone tonight after the order came through, but she was too busy to talk. Well, she can cross one agony off the list.

Along with contributing to my continued decline, this latest bureaucratic duel has frayed my relationship—another one
I'm not crazy about compromising—with Dr. Abrams, who is,
understandably, tired of the desperate phone calls and his new
role as insurance expediter. His mother didn't scrub floors for
this.

I get to the new hospital in the middle of the night to a
tiny room half occupied by a Latino old-timer who's asleep
propped-up and wearing a wool cap. He's got the window. The
night nurse settles me in and tapes the NPO sign to the door. It's
like I never left. Removal of food, removal of daylight, removal
of your own clothes. You can't help but feel that hospitals have
it backward, that they've made it their business to deny rather
than to provide.

I've come in during a quiet stretch on the overnight shift.
Nurse Sheila thoughtfully takes my comforter from the plastic bag looped on the wheelchair handle and spreads it over
the elevated bed. Despite many washings, kids' mess and picnic
grass stain the white cotton and crosshatched blue-and-yellow
diamonds. At this ungodly hour, Nurse Sheila strikes me as a
peach under a dyed mullet nest. She gossips about the price
of personal luxury in the celebrity wing across the atrium and
reassures me with a rundown of the procedures my team of doctors has scheduled for the morning.

"They've been expecting you," she says. "Dr. Abrams says
you're his sickest patient."

"I'm number one, baby," I crow.

I recline in the curtained bed through the sleepy hours before
morning rounds, cold in the Doris Day nightie that bares my

hairy stick limbs to the draft. I'm always a little homesick when I start in a new hospital room; it's an adjustment to a weird new place, like the feeling on the first day of camp. Maybe the ingrained anxiety comes from having begun my hospital tour a lifetime ago on a Thanksgiving.

I am relieved, however, to have finally made it to the right place. And I'm optimistic that whatever gremlin is sucking the crap out of me will soon be discovered. There's no clock in the dark room, but I guess it's about five. Christ, if only I'd crawled into their emergency room in the first place, by now I'd be home eating pound cake or sleeping. Stupid move.

Seven o'clock dawns, and I'm visited by Abrams; Eberhardt; Rothschild, my hematologist; and Klein, my urologist. They're concerned, but I'm heartened to see the doctors I know, and I hope that the worst is behind me. It's an abbreviated homecoming, and I'm wheeled away for a morning lab workout in search of a hole to plug.

Mount Save Me is colossal. I'm transported across sky bridges and subterranean passageways that connect a campus of massive, ugly steel and glass towers. First up, a sigmoidoscopy, a rectal poke that requires no exam prep this morning due to my perpetually evacuated state.

"Nothing like a good ol' snake up the arse to start the day right," I say to the nurse who's anesthetizing my insides with a local. It seems she's heard that one before. I'm actually looking forward to the day's tests. I want to believe in the trusted doors and their ability to figure out what's wrong. At the moment the exam nurse starts the drip, I feel like I'm on solid ground, like we're on the verge of an answer. It could be more functional denial, potent enough to erase history, but still. You start to think: *If only I could apply the power of denial to the rest of my life, I could conquer those challenges like a son of a bitch.* Denial isn't all bad. I'm not sure what good acceptance would do.

My head is pillowed on the table at an angle that allows me to see the monitor atop a wheeled cart, and I watch the reedy probe in living color. Looking at my internal organs clench and unclench like a slick puff pastry baking is entertaining for a while, until the choreography of probe and gut response plods too long over the same steps, and I want something interesting to happen. I'm waiting, the doctor leading the dance is waiting, but nothing suspicious shows in my glop.

"Do you see anything?" I ask.

"Nothing unusual."

After an hour, I get unsnaked and lose a little enthusiasm. However, there's still an upper GI series and small-bowel exam expecting me like old friends after the local wears off.

In radiology, I drink cups of horrid barium and hoist on a sliding table every thirty minutes or so to see if the radioactive fluid has worked its way down. The doctor is like a garage mechanic bathing a leaky tire, a glorified grease monkey. In between tire checks, I walk the rectangular perimeter of a glum adjacent holding room, trying to stir up the internal barium milk shake and accelerate its pour through my broken pipes. My walk cycle continues through lunchtime, around a group of beefy technicians sitting at a center table chowing on the hospital's foil-wrapped burgers and liter-size cups of Coke. They're jawing over the March Madness college basketball office pool. Hearing normal conversation about something other than pain and shit and insurance terror is refreshing, and I keep walking the loop, absorbing their received wisdom about North Carolina, Connecticut, Louisville, and Pitt.

"Can I get in on this?" I ask the round guy marking the chart with a highlighter, but it's too late. I didn't realize the tournament is already into the second round.

Every time I come to the end of the jog, I smell their food, dry meat and damp buns that sat too long under the cafeteria lamp, a cut above my radioactive pints. The bitter, gluey chalk of these barium shooters I'm gulping is the first "something by mouth" in me since the attack. They're not going down as well as a chocolate donut. After the lab guys finish their fudge-brownie desserts and deal a deck of cards, I start drinking from the third tray of tall cups and vomit standing up on my rag of a hospital gown. Smooth. The radiologist takes pity on me; he figures I've swallowed enough picture juice and helps me back to the exam room. I've been submitting to wretched GI exams for decades, and in that time of countless other medical advances, the GI procedures have remained singularly medieval.

I'm on my belly again, and the laconic radiologist is getting worn out looking for defined leaks in the viscous pictures. He takes off black-framed glasses and folds them in his pocket. "Turn to your left. A little more. Not quite so much. Hold it." Click, click, click, goes the shutter. "Breathe."

The barium vomit cakes on the front of the gown, and I'm nauseated by the overpowering, rancid smell. I have bathed, sort of, when disconnected from the IVs and catheters, wrapped in plastic baggies to keep the ports dry. But I smell bad. I smell like the hospital. It's a distinct, permeating, sick person's smell seeped into my skin, the smell of a state of being. It can't be scrubbed away, in the way that old people smell musty and babies smell sweet. When Teddy was a baby, he smelled like vanilla yogurt. I smell like rot.

There's nothing to look at in this dull exam room except the monitor behind the photo booth glass. I ask the doctor if he's picking North Carolina number one in the basketball pool, but he's not a sports fan, so the small talk dies. He has me flipping and flopping and holding my breath like we're driving past cemeteries. He finishes shooting the round and calls in another radiologist for consultation. Whoa! She's cute, dark-haired and olive-skinned with alert eyes, a poor man's Sandra Bullock, but she completely disregards me as a dying flounder on the slab. It's got to be repellent for women like her to work around guys with vomit on their gowns checking her out.

Oddly, in this basement chamber, my vomit, my odor, my scrawny frame, none of it cinches my self-consciousness the way things do in the outside world. Patients surrender their dignity upon hospital admission, and I'm as exposed as a new prisoner. Stripping down to try to sponge-bathe and shave my graying beard at the low sink in my room, I hunch naked, cadaverous, edematous, bedsored, pimpled, oily, unwashed, and bandaged. Capped tubing and baggies sag from every limb like power lines in an ice storm. It's a horrific sight, but embarrassment is, strangely, missing.

Too much of the time I've been excessively aware of my appearance, partly a consequence of the body issues that chronic illness compounds, otherwise because I'm vain. I'm not proud of it. Here, though, the clinical intimacy of exposing my body and confessing my pain stops me from caring about appearances, even in front of the cutie. I've never looked worse, and it really doesn't matter. Or, as I told Dr. Singh, the psychologist, during his velvet probing, "I used to be an asshole, then I got old and sick."

The two radiologists have the jointed camera arm bearing down on an area where I'm heavily bandaged, over the widest part of the open wound. I turn onto my belly, and they slide a wooden paddle on the table and have me roll on it back and forth. "Turn on your right hip. Back to the middle. Turn on your left. Stop breathing." Click, click, click. "Breathe." I'm reminded of the pizza maker at Totonno's coal-fired oven, paddling our margarita-fresh-basil-and-sausage pie. Teddy and Finn used to be too short to see the hole-in-the-wall oven behind the counter, and I would raise them up high, holding them the way tennis champs lift Grand Slam trophies. The radiologists' paddle presses deep into my abdomen, compressing the empty chamber like bubble wrap, and I bite down on my tongue. Well done, please.

At seven o'clock the next morning, Dr. Abrams enters my room and folds into the low-slung chair shoved between the bed and the bathroom wall. Preternaturally tan, he looks alive in the bleak light. It must be chilly out; he's dressed in a nubby wool overcoat that's unbuttoned down the middle and winged over the chair's pole arms. He opens my chart in his lap like a *Masterpiece Theater* host. His free hand rubs his salt-and-pepper brush cut, as if he's generating the internal energy to deliver a complicated story. We've known each other for fifteen years and, mostly, speak with the candor and trust cultivated by continuous treatment. When I retreat into clinical jargon,

I sound like a medical school dropout. He inhales and levels me straight in the eyes to deliver the exams' findings, but I can hear him parsing the diagnosis with conflicted reservations of hypothesis and sympathy.

"The small-bowel exam showed a fistula near the area of the anastomosis. Frankly, I was surprised by the report. This is not what I expected. I spoke with the radiologist last night and looked at the images. The fistula's there, and it's causing the diarrhea. It's like an open valve in a vulnerable area that's allowing your bile secretions to run through you."

He isn't the only one surprised. "A fistula? How could the surgeon have missed a fistula in the same area where I had the emergency surgery? I had X-rays. In the ER, they forced a tube down my throat for an emergency CT scan. I don't understand this, Gary." I reserve invoking Dr. Abrams's first name for moments such as this, when things seem particularly bad and I'm compelled to impress upon him my acute need. Informed, assertive patients get better care. That's an incontrovertible and unfortunate fact in a system where doctors see too many patients. If I am to suffer, I'll be damned if it's for lack of emphasis. My voice is sharp, and I'd slap the mattress if it made a louder bang.

But doctors, too, even one I can call Gary, have their own private code of conduct. Medicine is a brotherhood, and I've made an uncomfortable accusation: *How could the surgeon have missed this?* Dr. Abrams's tone formalizes by degrees into careful neutrality, perhaps to cover the opposing pulls of his personal doubt and professional protocol.

"I don't know," he says, his deep-set brown eyes lowering back to the chart. "The X-rays in the ER did not show the presence of a fistula when you were admitted. It's conceivable that it developed as a result of something technical that happened in the surgery."

"'Something technical?'" I pounce. "You mean a mistake? Something botched?"

The breakfast-cart rattle echoes in the hallway. Plastic-lidded trays are carried waiter-style past my door. A nurse speaks in a loud, slow voice to a confused old man at the station.

Dr. Abrams stays on the chart. "It's possible there was an inadvertent scalpel prick, or the tissue that the surgeon decided to keep didn't have the necessary integrity and a surgical staple came loose and punctured a hole. I really can't say."

My doctor is in an awkward spot between ignorance and finger pointing on the fault line of this latest unlikely calamity. I'm forced to respect his adherence to the boundaries of the brotherhood. Much as it would satisfy my anger, he has no business blaming another doctor. Dr. Abrams crosses his legs tightly over the bed corner, and I see that the braided silver clasps ornamenting his loafers are dulled from winter slush. They need polishing. What a thing to notice. He consults the three-ring binder in his lap and shows me the problem area on the X-ray film, circling the hole with silver ink. Another hole.

Knowing I've got his attention only a few minutes more, I resign my fury for the time being to focus on patching a hole. "All right, then, a fistula. I had the one ten years ago and Dr. Eberhardt closed it. I'm already here. He's here. I wasn't planning on more cutting, but he can do the surgery and fix me."

"We can't." Dr. Abrams says this quickly, as if he's been

anticipating my suggestion. His head juts toward me out of his coat collar.

"Why not?"

"I already spoke with Dr. Eberhardt. He's coming to see you again this morning, but he won't have much more to say than I have. The area of the fistula is too close to the anastomosis to operate now. There is swelling, the tissue hasn't healed, and you still have infection from the abscess."

A new Avocado Gal slings a steaming breakfast tray to my roommate's side. The guy hasn't done more than cough since I moved in, and the tray will go back untouched.

"But this diarrhea is killing me. They weighed me at radiology yesterday, and I'm down forty pounds. That's a new record."

"I know. I saw that." He flips the chart pages like a reporter's notepad and stabs one with a finger. "And your blood tests indicate plummeting protein and hemoglobin levels. I've asked Dr. Rothschild to look at you today. I'm concerned about the blood clots returning. Between the perforation trauma, the infection, the NPO, the fistula, and the active disease, you're wasting away."

Scrambled eggs, toast, and hash browns on the breakfast tray. I can smell the steam.

"Jesus, wasted syndrome, I've read about that. It's a euphemism for 'You're cooked.'" The prognosis confirms what I've felt since the chocolate-donut visions failed to appear when I expected. I'm fighting worsening illness with diminishing strength. A bout in the wrong weight class. I won't win. "How long can I last? When will the area heal enough for Eberhardt to operate?"

"It will be a few months. He thinks, ideally, three."

"Three months? I'll be dead before then. How's that going to work?" My knees are bent up to my chest, tenting the blanket. Chilled air blows through the gap in the yanked-out bedding.

I'm beginning to understand this as a pivotal moment when everything will change again, and what I know as normal will drown into memory, as though I'm in the water with nothing to hold on to, rushing toward the falls, unable to stop the current. I recognize this feeling—it has happened before: walking the hall to my HR manager's office, knowing I was going to lose my job; hearing my father's voice on the phone saying Grandpa Sid's heart died on the operating table. The repercussions fissure like veins. They are the before-and-after lines that map your life, redrawing the contours of a changed world. The moments stay with you, even the silly details like the dulled silver clasps on a pair of loafers.

What the doctor tells me is stunning.

"We're going to try something," Dr. Abrams starts with a cautious smile, his dark eyes back on me. "At this point, it's your only option. In order for the fistula to have any chance of healing on its own, of the tissue closing organically, your digestive tract will have to remain shut down. Between now and some number of months, the fistula may heal, and you could avoid further surgery. That would be best case. Or it won't heal, and Dr. Eberhardt will operate. I'm going to put you on TPN. I've already scheduled you to have a PICC line inserted this morning. A PICC is like a heavy-duty IV line that's placed in a vein in your upper arm and runs into your chest. In some patients, a PICC can last as long as four months. TPN is the nutrition you'll be fed through the line. It will provide the base level your body needs. At the same time, we'll augment the TPN with octreotide, which will essentially shut down the bowel and could help the fistula heal. You'll start TPN in the hospital. If you tolerate it, and when the abscess clears, you'll go home and continue the therapy through the PICC line with a portable pump."

"What happens if I don't tolerate it?"

"We'll talk about that if we have to. I'm sorry about this."

Dr. Abrams notes the conversation in my chart and leaves, taking off his overcoat for rounds.

TPN. Total parenteral nutrition. Base-level nutrients through a hose in the arm. I can't believe it. As of this morning's holey report, I understand the problem, but this isn't much of a solution. I'm reminded of the severed fish heads tilting in the pot of *callaloo*—they're part of the recipe but grotesque and utterly inedible. My cell phone has rung several times since Dr. Abrams left the room, and I haven't answered. My mind is elsewhere, back to the moment of the attack and the days leading up to it, searching for some clue to figure out what could have caused this to happen. It's a bad habit of mine, living life in the rearview mirror, wanting to understand what cannot be understood, to change what cannot be changed.

What's done cannot be undone. I know that, and my failure to accept it is the problem. It's been an issue between Susan and me that drives her mad. "What good does that do?" she'd say, her voice rising and impatient. Life is uncertain; life is random; control is an illusion. In my condition, though, I sure as hell don't want to believe that. I fear what uncertainty could mean for me. Another surprise shit storm, and poof. Yet here I sit, still-living proof of uncertainty.

The rupture doesn't make sense. But I need to know why this happened for my own future preservation, if there is to be any.

Ironically, the last thing I finished before the explosion was the weekly grocery shopping. It's a routine I never would have imagined when my working days were spent writing creative bullshit and deforesting the earth.

Twice a week I walk down Broadway straight after dropping off the boys at school and shop in a neighborhood supermarket hours before the mad crowds turn the aisles into the stock exchange. It's just me and the turnips. The rows are jammed to ladder height with everything I need and more—kale, broccoli, tomatoes, blood red beets and grapefruit, organic eggs, peanut butter, berries, fresh baguettes, hunks of cheese, green olives, turkey breast, rotisserie chicken, pecan pie, marble pound cake. The store is a foodie's paradise, and as a mere novice of a cook, I'm sometimes overwhelmed by the abundance of choices and puzzled by the food that still mystifies me. To make peanut noodles, do I want the anise or the star anise, or are they the same thing? What would I do with a parsnip?

In the eighties, I knew a writer named Yuri who was a poor defector from Soviet-era breadlines. The first time I took him to a—relatively Spartan, urban—American supermarket, we stood in the cereal aisle under a tower of brands, and he cried into his blunt hands. What would Yuri do if he saw the terraced sixty barrels of coffee beans where I stand to order Susan's favorite Danish blend? It looks like a conga band and smells like a plantation. The beans glisten under lamps, especially the dark ones, moist like moonlight on the water. I'm always tempted to dive in headfirst.

The empty supermarket is also conducive to kibitzing with the counter guys, and I have my check-ins with Frankie the deli cutter, Rafael the fishmonger, and Eduardo, the rotund cheese-monger with the rumpled white coat and mango face who indulges my high school Spanish.

"*Hola, mi amigo. ¿Cómo estás? ¿Bueno?* I see the price on your Swiss Gruyère is down two dollars. Bien. I'll take half a pound, sliced. So, did you see the Knicks lose last night? They stink worse than this smelly cheese you're selling me. *Que lástima*. No shooting, no speed, no defense in the hole. You'd be better at the point than what they have."

Eduardo smiles and slices the log of white-yellow cheese into a stack. "They cannot win with the players they got. No play-offs this year. This what I think."

Eduardo's crazy for American sports, and the latest New York win or disaster starts our conversations. His predictions are usually right. He hands me the wrapped and sealed package.

"All right, my man, the schools are closed for winter break, and we're going away for a few days, so I'll see you next week. I'll call the Knicks and tell them you're available. Adiós."

Since Susan and I swapped roles, food shopping and cooking consume an unyielding chunk of my time, responsibilities for which I was shamefully ill prepared by the legacy of ten thousand tuna casseroles permeating my formative flavor years. I've had to learn under fire what I should have already known. My evolution from "eat to live" to "live to eat" demanded emancipation from a no-frills food culture boiled down since the advent of Minute rice. Frozen and processed food emancipated my mother's generation from the kitchen and allowed more time for careers but, ironically, shackled me with ignorance about the basics of cooking and nutrition, information that's become crucial to me since my career vanished.

Now I try to undo personal history. Good-bye, frozen fish sticks, hello, poached salmon. I am our house's chief of food police, vigilantly prohibiting agro-corporate-additive "food products" from our diets, guarding the kids' health against sugar-induced comas, and expanding the menu to encourage experiments when we tire of the staples. In the process, my cooking skills have risen from TV-dinner reheater to passable truck-stop cook.

Disease, however, complicates matters, as shopping and cooking are mixed up with my private obsessions of monitoring and maintaining weight and blood levels. Pleasure is always adjusted by the vital numbers on the dial. All the practical boosts of food and drink—nutrition, absorption, calories, energy, excretion— are the disease's leading indicators. People like me are foodies, though not the garden variety. I'm a conflicted omnivore: I love to eat, but food is fickle medicine, and I'm at its mercy.

Ten pounds of sugar in a five-pound sack.

I'm in the kitchen nibbling at a Tupperware of leftover spaghetti carbonara as I unpack the eight bags of groceries from the morning shopping, clearing space in the fridge. Our galley kitchen mandates a Stalinist approach to space allocation, and I begin the unpacking process with a visual survey, implementing the organizing principles I've established, without which the food just won't fit. My method requires that I first function as a human garbage disposal. A pair of softening Spanish clementines, a calcifying wrapper of goat cheese, Twizzlers, it could be anything so long as disposal will clear precious real estate and save me the guilt of dumping any stray morsel shy of a posted or inferred expiration date. "I need space for the yogurt. Let's see, now, this turkey still smells safe enough to finish."

At this hour of the morning, while most people are out making a living, I'm earning something less stacking cans of tuna on a shelf littered with chopped walnut crumbs. In the silence of a stay-at-home's invisible daily triumphs, stocking the kitchen with fresh food is a personal reward. It's one of my more essential duties—if I don't shop, we don't eat—and defines my role. Meal planning is one thing I have control over, and it beats the weekly charade of sending résumés down a black hole. It's unfortunate that grocery lists don't have a very long shelf life in your portfolio. The reward disappears faster than the week's soy milk, and I'm back to the supermarket.

The carbonara in the Tupperware is still good. I grate a Parmesan wedge on the leftover pasta, bacon, and eggs, nearly fresh to my chew. Food that tasty can't be what did me in. Forget about fickle medicine; that would be downright punitive. Then what?

For close to a year, I've enjoyed an astonishing run of good health, and I think I'm on to something. I feel like a healthy person must, without the disability or anxiety of illness. No bouts of abdominal pain, no fever spikes, no nausea, no malabsorption, no protein deficiency, no anemia, no diarrhea. After years in the culinary wilderness, I've eagerly grabbed a seat at the global banquet table of eaters. The bounty is displayed most prominently by unprecedented twenty-five-pound weight gain, excellent fitness, and rich blood levels directly attributable to my body's staggering ability to properly digest and absorb the calories and nutrients I shovel in like coal into a furnace. For the first time in two decades, I can—and do—eat anything I desire. The chance to savor flavors, ingredients, dishes, and whole meals long stricken from my menu is a sensual delight I can equate only with passionately sustained sex. When you've been restricted since the Reagan administration from forbidden fruits such as a luscious, chewy, fragrant fig, its reappearance in your mouth arouses sensations of delirious pleasure. Figs, red D'Anjou pears—ordinary perennials shined by my reawakened freedom—sushi, wasabi peas, coq au vin, flourless chocolate cake. My appetite grows proportionately with our grocery bills, and I dream like a parolee of exotic flavors to be discovered and proffered to my salivating buds. I will eat forever!

I am also living by more than bread alone. My reunion with alcohol after suffering years of self-imposed abstinence is especially humanizing. At every dinner, I drain a lovely glass of wine that complements the meal's petitioning flavors. A beer with Saturday lunch is a frosty intermezzo to more food. I'm passing for normal, and the slight arc of an embryonic drinker's gut is a measure of recovery that I relish, though I imagine it's a growth most men can't fully appreciate. When I glimpse my reflection in the supermarket window by the checkout, I'm no longer depressed by a hunched clothes hanger but delighted by the sight of a solid man without the shadow of illness darkening hollow cheeks.

I can't imagine going back, and there seems no reason to

worry. The doctors are at a loss to explain the mighty surge in my power of absorption—nothing has changed in my course of medications and supplements—and conclude that their medical intervention has absolutely zero relationship to my restoration. I attribute my newfound good health to the Drinking Cure, a name I propose to introduce into the medical literature. The stumped medical team encourages all future gorging, and I circle the kitchen wall-calendar page months ahead for the debut of Beaujolais Nouveau. Serious wine drinkers dismiss the Nouveau as immature, "like eating cookie dough," but I value the grapes' sprint to my mouth. I *like* the fact that it's intended to be drunk immediately. After all this time, why wait?

August comes, and as the purple Gamays are being hand-plucked in Beaujolais, Susan, Teddy, Finn, and I return from Maine and prolong our summer escape on the east end of Long Island, vacationing for cheap on the beach. Fortunately, the boys are conditioned to be thrilled by the avalanche of a hotel ice machine, so they don't expect a yacht with their sand. The best thing about being unemployed, maybe the only good thing, is being unemployed in the summer.

On a perfect, cloudless morning, a family of locals recommends that we breakfast at a legendary pancake house. Judging by the long line tailing out the restaurant's front door when we arrive, we won't be disappointed. It'll be forty-five minutes for a table, and with the prospect of good eats to come, Susan and I get comfortable on the sidewalk while the boys chase each other like terriers in the sun. Sated eaters amble past us, slow and smiling, looking like they're heading for a nap. I'm already envisioning a lazy, lovely sleep on the beach under the umbrella.

Reading the restaurant's paper menu taped to the cluttered front window, I recognize a familiar face of brown doe eyes and gleaming white teeth. I am surprised to see Ms. Jordan, who will be Finn's teacher in September. She remembers us and is quite gracious, mixing milk and meat on her summer vacation, asking Finn about school and introducing us to her good-natured banker husband. They're fifteen or more years younger than Susan and me, a calculation that still stuns, and they share newlyweds' enthusiasm for the chocolate-chip pancakes. "It's your first homework assignment, Finn," she says, and charms him with a giggle.

He gets uncharacteristically shy, filing behind me for cover, and I'm relieved that the devil inside him will wait until school starts to make itself known. "Chocolate-chip pancakes? Excellent," I say. "I'll have him write a research report."

Finally, we get in and sit two across in a booth by the flapping kitchen door. The room is humming. We're famished and excited by the freighted plates sailing by. I know the boys won't finish them, but the price is so low that we let them order individual plates of chocolate-chip pancakes. Susan goes for eggs, toast, bacon, and coffee. I decide to try the corned-beef hash and toast. It's starred as a house favorite on the chalkboard over the cash register. When in Rome.

On our trips to visit Susan's family in the Midwest, we've become accustomed to the super-sized portions that restaurants have made standard in their quest to stuff insatiable Americans. However, even by that more-is-better measure, the pancake-house servings are big enough to choke a horse and the horse's fat groom. The pancakes are twelve inches across and stacked half a dozen high, like records in a jukebox. It takes me ten minutes just to cut the spongy cylinders into pieces the boys can actually fit in their mouths. Susan's breakfast covers three plates. My corned-beef hash weighs at least eight pounds, and I dare the boys to lift it.

"This is all going in me," I declare, and tuck a paper napkin into my shorts.

The corned beef is good—salty, lean, chewy—and they've browned the toast to the right consistency, so it sticks to the pile of meat and makes unbroken slabs for pushing in load after load. After nearly a half hour of solid eating, I finish the entire plate, gulping glasses of orange juice and water to neutralize the salt flats curing in my mouth. Between them, the boys leave over a full stack of pancakes that would be a shame to waste. It's the restaurant's signature dish, and hey, they're already cut into bites. I clean another plate.

We waddle out of the place around eleven and drive our rental car to a gorgeous ribbon of beach bordered by dune grass and gentle, sparkling surf. There are only three other groups of people in this secluded paradise. The day looks to be terrific, and I start unpacking the beach umbrella, blankets, towels, pails, shovels, baseball gear, football, Kadima paddles, and cooler that comprise our light packing. The boys dig an umbrella hole in the fine-grain sand, and I spread the blankets and towels behind.

Suddenly, I begin to feel strange. I'm sweating and going green at the gills. I double over at the sand hole, nauseated.

"Dad, you look bad. Your neck ball is shaking," Finn says about my clenched Adam's apple. "I could play tennis with that."

Susan has lain down on a blanket, and I see that she's suffering the same post-pig-out symptoms. On my knees, I plant and raise the umbrella and collapse on the blanket next to her. "I may have eaten too much," I belch.

"I feel sick," she says, rolling into the circle of shade. She hasn't taken off her capri pants and top. Her eyes are shut. "What were we thinking? Why did you make me do it? You get out of control on vacation. That was so stupid."

"But it was so good. It would have been a shame to pass up. People eat this way all the time; the place was packed, you saw them. We're just wimps." Lying flat out, I unbutton my popping shorts, gross and moaning like Uncle Richard on the living room rug at Thanksgiving.

The boys build a fort at the water's edge and, mercifully, occupy themselves by the languid tide. Susan and I quiver like dying beached whales and spend the sunny afternoon comatose and drooling, lightweights wiped out by nothing more than a hearty American breakfast. We can't stomach the thought of lunch.

I know the plates in me will digest, however. I have been feeling great for months. I've crossed the threshold into corpulent normalcy, and no Jew-hating gastric menace is going to take me back. There's nothing to be afraid of. I'm one of the people now. I'm an American. I'm a man.

Indeed, Susan and I laugh over our gluttony at dinner that night, eating juicy fried clams and drinking tall cups of beer at a roadside shack that—whoops—takes only cash, so we split the chowder. Susan finds a last cruddy bill buried in the sticky mess of her canvas bag. The boys throw rocks in the gravel parking lot and get us kicked out. We push on for ice cream.

It was fun while it lasted.

Now I'm back in the hospital bed with an IV needling my arm like an NPO piercing, wondering what put me here. It wasn't the corned-beef hash I ate last summer. It wasn't the spaghetti carbonara the morning I unpacked the groceries and exploded. It wasn't the tuna sandwich I finished the day before that. It wasn't the apricots I sniffed in the paper bag on the kitchen counter. What was it?

———

"We can live with that. Think of it as a white-noise machine. Like the one we kept by the bed in the old apartment." Susan offers this constructive comparison from the chair beside my hospital bed, where she sits with her heavy school load. She's having a first look at my food pump.

I don't respond, but my pitiful expression is bracingly clear: Are you kidding me? The grinding, the clicks, the reset beeps— it's like living in a blender. It's all so mechanical. NPO: nasty pump on. I don't mutter a word because the day nurse is here, stringing up my inaugural TPN meal. She's rushing like a diner waitress to serve me and finish logging the chart before the seven o'clock shift change.

Susan is late to leave for home and has her down coat zipped. If I say something, it will only provoke exasperation and another joyless exit. I've already subjected her to a ranting version of the prognosis laid on me this afternoon by Dr. Murdoch, the endocrinologist recruited by Dr. Abrams who pitched the pump. Murdoch sold it with more enthusiasm than I felt like mustering in the retelling. He doesn't accept our insurance, and neither does the home nursing service he insists on using, which should make for a party come bill time. Susan is working at her particular teaching job for the health insurance as much as anything else—when she went back to work, she was offered less difficult positions but with poor benefits—and I worry the food pump will have a meter running, like at a gas station. Fill me up with regular.

Dr. Murdoch wears a getup of patterned suspenders and tie, an immaculately pressed striped shirt, and chunky cuff links. His smooth face and slicked brown hair read too young for him to still sport the Gordon Gekko look out of habit, but the braces accessorize a fashioned trader-like cockiness in the guy. I'm wary of the ease with which he dispenses the several-months trial of hunger. Unlike psychology, where submission to analysis is a requirement of medical training, the study of endocrinology does not demand starvation as a condition of residency. It all sounds too easy, too perfect a solution for something with so many moving parts. The doctor speaks fast. He says he's prescribed this Erector-set concoction hundreds of times, and I wonder if his speedy delivery is intended to obscure the difficult bits, to dazzle me with shiny objects and discourage scrutiny. Sure, I want to feel confidence in a doctor when he's going to cut into me or hook me up to a mechanical stomach. But this brand of confidence is suspect, as if the pump is a late-model Impala and he's got me cornered in the parking lot. Dr. Murdoch talks quickly up to his sign-off, a man in a hurry. "I'll write up the orders and have you running on TPN by dinnertime."

In graduate school, I taught in a building where space was loaned to my department from the veterinary school. There was

a shortcut to my classroom through the barns where the vet students did field research on animals. The star of the barns was a
Holstein named Oreo who'd been outfitted with a Plexiglas skin
over her carved-out middle for an academic view of the complex
working of her stomach's four digestive compartments. The window stapled to her hide was creepy, but all in the name of science, and Oreo seemed to be treated well enough, though she was
not particularly friendly. Occasionally, when class ended, I would
stop in the barn and visit the transparent cow. Her mash of guts
pressed against the smeary glass looked nothing like the corresponding, cleanly engineered, color-coded GI diagram hung from
a beam over the stall. The poster was finely detailed; it could have
been the rendering for a steamship's engine room. What was so
clear and logical in the tubular drawing was a mess in reality,
gloppy and congealed and bloody, like overcooked spaghetti.

I stare at the pump, my new stomach, clamped like a barn
door to the listing IV pole, and wave Susan off before I start
griping. The nurse heads out to her station, and I recline at an
uncomfortable angle, ready to receive liquid dinner. It's true
what J.P. said about hospital food getting worse. The tube loop-
ing from the pump into my left arm is dodgy, for starters, and
the milky food supply clogs around an air bubble the length of
a cigarette. The pump jams and sounds its alarm. "Nurse."

On the bus home from the gloom of the hospital, Susan real-
izes that she forgot to take the chicken breasts out of the freezer
before leaving for work in the morning. She'll have to improvise
something for the boys' dinner, then plow through homework,
baths, and story time. Keeping to the routine seems the best
defense against the chaos my situation has inflicted on them.

She makes do with what's left from the dwindling groceries ordered online Sunday night after the boys went to bed.

In my hospital cell, I'm frozen out of the chicken story and the disturbing episode that follows, like one of Grandma Jennie's plucked birds. It's only later that I learn of my family's anguish and lasting fears. Susan swallows the details of these incidents in our increasingly tortured hospital conversations, sheltering me from their anxiety but furthering my oblivion. It's a no-win situation for both of us. I'm becoming a ghost at home, a pair of empty slippers left under the bed. My spectral look doesn't even come with a *Heaven Can Wait* view from above. I feel like I did that day lying on the living room floor, sealed off in private misery. Living in isolation is its own kind of death.

"Boys, I'm in the mood for hard-boiled eggs, ham, and carrots," Susan calls from the kitchen hopefully, taking the found food from the refrigerator to the counter before Teddy and Finn can object. "Does that sound good to you?"

Dinner in our home has always been a standing reservation for four, a nightly occasion engineered by common rituals. The meal is cooked or, even better, reheated; the table is cleared of mail and backpacks and set with place mats and cloth napkins (filthy by the middle of the week); two long tapers are lit; the television and phones are silenced; music is played; two glasses are poured from a bottle of red or white wine, with water in real glasses for the kids. On a good night, the cook is even thanked. Overlooking the ground-in residue of meals past that grimes the table and chairs, we strive for a semblance of dignity. We encourage table manners and actual conversation about subjects besides farting, fighting, and SpongeBob (mostly, we fail). Dinner is an important custom, and though the boys typically destroy its intended sanctity with trapped-animal frenzy, we cling to the civilizing fantasy of the meal as a brief escape from the noise of day—one that binds our family together through the shared effort and pleasure of meal-time. In actuality, we operate a no-star restaurant.

Half a dozen eggs are boiling on the stovetop. Susan lights two candles that are burned down to stumps and asks the boys to come set the table. They complain. Before it escalates into a battle, she meets them halfway, handing them napkins and silverware as she tells them the news. She ignores their coats and notebooks thrown on the living room rug.

"Dad's doctors think he may be able to come home from the hospital in a few days. He's really excited about that."

The silverware is large and weighty, bought in a big-box Indiana store where abundant shelf space is the norm. It's scaled for a McMansion and makes for clumsy setting. A knife and spoon slip from Finny's hands and clang to the worn wooden floor, scattering breakfast crumbs. Susan picks up the silverware.

"Will he sleep in your bed?" Finn, a natural leader, asks.

"Yes, honey. Why?"

"I thought he has to be in a hospital bed that goes up and down."

"No, not when he comes home. But when he does come home, he won't be able to eat. The doctors think Dad will get better if he doesn't eat food for a while. Instead of eating food with his mouth, he'll have a food pump that'll give him nutrients through a tube that goes into his arm."

Susan is spent and wears the strain of a brave face. She tells the bizarre pump details in a matter-of-fact way and smiles with the anxious tenacity shown in her sorority photos buried at the bottom of the cabinet in the hall. The news is weird, she knows, but she hopes to get through the night without another explanation. Her voice is frayed and sounds like she has a cold. She's tiring of being medical reporter to the kids, to my parents, to my sister, to her parents, to her sister, to the parents at school, to my old friends, having to meet their concerned, tentative questions with the mask of optimism. It's draining—standing upright rather than succumbing to misery. Someone has to be strong for the kids. However, medical reporter is a job she never asked for. Why doesn't everyone just call Jon and ask him themselves? she has thought lately. He's got time.

She hears boiling water dousing the stove's gas flame and moves to turn it off before it blows.

"Dad can't eat?" Teddy deadpans from the living room couch, his voice flatlined to a monotone, another consequence of the unfortunately early arrival of pre-adolescence. It's a phase.

"He will eat. Just not when he first comes home." Susan is rushing to peel two cracked carrots. It's getting late for homework, and the boys skipped baths last night when the time got away. Finn's hands are sticky from an afternoon granola-bar snack, or maybe something irresistible he mooched at the playground.

"When? When will he eat?" Finn demands, joining Susan in the kitchen.

"The doctors want to try this for a couple of months. Dad showed me how the food pump works. He said you could help him put in the batteries and program it." This is a generous lie. My grumpy instructions about the food pump did not include a bonus section for family fun.

Finn is crying. His fair complexion blotches red at the cheeks and chin, and his nose snots. He's so tall for his age, tears come as jarring reminders of how young he really is.

"What's wrong?" Susan worries. She leaves the carrots and comforts him, moving to the couch.

"I don't know why he can't eat. And every day when Miss Jordan asks me how Dad is, my face gets hot and I have to go to the bathroom so no one in class sees me cry."

Teddy, pushed by his younger brother's confession, breaks down, still brittle and just nine under the cool-kid pose. "Today I got sad in school and started to cry, and Sophia saw it and started to make fun of me, so I had to pretend that I hurt my knee in gym." He buries his head in Susan's lap and bawls. "Is Dad going to die?"

She strokes Teddy's mop of righteous teen-idol hair, the same leaf-brown she had as a kid, and wipes the tears falling from Finn's lovely blue eyes, just like his mother's. The boys look nothing like me; their faces are descendants of her curved, pretty angles.

"No," she answers, and her fragile guard collapses. Her hands pull tight around the boys' bony shoulders, and she cries in a jag, dropping fat, wet tears on their heads. Susan has spent so much energy being cheerful for the boys, keeping their schedules as intact as possible, getting Teddy to piano and basketball, treating Finn to movies and sleepovers, shielding them from the despair of the hospital. But they know what's happened. Susan and the boys sob on one another, folded together like wet paper. "It's okay, honey, it's okay to be sad."

Now it's the three of them holding on. It's a mess. And I am in the bed that goes up and down, with a weight-loss show blasting from the other side of the useless hospital curtain, as my roommate's visitors shout out scale predictions.

The doorbell buzzes and startles them. Her face puffy and slick, Susan answers and is surprised to see our upstairs neighbor, Sheryl, a competitive litigator to whom we owe more dinner invitations than we'd like to count. (Their apartment has space for a formal dining room. It comes with the territory.)

"Are you okay?" Sheryl asks, cautioned by the evidence of a breakdown as the boys continue crying on the couch. From the looks of Sheryl's floured T-shirt, she's been cooking or baking. A border of perspiration lines her black headband.

"Oh, we're all right, just having a family cry." Susan sweeps hair off her smeared cheeks. She looks anguished in the white hall light that spills into the small entryway.

"I came down to invite you to dinner. I know it's late, but I made more food than the three of us can possibly eat. I thought you might like the night off."

Susan slows her shallow breaths and summons her gratitude with a relieved smile. "Sheryl, that sounds wonderful. Boys, let's go have dinner upstairs with Sam's family."

Penne alla vodka and broccoli rabe are served on speckled plates at Sheryl and David's long farmhouse table. Sheryl is an excellent cook. Susan savors the food and appreciates Sheryl's thoughtfulness, a trait sometimes obscured by her hard charging. For a short while tonight, Susan can escape. She can have an adult conversation and forget about a sick husband. She can put off making school lunches. The meal tastes delicious.

Finn picks at the greens, and Susan whispers, "Take a no-thank-you helping" in his ear. He halts the conversation with a headline to the table: "Dad can't eat."

PART
TWO

CHAPTER 4

I must lick this french fry. It's calling me, and I have no choice. I'm not asking to *eat* the fry; that would be a mess. I just want to lick it. Taste its salt. Have it in my mouth and melt into me. Just a taste, man, that's all I need. I'm standing in our kitchen, home from the hospital—hiding, actually, from Susan and the boys at the dinner table—wooed to the stove by the smell of cooked hamburgers and french fries. The smell should be a draw to a real meal, the satisfying act. In the sensuality of eating, the nose teases and the mouth consummates. The intensity of the dinner's aroma is playing havoc with my senses, as so many smells have lately, and I'm transported.

The chestnuts smelled like this.

When my grandparents Sid and Marly were alive, they were the extended family's Thanksgiving hosts, cramming two dozen people around their bulky dining room table covered by protective pads, and the satellite folding tables that stepped down from the big one like Lincoln Logs. These annual feasts lasted well into my twenties and were as memorable for the menus' cultural idiosyncrasies as for the plentiful if clashing meal—a loaf of seeded rye that Marly chainsawed, beside a cut-glass bowl of half-sour pickles, a tray of conventional sweet potatoes, and two dozen bitter yellow grapefruits topped with maraschino cherries and tied in wax paper babushkas. Their 1950s Long Island tract house had a tiny kitchen and an electric stove for cooking the mismatched food and unstringing the white gift boxes of Italian-bakery desserts.

Grandpa Sid and I parked on the crowded kitchen's aluminum chairs to roast chestnuts. We would start in the morning, counting out nuts from a burlap sack, slitting small Xs on their brown bellies and spreading concentric circles of beauties X-side-up in four dented tin pans. By the late afternoon, after the turkey had been (over)cooked and devoured, Sid and I would wrap our hands in damp dish towels hanging from the neck of the kitchen faucet and slide the full pans onto the hot oven's center rack. Roasting lasted about half an hour. We'd wait on the brutal chairs by the stripped turkey carcass as the kitchen air swelled with the profound scent of cooking chestnuts.

As the oldest grandchild, I alone had been entrusted with the chestnut ritual, an ethnic stab at Currier and Ives Americana in the cookie-cutter built on plowed-over potato fields. To pass the roasting time, Sid whistled old songs that I'd heard him jangle on the mandolin. He was an orchestra behind clenched teeth, his fleshy lips pulled wide under a trimmed mustache. The chestnut air turned warm and fit me like dried laundry, and I had the best seat in the house. In those moments, the harsh linoleum-floored kitchen felt like a concert hall. Every few bars of "My Blue Heaven" or "Mairzy Doats," Sid would break from whistling and inhale the perfume wafting out of the oven. "Oh, that's good. You smell that? That's *something*!"

"That's something!" was his all-purpose expression, and I grew to understand just what he meant. The roasting chestnuts were more than a nice smell. There was magic in the air, a *something* beyond our making, beyond our control. He wanted me to know.

Sid had abundant cravings and fed them impulsively, even recklessly, darting like an excited dog to the things he wanted— cars with big trunks, zoom lenses, a deep-sea fishing pole, barley soup, stuffed cabbage, chopped liver, roasted chestnuts, and all the restricted fatty food that got his hand slapped—any *something* he believed he needed to scratch his itch. I once saw him climb into the trunk of an elephantine Plymouth Fury sedan he had his eye on, just to prove how big it was. Cravings drove him.

Sid had a tough childhood—born premature and undersize on New Year's Day 1913, grew up poor, destitute after his father died, and left school at eleven to work and keep the family in their tenement. As an adult, he worked as a window trimmer, bent on hands and knees, dressing mannequins and environ- ments in Bond's department store displays, under the beckoning TWO TROUSER SUITS marquee in the chain's Times Square flagship store. On weekends, Sid worked a second job photographing weddings and bar mitzvahs. He developed the posed pictures in a slop sink in the house's clammy basement. Occasionally, if I nagged persuasively, he would let me join him to witness the pictures develop in the basin: boxy tuxedos and shiny yarmul- kes, lumpy satin dresses, cheesy grins and pork-chop jowls and strobe-flashed eyes emerging as black-and-white biographies written in the chemical bath.

"Look at this *chazzer*, he's so fat from eating off everyone's plate," Sid would snap, removing his Coke-bottle glasses to get a closer look at the fresh picture, and clothespin the slick paper to a laundry line. "Florence Gluckfeld, she killed her husband, poor bastard. Always with a puss on, that one. What a *kvetch*."

Sid rarely had a puss on, despite his hard life and a first heart attack at fifty-six. Discipline didn't come naturally but was imposed on him, first by the demands of poverty, then by the middle-class ambition of his determined, fearful wife. Marly tore paper napkins in half and hid money until the day she died. She once had to be stopped from peeling and eating the orange that had cooked inside the cavity of the Thanksgiving turkey. Sid was her opposite and a lot more fun. If left to his own impulses, he would have raided their savings account ten times over for a car with a bigger trunk. The yearning for *something* kept him going, ahead of the hardships sucking from behind. Cravings made his confined life in the window worth living. Sid's desire index reading was off the charts, even if the lure was as ordinary as our tins of cooking chestnuts. His wasn't a complicated approach to finding happiness, and if discipline had to be dug like a channel to meet his cravings, at least the air smelled good.

During the chestnut incubation in the hot kitchen, I mostly listened to his running spiel. I didn't know much about cars and cameras, though I shared his excitement for the nuts. We stayed on the spoked chairs, the time passed with charged zeal, and I stared at the kitchen timer turning in one-minute clicks back to zero.

When the timer finally buzzed and we cooled the heated tins on cardboard trivets my sister and I had painted, the anticipa-

tion became unbearable, and Sid and I would burn our fingertips peeling the nuts' hot shells by the curled tops that looked
like jester shoes before the meat stuck to their skins. It never
occurred to us to fashion some shelling tools from the tangle
in the drawer. Despite the sting, it was more fun to tear out the
flesh with our bare hands.

The chestnuts didn't taste very good. In fact, they were basically inedible. My outrageous jonesing was deflated annually
by the dry, fuzzy meat, like eating a burnt spider, so dry that I
would gag and search the emptied refrigerator for a remaining sip of cider in the special silver pitcher. The lousy taste
was a disappointment we never confessed, though. We'd force
ourselves to eat two or three arid nuts, and Sid would crow to
Marly about how great they were and what a *something* she was
missing. "Molka, stop working and get in here. They won't last!"
My grandmother would transfer the awful chestnuts to a gold-
rimmed plate and serve the pile at the big table. The nuts would
end their day in the kitchen trash pail, like souvenir beach rocks
that belong back on the sand.

In my kitchen now, the smell of Susan's dinner is overpowering like the chestnuts, but my french-fry-licking craving feels
so illicit. And stupid. I cower behind the greasy wall bordering
the stove, away from the family just on the other side of the
open doorway, enjoying a sumptuous dinner like eaters do—
devouring what's delicious, picking at what is not, saving room
for dessert—while I starve. I can imagine burning my fingertips
and more. Lousy as the chestnuts were, I did get to eat them.

There's been nothing by mouth for two months. No food, no
drink, nothing has passed my lips except the air I keep suck-

ing. It's an exhausting endurance test, like trying to stand in place in the ocean tide, and I'm in a state of prolonged inertia. I've come home from the hospital, I've changed into my own clothes—dressing every day like a hostage in a gray hoodie and the same pair of elastic-waist black running pants to conceal my weight loss—but the NPO diet is the same as in the hospital, and my health hasn't improved. Despite the calendar change, the weather is also stuck in dreary, wet winter, a season on perpetual hold.

In one sense, I should be used to this. Since I lost my last job, we've been living month to month on Susan's salary, unable to bank money for the future, a family of four subsisting on a teacher's income in the most expensive city in the country, and we're into year four of this financial grind. We've been living in the moment, while wondering if life will ever get easier: money for kids' clothes, summer camp, orthodontia, college tuition, a second bathroom, a third bedroom, a real vacation, some new music, an occasional dinner out—all the things that seem impossible. Living in the moment is supposedly a state that provides a breakthrough to personal happiness. I'm waiting.

I'm not unfamiliar with cycling in place: in healthy times, waking at six to shower and eat and dress and make the boys' breakfast before I get them up at seven, then chunking the rest of the day into logs of scheduled chores. The routine is monotonous and occasionally soul-crushing. Cultivating a structure can give me a sense of comfort, though, days that are predictable and controllable, a lattice bolted upright against the free fall of unemployment. By nature, I'm a creature of habit; as much as I growl about routines, I rely on them. But the particular oppression of the nothing-by-mouth structure has me feeling trapped in a routine that regiments my days and nights, a state that has nothing to do with comfort.

The rigid TPN schedule is nothing, so far, if not predictable. However, unlike choosing to wake at six and shower, or make the boys' next-day lunches when we get home from school, or do the laundry midweek when the basement washers aren't busy, TPN is a routine of mechanical tyranny, controlling me beyond even the illusion of personal choice. It's difficult for me to leave the apartment, bending the schedule is potentially dangerous, and the food pump calls the shots—TPN, the pump nags.

All the moving parts and the heavy TPN feed bag reside in a backpack slung over my shoulder like a nylon camel hump. Tubing is threaded from the TPN bag through the backpack's interior loops and out to meet the PICC line porting in my upper arm. TPN sustains me, allegedly. Total parenteral nutrition is the product name for the mixed bag of nutritional fluids that filters through the umbilical cord snaking through a vein in my left triceps into my chest, where the soup is doled out. I run the pump fourteen hours a day, plus another four hours of medicinal octreotide and saline solution that drip from bags hung IV-style on an aluminum pole. Disease has always intruded on my life and the effort to live a normal one; now it has taken over.

While I was empty and miserable in the hospital, I wasn't ever hungry. I was decimated but not starving. The desired visions of chocolate donuts and crispy pizza never came on like heart paddles to stimulate me. Of course, I wanted out of the hospital because I couldn't stand the depression of being confined there any longer, let alone dying there, but all my thrashing didn't register a blip on the desire index. My appetite, my libido, my heart flatlined. Other than the blues, I never felt anything. More to the point of living, I never *craved* any something.

Now I'm bent in a twisted position by the kitchen stove, and the hunger is driving me mad. I crave food more than sex. The smell and touch of food in our apartment can drop me to my knees. I think about it constantly, more desperately as the months wear on, an obsession that magnifies a craved bite of the ordinary into surreal portions. A simple french fry like the one I'm squeezing under the joints of my closed fingers is a wonder; an uneaten crust of whole wheat bread found in Teddy's lunch box salvation; something as unattainable as the fried-egg sandwich Susan made for herself Sunday afternoon, life itself. People with chicken pox wear cotton gloves to help keep from scratching their itches. What is there to prevent scratching for food?

The apricot bag is still here, rolled down as I left it, in the kitchen cupboard. I discovered it yesterday.

I'd decided to make the kids' school lunches, to do something to help in the house. I searched for the small boxes of organic raisins I pack as a no-labor fruit when I don't feel up to chopping apple slices for the eight millionth time, but I couldn't find them. Susan either didn't buy the raisins or put them on a different shelf. I grumbled and was about to get grouchy with her when a vision revealed its lovely self: the apricots, at eye level, pungent and available—they'd been here waiting for me the whole time. *Why did you eat them all? Because they tasted so good.*

My obsessive food trance isn't healthy or normal, but nothing I do fills my empty gut and conquers the hunger, and there is nothing to be done by anyone else. When cravings have no chance of being satisfied, you either find a substitute or they snatch you and isolate you against other people. I haven't found a substitute. Living without food, my craving for it has overtaken me, like the craving has reduced me to a pod person. Hiding in the kitchen clutching a french fry can't be healthy, but what else have I got? There's no way to share the pain or accept relief for my hunger, which is driving away well-intentioned people, discouraged and frustrated with me.

At mealtimes, while dinner is playing out on the other side of the wall, I unpack bladders of laboratory-made nutrients that take the place of food. I fill syringes. I prime the pump that shoots the food bag full of fortifiers into my vein to keep me alive. Nothing in that synthetic bladder relieves the hunger. I knew there was a reason Dr. Murdoch spoke so fast, eliding the fine print. He neglected to mention that TPN wouldn't be able to outsmart my body and mind, which have woken up to what's missing and won't be misled by the weekly lab shipments from Deerfield, Illinois, that Sal the UPS guy delivers.

Meanwhile, the apartment is infused with an essence-of-diner odor that I dearly miss. The Metro, the City, the New Wave—that's my Manhattan Michelin Guide. The mini-hamburgers and fries are Susan's slumming treat for the boys. The apartment windows are shut against a chilling rain.

"Dad, you've got to see this," Finn calls from the other room. "Dad, what are you doing?"

I close my fingers tighter around the oily fry and move to the cracked love seat in the living room, keeping company with the food pump. The table on the opposite side is set with candles and a blue glass bowl of precious winter fruit, two of my beloved red D'Anjou pears and a galaxy of clementines mottling candlelight reflections on their orange skins. My customary end chair is unoccupied. For the first meals after I came home, I tried joining in at the table, a happy-meal family, but my starving presence disturbed the kids, and I've been marooned on the love seat or exiled to the bedroom ever since. There isn't enough room in our apartment to get a good game of hide-and-seek going, but mealtime now comes with regular servings of separation anxiety.

Finn holds up a silver-dollar-size burger in a petite seeded bun, excited to show me his novelty dinner. He and Teddy yammer with mouths full of food, their speech garbled by chewed meat and bread soaked in warm juices. As the pyramid of sliders falls, I can only watch the plate get swept clean. Finn kneels on his chair and turns to me, presumably to show off his open-maw carnival. His mouth is a juicy mess, but he trains me with a severe look. "When will you eat?" he demands in a six-year-old's voice complicated by vulnerability, the involuntary condition that afflicts all children whose parents get sick.

"Soon," I lie. "Tell me about the burgers." It's a lame attempt to take his mind off the skeleton father before him, the kind of diversionary tactic whose power diminishes in proportion with each year of the kids' advancing ages. They probably don't believe the "everything's fine" ruse they've heard a lot of, either. "Do they taste like White Castle?" I ask Finn, steamrolling. "Mom spent most of her college years there. That's where she got the recipe."

Finn doesn't respond to my lead, and I realize the boys have never been to White Castle. There is nothing for them to be reminded of. Nothing for them to miss. I abort the food nostalgia and don't dredge up the triumphant old epic of eating fourteen sliders in a ravenous two-in-the-morning binge. The conversation ends. Finn looks at me curiously, wipes his strawberry-blond bangs across his forehead, and goes back to savoring the food like a lion on a carcass.

The plate's empty.

"Mom, these are so good. Can I have more?" Teddy breaks in. The minis have conquered his usual pickiness, and Susan is up from her chair before Teddy's real-food urge dissolves into nagging for a sweet dessert. On her way to the kitchen to replenish, she regards me with a silent, sorry look. After everything Susan and the boys have had to put up with, their lives made frightened and insecure by my health, by me, I should be pleased by the sight of their shared simple pleasure at the table. But I'm too far withdrawn into the abyss of my gut, plagued by the dismal diet of cravings frustration. And I'm carrying. I've got this concealed fry bleeding in my hand. I better do something with it before I'm found out and forced to cop to fryjacking.

Susan comes back with a square plate full of burgers, and I slip into the kitchen ready to do the nasty, leaving the carnivores to their assault. Pressing out of view, tight against the warm stove, I unclench my hand and let go of the contraband, then touch all ten fingertips to a fallen nest of fries scattered on the baking sheet resting on the stove's two front burners. They are crisped and stinging hot to the touch. I pick up a handful and bring it to my nose. Food has not passed my lips for so long, and the prospect of the near, oiled, salty fries excites me. I draw a stiff and crispy one to my mouth and lick it. The texture is wicked—coated and crunchy as I had fantasized. However, the salty taste that should open like a flower in my mouth is frustratingly absent. I lick again, doggie-style. Nothing. Exasperated, frustrated, horny for flavor, I bite off an end piece and nestle it into my tongue, sucking for salt. Absolutely nothing, like I'm draining saliva in a dentist's chair. I bend forward to the stove's mirrored top for an oral inspection. I see. My tongue is as shiny smooth as a porpoise. I curl the tip and poke and confirm: My taste buds are gone. Sheared right off like rotted wall tiles. Atrophied. Jesus shit, when the hell did this happen? What does that mean? Are they coming back? I spit the mangled potato into the trash. Just then Teddy appears, no doubt leaving burger heaven for the last three-berry-pie triangle in the tin, and catches me midspit.

"*Dad,* you're not supposed to *eat,*" he scolds in a disgusted voice, the soulful eyes boring insistent and hard. The food police, they come in all sizes.

"I didn't eat!" I object. My brittle, defensive burst is incriminating.

Teddy examines the evidence in the pail and the awful expression on my face, troubled by the pathetic sight. "Da-ad," he pulls long like a boat horn. "You can't eat that french fry."

How right he is. Teddy plates his pie and grabs a fork, slumps his shaggy head to his chest, and leaves me caught in the kitchen.

"Really, sweetheart," I call after him, modulating my voice to something lighter than tormented guilt, trying to sound more dadlike, more like the man I was before the hunger came to stay. "I didn't."

I have become "The Man Who Can't Eat" to him. We're going in opposite directions, and neither one of us likes his new role.

After dinner, Susan and the kids settle in for their *American Idol* fix, a school-night exception for an hour of relief in their strained lives. Typically, I watch Simon's filleting of the fish, but I've removed myself from the room and lie in bed. The *Idol* judges would call my TPN pump noise "pitchy," and rather than override the show's lineup of power belters tonight, I've left the competition. I tried sitting apart from the family's huddle on the couch, sequestered on the love seat, but the turning gears of my TPN pump prevailed.

Our once peaceful bedroom has been kitted out like an infirmary. I get up from the bed to take inventory of the supplies. In the morning Nurse Patty will come to place the weekly order with the pharmacy service. I count four packing boxes of pre-loaded heparin flush and saline flush syringes, empty syringes, hypodermic needles, bandages, surgical tape, surgical gloves, gauze pads, alcohol wipes, saline solution, batteries, and packets of plastic tubing. The jug-handled sharps container is full of used syringes and will need to be collected by the hospital. In the corner by my dresser, I open the door of the mini-refrigerator holding the liquid ingredients that fortify the TPN. The wood-veneered cooler, which once housed beer and hash brownies in my college dorm room, is packed like an astronaut's freezer with bladders and vials of octreotide, thiamine, folic acid, famotidine, and insulin. Total parenteral nutrition is complex. And expensive. The three-thousand-milliliter bag of solution, a slippery load that I fetch from the fridge, constituted by a base formula of dextrose, Travasol, Intralipid, selenium, chromium chloride, and a dozen other chemical-lab seasonings, runs eight hundred dollars or, in my case, one dollar per juiced minute.

"Whatever you do, don't puncture a hole in the bag or contaminate the ingredients." Nurse Patty impressed this upon me on the first day of home-care instruction, the official warning issued through the bright frieze of her disarming smile. She's a formidable redhead, big-boned and curvy like an Updike woman, sexy in an old-fashioned way, who fixes herself with the discipline and recall of the air force nurse she was for two decades. "Begin by clearing your workspace, then lay out all the items on the checklist," she said to me. Having passed basic training, I am responsible for mixing up the medicine.

In no way can TPN be confused with actual eating. Pulling on rubber gloves and laying out potions and needles on beds of sterile wipes across my living room table, injecting the compounds into the big bag's tiny rubber-tipped port, I feel more like Owsley Stanley producing kitchen-clean LSD for the Mercy Pranksters than the passable cook I used to be.

The TPN regimen is a pain. What made sense in the abstract of Dr. Murdoch's pitch—relying on a battery-powered hose for nutrition fourteen hours a day—reveals its glitches, shortcomings, and impractical demands in practice. No doubt, this discrepancy between the theory and reality was the fissure behind Oreo the cow's similarly shitty disposition.

The programmable food pump is about the size of a jumbo foundry brick and weighs as much as two. The pump's motor grinds in continuous cycles of whirs and clicks, parsing the thin white stream of medical milk nursing me from four in the afternoon to six in the morning, and requires a klutzy midnight

battery change to continue through the night. My hassled movement in the apartment from bed to toilet to living room couch
is accompanied by a continuous-loop soundtrack, my entrances
heralded by the sump-pump equivalent of horns blaring: The
Man Who Can't Eat has arrived! The ceaseless engine racket is
a loud party to conversation, television watching, sleeping—as
sweet as birdsong—and I'm often compelled to leave the room.
From bed, I hear a unanimous appeal to the TV from the living
room *Idol* judges.

Susan and I have switched sides in bed for me to be able to
set the moaning backpack on the night table, and so I have a
shorter path for lugging it to the bathroom. There's almost no
slack in the line from me to the mechanical cow, and I'm tied
down for the night like a boat in a storm. When the position
gets uncomfortable and I roll over in my sleep, I'm awakened
by the wallop of gear crashing from the night table to the wood
floor. Susan seems to sleep through it, getting her usual eight,
though she claims otherwise. To her, maybe the pump does
sound like the white-noise machine in our old apartment. I call
the pump Oreo.

These bedtime adjustments are minor compared to the two
involuntary nocturnal reactions that TPN is triggering in me—
pissing and sweating. Every night, within an hour of nodding
off, I am swamped by the dew of a night sweat. My T-shirt is
soaked, my head slimed by perspiration, my shorts damp. From
then on, I'm sweat-showered at one-hour intervals, which
kills the prospect of prolonged sleep and forces me out of bed.
Changing my shirt is loopy, as the TPN umbilical runs through
the T's left armhole. To put on a dry shirt, I peel off the wet one

and slide it down the line, sagging the cord between me and the backpack like wet wash. I sleep on a beach towel spread over my switched side of the bed, trying to keep the pillowcase and bedsheets dry, but the terry cloth's pimpled weave heats my body and wattles my face.

The pissing, incredibly, is worse than the sweating. Also hourly, my bladder fills to bursting, and I wake to drag the pump to the bathroom for a Seabiscuit-size stream. After it became clear this was the pattern, I spoke to Dr. Murdoch. He told me this is just the way my body is reacting. Everybody's different, and there's "nothing to be done," he said, in speedtalk.

Nothing to be done?

I haven't slept more than an hour straight since the surgery. Food never did this to me. Take away food, take away sleep; isn't that covered in the Geneva conventions? Cheney must be behind it. I believe I have earned a dubious achievement. I've surpassed the acknowledged rock-and-roll record for sleeplessness — Keith Richards's nine consecutive all-nighters. I've got ol' Keef beat without the benefit of heroin. Was his while recording *Exile on Main Street*? Open up and swallow.

The interrupted nights make for exhausted days. Patty and the other nurses arrive every morning following completion of the TPN meal to draw blood specimens; take my blood pressure, pulse, and temperature; tape-measure my achingly slow-to-close wound; and watch me clean the crater and change the dressing. My daytime is spent mostly preparing for the next round. If this keeps up, I'll soon be making ashtrays and asking for Bingo.

Tonight Susan gets the kids to bed and passes out after *Idol*. She's too tired to talk about what I missed and shrugs me off.

I'm in no hurry to start the sweating-and-pissing marathon, and I get up to watch TV alone in the living room. Jon Stewart and Colbert are dark this week, so I turn to *Charlie Rose*. Ferran Adrià, the celebrated Spanish chef of El Bulli, his Catalan restaurant with a thirty-five-course taster's menu, is the headline guest, animated by a visceral philosophy: "Eating is the most intense experience in the world. There is no other creative moment that uses all five senses," he says through a translator. "Breathing and eating are the only things that we do from the moment of birth and for the rest of our lives."

Adrià's back-of-the-throat consonants and diphthongs clear his speech for what sound like ancient truths. He explains that human beings have a complex relationship with food—through previous experience, the context of eating, of memories, of traditions, associations both regional and personal. *Tell me what you crave, and I will tell you what you are,* he seems to be saying. In my living room illuminated by the bright image of the knowing chef, his declarations penetrate the gloom with profound insight. Nothing by mouth has eliminated more than the function of eating. The day-to-day cooking, shopping, and nuclear-family provision that defined my caretaker role has been placed in suspended animation, along with the occasional dinner-date prospects that inspired Susan and me to remember why we married each other. Food has been a partner in the substance of life, making and filling the experience. Its absence has alienated me from who we were. Nothing by mouth has alienated me from myself.

The Man Who Can't Eat. My identity is defined by a negative, by what's been lost. Why not add to it the Man Who Can't Work, and the Man Who Can't Play, and the Man Who Can't Sleep, and the Man Who Can't Think? Captain Hook had a more positive nickname.

My brother-in-law the physician told me that instead of blaming the surgeon and being angry with the pump pusher I should appreciate that not all that long ago I probably would have died from the rupture and that the technology is keeping me alive. Put it in perspective, Reiner. He's right, of course. But sterilizing my TPN bottles doesn't quite cut it as a substitute for the feeling of self-worth that came from figuring out that chopping chicken breasts into nuggets excited the boys enough to actually want to eat them. Or celebrating a low-rent wedding-anniversary lunch with Susan last summer, getting a little drunk and flirty over lobster rolls and draft beer in the salt air and seagull noise at J's Oyster. Susan and I can't even think about going out to a restaurant together now; though it suddenly occurs to me that she could go without me.

When we were first married and both working, we invested in a Zagat guide and made every Friday night a journey to a different neighborhood, a different restaurant, a different style of food. Friday nights became a hunt to look forward to, fresh and fun. We were new to the city, new to each other, living in a five-hundred-square-foot nineteenth-century walk-up we thought was charming, and our fortunes were ascending. New York, too, it seemed, was blossoming with the collective optimism of new marriage. Every empty storefront and warehouse was being transformed into a bistro we'd explore on our Friday-night treks. Their brick walls and pressed-tin ceilings looked like our tiny apartment, and we brought home doggie bags of ideas from the restaurants to try during the week in the matchbox kitchen.

Susan is an accomplished cook and an adventurous eater. Discovering her new flavors in my mouth introduced a body of experience I didn't have and illuminated the bewitching person sitting with me at the table sharing my life. We led this new-lyweds' feast for several years of successive Zagats, capping chicken curry on East Sixth Street or grilled pork in Gramercy Park with a late-night cocktail and lovemaking and passing out in bliss. It was all so easy.

Of all the Zagat listings, there's one that still stands out for me, a headliner of the CAPITAL LETTER crowd, a restaurant called Chanterelle. They serve French cuisine in a simple honey-colored dining room with tall windows opening to a cobble-stone street in TriBeCa. Chanterelle started in the neighborhood years before it became overrun by hedge-fund doughboys, so the restaurant is elegant without being stuffy, and the food, such as their signature grilled seafood sausage, is distinct and superb. Or so I read in Zagat. It's a special-occasion restaurant, our local El Bulli, as expensive as its CAPITAL LETTER rating, and Susan and I kept waiting for the occasion special enough to justify the cost. Our occasions and finances never came together to make a dinner reservation. However, until I went nothing by mouth, we talked about Chanterelle now and then and held it out like a Holy Grail.

When I was working, I sometimes had meetings in an office close by, and I would divert my walk back to the subway by way of Chanterelle's corner for a fantasy leer. I'd stand at the plate glass, looking through the gap above the sheer curtain, transfixed by the courses of cheese and fresh scallops and beef carpaccio with black truffles and petits fours served at the white tables, walled by arrangements of lilies and forsythia in unadorned columned vases. Even on the wrong side of the window, imagining their sweet aromas transported me, like marveling at the sparkling blintzes orbiting Ratner's dining room when I was a kid. I watched Chanterelle's waiter-philosophers, who famously doused the room with personality rather than starch, fanning the funky menus designed by the downtown old guard. The space between the square tables was generous, like at a picnic in the French Alps. As far as I know, Chanterelle is still in business. The last Zagat on the bookshelf by the window is from 2001.

Maybe the most vivid side effect of total food deprivation is that everything conjures food, and I rarely see it coming. Sometimes when I look at Finny's basted kid legs stepping out of the shower, I half expect him to morph into a pluckable chicken bobbing around the room.

Deranged by hunger, missing the filters of reason and moderation, I have received personal messages from many unlikely sources. The Spanish chef on *Charlie Rose* delivers his penetrating words directly to me—only me—like Don Quixote. Yes, "breathing and eating," I hear what you're telling me, Señor Magic. The apartment is empty after Nurse Patty leaves, and I'm listening to an old Bob Dylan album I have heard a hundred times, and the line "I've got a hole where my stomach disappeared" jumps from the speakers like divine prophecy. Testify, Bobby! I come upon the rerun of a creaky *Odd Couple* episode, circa 1971, with Felix and Oscar starving at a fat farm. The script is peppered with shameless borscht-belt jokes and corny shtick, and the fact that the clinic's director is a Teutonic scold named Burger strikes me as deep received wisdom. I've got to get out of the house.

Along with my physical illness, I'm plagued by this clinical cognitive myopia, a twisted condition that further isolates the patient and aggravates unfortunately proximate loved ones. In addition to exhausting good people's patience, this warped perspective melts the patient's ability or willingness to distinguish what's meaningful from what's merely self-indulgent. My own volley of despair and hope, and the compounding tension's cannibalizing madness, is fired by the nightly match between the eaters at the dining table—filling their mouths, sating their hunger, gaining weight, growing healthy—and me, shrinking and watching from the sideline. Aside from driving me and them crazy with the irreconcilable differences dividing us, this medieval "therapy" of TPN I'm absorbing has reduced me to less than whole.

I've brought the saline, sterile wipes, surgical gloves, gauze, tape, garbage bag, and scissors to the living room tonight to change my wound dressing during *Charlie Rose*. I strip my pajamas off around the pump to start. I'm responsible for changing the dressing twice a day and have gotten accustomed to the grisly process of peeling off the surgical tape that has congealed to my irritated skin like old wallpaper. The complete dressing is a matrix of four gauze squares taped together and interlocked like two-over-two windowpanes to provide a large enough surface area to cover the wound. I did end up like Oreo the cow.

Nurse Patty wouldn't be pleased with my work environment tonight. I'm sitting in front of the TV naked on the unvacuumed rug, and the supplies share the adjacent coffee table with three days of newspapers and granola-bar wrappers. I have to be deliberate to keep all the pieces sterile. Tossing the crusted bandage in the garbage bag, I decide to give my body a few minutes of al fresco luxury before taping a fresh window on my gut.

I'm sitting close to the TV and can see my reflection in the screen's black sidebars, on the margins alongside the pontificating chef. Generally, I avoid looking at myself in the mirror these days, unwilling to register my bony body for what it is. I'd rather not regard the loss of bulk from my remission-era days of food-loading and pricey Ensure supplements and gym workouts. Even during the reign of the drinking cure, the dedication required to gain a few pounds—the constant calories, staying ahead of hunger, the money it cost to feed like a pre-hibernating bear—was all-consuming. To see that investment washed away is discouraging, a frustrating roll back down to the bottom of the mountain. The person mirrored on the TV border is stunning: haunted eyes and a narrow head like a railroad apartment; a cadaverous figure punctured in the middle by a bloody hole. Like Sid Vicious in his last days at the Chelsea Hotel.

I inspect the toll of the illness on my body. Since coming home from the hospital, the days' small, silent victories have declined from, formerly, getting the family's groceries shopped and unpacked to the current low bar of bathing and covering my wound. Seeing the stark image of my skeletal form on the screen makes questionable even the nominal goal of getting through another day, a flight of fancy to a dwindling future. Look at me. I've been deluding myself. It's foolish to think about a future. No wonder I can't get out of the past.

I look deeper into the hole in my gut. Face it: You're never going to see Thompson Lake again. The cut is still big and grue-some on me, a map of my lake like Lyndon Johnson's Vietnam scar, the open wound that won't heal. The crater of missing flesh is a personal history I can't ignore and, it seems, an end.

Thompson Lake was my escape, the valve that released the pressure of daily life.

My family first arrived in Maine not even by steerage class but by thumb. Grandpa Sid hitchhiked there in the summer of 1930 on Rudy Vallée Day, an unemployed kid with nothing to do, bumming rides from Brooklyn to Canada with his buddy Sam Yates. Turned away at the border as indigents, they came back south through Naples, Maine, and Long Lake, and, so the apocryphal story goes, Sid was cast under the spell of the magic water and pledged to come back. Actually, there's proof. Under the map on the boys' bedroom wall hangs a present-at-the-creation Brownie photo that Yates shot. My grandfather sits in profile on the throne of a sloped boulder at the shoreline, unrec-ognizable to me as a skinny seventeen-year-old with a forelock arcing from a crown full of hair, a boy king at sea, looking out over all that water. He did come back, first to a primitive camp on Long Lake with Marly and my mother and Uncle Richard. When my mother got married, she and my father moved up to a slightly better camp with running water, where my sister and I were indoctrinated, and then, decades later, to a real house on Thompson Lake, where Teddy and Finny think nothing of hav-ing an Internet connection.

Normally, it's the place I dream of nine months out of the year, knowing that everything will be waiting, unchanged. It's the place where the outdoor grill stands, and as I tilt my head back to rest on the couch cushion, I am suddenly there. Boxed in our city kitchen during the year, I yearn for sparkling summer and my station at the grill. Greatness comes from that grill. Fresh shrimp, scallops, clams, lobster, peppers, sugar and gold corn, burgers chocked with onions, Katz's franks driven up from New York. Me in my Katz's apron like the cutters behind the tall counters.

When I was a kid, my father and I would make a special trip to the Lower East Side at the end of the school year to provision for the lake, and as an excuse to split a hot pastrami lean on club, the mountain of briny, smoky brisket dripping with spices. Standing under the hanging salamis, we'd count the linked dogs as the Katz's counterman layered pounds of them in sheets of brown paper and spooned pints of mustard into the recycled yogurt containers. The lusty Jewish-kitchen smell of the hot dogs filled our Country Squire station wagon as we made our way up to Waspy Maine to feast all summer long.

My father is in his late seventies and still makes the frank run to Katz's before he and my mother head up for the summer. The counterman enjoys when my dad comes in for the annual pilgrimage, showboating to the other guys, "Twenty pounds of franks for the man from Massachusetts." Geography is not their strong suit. But Katz's still makes the best franks north or south of Houston Street, an indisputable truth confirmed seasonally by our gentile neighbors on the lake, who shun their rubber New England red hots for the Lower East Side's cased salty dogs.

Oh, my grill, my grill!

Whatever the meal I'm cooking, opening that grill's heavy lid and releasing the smoke and smell of dinner makes me giggle with the delirium of a vacationing idiot. Glass of wine in one hand, burnished spatula in the other, my trunks dripping from a quick swim while one side of the fish grills—that's Thompson Lake. I see, however, that it's all in the past. Stamped as it is on my gut in permanent ink, the image has a different connotation, and my Maine reverie is broken by the portrait staring back from the TV screen. Jon of Gaunt, I am a starving man. The hunger rages in the middle of my head.

Ferran Adrià is still gushing like a Romantic poet about the fundamental pleasures of the five senses we should all enjoy on a full plate. I pass out slumped against the base of the couch.

I am revisited by the nightmare from the hospital. I'm alone again in the apocalypse, suffering the torture of fear, the towers are burning and colliding, the streets are vacant, there is no food. I'm sinking in the hole of the crumbled pavement, and the menacing figure appears in view and approaches, ready to strike again. The figure's form is that of a man now, but the face is still blank. It raises a fist. I'm paralyzed and can't move. I stretch my mouth open to shout him away, but there is nothing. Nothing comes out. My mouth pulls wide and empty as a chasm. The fists come down on me, hammering and breaking me down like a cut of butchered meat.

"Yaaaaaaaaaahhhhhhh!" I awake screaming. I'm in the living room. The scissors and tape are still on the coffee table. I'm naked on the rug. The TV is blaring. Ferran Adrià and Charlie Rose are gone, replaced by images of enormous eaters in droopy shorts and bare chests like wet bags of lard weeping on scales that top five hundred pounds. I struggle up from the floor to shut off the set, cutting the room's light to smears of ambient nighttime glow on the wet windows.

I need a cold drink to shake off the nightmare. Instinctively, I stagger to the dark kitchen, cradling the Oreo pump and my clothes hung on the line, and open the refrigerator. The door is heavy, loaded with colored bottles and jars. I see the shelves for the first time in months. They are double- and triple-stacked with full meals and leftovers, filled so deep they shade the refrigerator's interior light. A golden-hued cheesecake looks ready to tumble from its high perch on a chocolate-pudding six-pack, and I feel something like the sting of a phantom limb. I've got to have a drink; my mouth is so dry, I can't swallow, I can't breathe. I grab the top-shelf pitcher of filtered water and bring it to the counter to pour. I'm so thirsty. I take a glass from the cabinet. The water spills in the cup. Then I remember. I'm NPO. Nothing by mouth. I can't have the water.

I return the pitcher to the refrigerator and come to the couch, shaken, drenched in the murk of nightmare and TPN, filling with dollar-a-minute piss. Again I pass out in the dark, wake with a bursting bladder, and repeat the draining cycle, stuck on an endless loop in the all-night funhouse. *Play Fascination. What a sensation. World's greatest creation. Thrill of a nation. Across the street from the BMT station. Play Fascination* . . . The days and nights are all like this. The pump is a despot, laughing at my body's rebellion and imprisoning me. I'm unfit to live with the others in this home.

That cheesecake. The stocked refrigerator shelves I saw in the dark once would have been a grand measure of my domestic duty. It doesn't belong to me now. I've been replaced.

Ironically, at the same time, the golden cheesecake and three-course meals are the stuff of something painfully beautiful happening here. A parade of food has been coming to our door, offerings that add a sixth sense to Ferran Adrià's philosophy. What I've witnessed is nothing short of astounding.

A dear group of school parents, neighbors, and old friends organized themselves immediately after my surgery and channeled their collective desire to help into a wonderful service: home-cooked delivered meals. They launched an online meal-calendar spreadsheet and have volunteered to cook and transport dinner and dessert every night since then. The meal slots are currently booked through April. Skirt steak and fried potatoes. Lamb stew. Lasagna. So much for the popular slur that city folk are hard and uncaring. That's a lie told by people who watched too much *Kojak*. City dwellers live on top of each other; how could we not be in each other's business?

For Susan, this kindness has been a godsend, saving the family from a spiral into three-day-old KFC. The meal blessing is in addition to Larry, a dad from Finny's class, taking the boys to school in the morning along with his own kids; and Kelly, a class mom, hosting Finn for after-school playdates, serving him dinner, and bringing him back to our apartment despite four little kids of her own at home; and Sharon, another school parent, taking me to doctors' appointments; and my mother driving in from New Jersey to scrub our apartment and bring the boys home from school; and many, many more inspiring gestures of help. In the hospital, I was lifted when Susan told me about the compassion and support from our treasured community of people. It should be life-affirming for me to see their charity on a plate.

Shamefully, I can't appreciate the full meaning of our friends' humanity in my confused, self-absorbed state. The family food bank is salvation for the house's eaters, but for the starving, the generosity of spirit baked in the bounty is ruined by my tormented cravings, unrequited desires that get whipped up by the presence of so much damn fantastic food. Frustration is an unintended ingredient blended in to the Adrià principles of these generous meals. That refrigerator is a tomb.

Anyone who's ever starved for a day, for medical or religious or financial reasons, knows the torture of moving along the sidewalk and having every pizza aroma within five blocks knock you down blind. Imagine getting provoked every day in the confining walls of your own home with meat, vegetables, sauces, and brownies coursing the plate.

I'm reduced to a thing that wants what's gone, I think. How can I be envious of the people who are trying to help me? How low can I sink?

The following night, I languish at dinner, cuffed on the love seat by the incessant Oreo, while at the table, the others chew on the gift of another well-made meal. This one came long-distance: roast chicken, mashed potatoes, and cucumber salad ordered up by our old friend Ellen in Washington. The browned chicken reminds me of my grandparents' table.

Finn, ever the hedonist and a raw nerve of id, reacts once more to my exile with the question we'd all like answered. "When will you eat?" he screams, his chin bearded in fluffy potato.

"Soon," Susan answers in the soothing voice she punches up from her emotional speed dial.

This time I don't bother to agree. I've watched the food come in night after night, provided by thoughtful friends to comfort the family, and it has become like an extended secular shivah. (Shivah is the first known example of the Jews squaring bereavement with food.) Even in the most observant houses, shivah lasts for only a week. In our apartment, the grieving feels eternal.

In the ritual's custom, providing food is considered a mitzvah, a good deed of kindness and compassion, but also—in the yin and yang of gift and loss embroidered on the Chosen People like the sleeve on a Torah—an expression of consolation. That's the conflict that has me as I watch by the living room window. The online dinner calendar and home deliveries are the milk of human kindness, but they exist *because* of my separation from eating, separation from the family, separation from the living. When the doorbell rings and another meal comes in, it's like I'm not here, like I'm already gone.

I remember the shivah in Marly's house when Grandpa Sid died. He was the first to go among the retirees from Bonds' window, and the curtained downstairs rooms were livened by plates of roast chicken and Tupperwares of kasha varnishkes and the old-timers telling stories about Sid, like when a fat lady at a wedding shoot sat on the mandolin he'd left on a folding chair, crushing it to splinters. George Kaplan, Sid's boyhood friend, a beaming smile and a Buddha's bald head, recalled when they were ten and Sid came downstairs to the tenement stoop to say that his father had just died. I talked about the Thanksgiving chestnuts. The shivah was emotional, happy, a moving celebration, except Sid wasn't there with the living to enjoy it, and to eat the food.

A knock comes at the door. It's our upstairs neighbor Nancy, a concerned woman whose exquisite, moist brisket has actually compelled me to a Passover table. I'd wear a yarmulke for a month for a forkful of that tender, falling meat. Nancy is wearing a striped apron over office clothes, and she enters the apartment carrying a chocolate Bundt cake that has been soaked in rum, spraying the air with an intoxicating scent.

"I hope you like chocolate cake." Nancy smiles at Teddy and Finn, who are fussing on each other's laps at the table. "Isabelle and Naomi helped make it." Her daughters are around the boys' ages.

"I bake, too," Finn says, and his messy face serves up its engaging dimples under the cheeks. "How many eggs did you use?"

"Four. I didn't have enough, so I borrowed two from Sheryl. I guess this is really a building cake." Nancy's tawny skin is radiating a warm glow. She's suffered her own serious health problems—breast cancer and other invasive surgeries. Sometimes, perhaps understandably, she can drive people crazy with worry, but she's been exceptionally kind to me. One holiday, she even cooked an extra brisket, and her husband, Ben, made his specialty potato latkes just for us. Fried ecstasy.

"Nancy, this smells heavenly. Doesn't it, boys?" Susan says, taking the cake plate in her hands. "You're so nice. Please sit down and join us for a piece."

"Ben isn't home yet, and the girls are alone upstairs, so this will be just for you. Finn, let me know if you think I used enough eggs."

Susan cuts three pieces in the kitchen and brings them out to the table. I watch the plates of donut-edged slices float by. The boys stuff their mouths vigorously with the dark cake, barely using forks. Rum-saturated whiffs from the air around Susan's path raise me furtively to the kitchen. I plow my nose down like an anteater to the cake on the counter and inhale. Woozy on the fumes, I breathe deeper. I smell it all: Mount Gay or the jivey Captain Morgan that you always see splashed on subway ads, it makes no difference; flour, butter, sugar, the pair of borrowed eggs. Crumbs sprinkle my forehead. I'm aching to jump in the center hole and bury myself in the cake.

Smell isn't enough. I touch the wet cake with clumsy fingers, running them through brown chunks that crumble impossibly. It's like chocolate rain falling in a desert, and I need a prospector's pan to catch the dropping treasure. I plunge my hands into the mound, and then Susan walks into the kitchen. I should be embarrassed, or at least try to hide what I've done, but I am too far gone. Susan is stunned by the mess I've made, bothered by the violation of the family's dessert.

"What are you doing?" she asks urgently and hushed, so as not to alarm the kids in the next room, her face betraying both pity and scorn. Her hands fly from her sides, maybe an impulse to try to put the crumbled cake back together, but it's futile, and she waves them at me. The joy with which she received Nancy's gift of friendship is spoiled. I look at her, shake my head, shrug, and laugh weakly, the chocolate caking my hands like blood. Here's a spot. Damned cake.

Selfishness is not an answer. Increasingly, it seems, we're closing in on the end of our patience—with each other, with my sickness, with my attitude, with me. Chronic illness, always lurking, has become the handmaiden to my checklist of life's larger failures and what seems like inevitable doom. That's my affliction. But failure, desperation, defeat do not come naturally to Susan. My descent into the hole of food deprivation, my plummet into the Bundt cake, clashes with the faith of her innate optimism. She's got no interest in plumbing this depth of hell with me. Her soft face tightens with anger, but she has a deeper message for me.

"I just can't be everything," she says, her emotions breaking loose. "I can't try to be happy for the boys and me and serve your every need and be alone doing it. There are limits to what I can do. Maybe some people can, but it's too much, *this* is too much, and I can't anymore."

The misery of my relentless hunger has contaminated her once unshakable belief in our happiness. It's a Friday night, I think—our old dining-out night. *Tell me what you crave, and I will tell you what you are.*

Why did I destroy your dessert? Isn't it obvious?

CHAPTER 5

The egg in the basket sizzling in the iron skillet sounds like fire-crackers and glistens so real and gooey on screen I want to eat the television. It's after three in the morning, and I'm alone in the living room, watching *Moonstruck*. Olympia Dukakis is in her housecoat at the stove, cooking breakfast. The scene opens with a close-up of the one-handed egg-crack-and-drop into the fried bread's basket hole, but I wish the director had started earlier and shot the whole one-eyed-Jack concerto that brought this dish to the brink of perfection. I imagine Olympia carving the half-dollar-size holes in the two thick cuts of bread with a cookie cutter, then buttering the four sides with the stick soft-ening on the granite counter of her cook's kitchen. It's a tiled room big enough to seat the entire cast. They live in a brick house on Cranberry Street. Frying the bread in the black pan's olive oil coating, Olympia flips the slices, and the egg and the yolk conjoin like twins in their swimming holes. This is no ordi-nary egg in the basket—it's something!

I know all the food in this movie. There are spicy peppers seasoning the egg in the hole; missile-size bread loaves cooling on metal racks at the Cammareri bakery; manicotti and minestrone soup served at the Grand Ticino restaurant; two martini olives Olympia bites from a toothpick; a Parmesan wheel Uncle Raymond splits on his grocery-store counter; the fried steak Nicholas Cage cuts like a wolf with the cleaver in his fist. Food or drink fills practically every scene ostensibly about romance and submitting to the randomness of fate. I've got the whole movie in my head. It's one of Susan's comfort foods, and we've watched it together so many times that I know what scenes have been chopped over the years for commercials. If the egg-in-the-basket close-up ever gets cut, that will be it for me. All of it looks delicious, right up to the end when Nicolas Cage and Cher's engagement is toasted at the breakfast table. White sugar cubes are dropped into flutes of Brut Champagne. *"A la famiglia."*

Tonight I'm watching *Moonstruck* alone because Susan and the kids have left. The apartment is empty. It's spring break, and they've escaped to her parents' house in Indiana. Land of big houses, big driveways, big cars, big box stores, big kitchens.

Susan has a hard, sometimes thankless job, teaching reading to Hispanic kids in a pressurized city school. She's responsible for educating teenagers who bring to class all the challenges of poverty and immigration during a cycle in American history when politicians prefer to blame teachers for the classroom consequences of the deeper societal challenges of poverty and immigration: "Just decertify the teachers' union, and the level of learning in this country will soar." Sure, tell me another one. It's a demoralizing climate for teachers, on top of the budget gutting that is eliminating positions in spite of greater performance expectations. Susan's an intelligent, educated, committed professional working under unreasonable conditions, and she's forced to hear grief from suits who've never spent five minutes in front of a classroom. Not so different from getting harangued by the rants and accusations that yoke her with my insoluble misery. This is her vacation week, and she'd rather not spend the time off from work with the other source of her problems. Smart girl.

A nasty fight sparked between us the night before their flight, punctuated by the kind of language that explains divorce. Apparently, I haven't been the only one contemplating the future of the family unit without me, and the scenario of our marriage failing lurks in the room, the endgame of degenerative distress. We've both been tried by these months of hunger, devoured by an emptiness neither expected, and I haven't shone as the kind of husband needed to hold together a marriage in crisis. She needs time away from me and the poison I've spread.

I understand that—my behavior is insufferable—but I'm angry at being left alone. Inside this void, I feel like there's nothing else and that no one can bring me out of it. I'm in the shackles of nothing by mouth. It paralyzes everything.

I've stopped believing in the future. Some people believe God works all things for our good, even if we don't understand them. That's a premise of faith. But I'm separate from God. Faith in what? I don't know that I'll eat again, or that I'll ever be liberated from this gnawing chronic illness. I don't know how I'll do anything interesting again, how I'll provide. Teddy told us he wants to go to sleepaway camp this summer, and he should, but how? The kitchen cabinets' cheap veneer is peeling off like dead skin, and the garbage disposal has started leaking great gobs of dirty water. When we bought this place we thought it would be good for five years. This is year ten.

My hospital roommate J.P. has left two messages. I haven't returned the calls.

Saving the worst for the people closest to me, I direct my litany of complaints and anger mostly at Susan. Rages to validate my pessimism: "You can eat; I can't. You feel healthy; I don't. You are alive; I'm not." I'm screaming at her like crazy Nicholas Cage—"I lost my hand! I lost my bride!"—looking for someone to blame.

The tender triptych cooed off my tongue as Susan packed for the trip, her eyes weary. Her openmouthed duffel bag sat on the sole corner of our bed free of the vials and syringes I was prepping for blood-thinning and blood-boosting injections. She grabbed a sock from her dresser drawer and flattened it between the bedroom door and its chipped jamb to force the door shut. All the apartment's doorknob latches are broken from the boys' slamming rounds of wild chase, and the only way to keep a door shut is to shove a sock in the gap. The toe end of Susan's sweatsock flops down like a strangled puppet.

"I don't want the boys to hear this," Susan snaps in a whisper by the door. "How many times have I said 'Keep your voice down'? You don't think they hear this?"

"Then when exactly am I supposed to talk to you? You're leaving." I sit upright against the bed's cherry headboard and bull's-eye a hypodermic needle through the rubber port of a B12 vial. Fluid draws out into the syringe cartridge like a draft beer heavy on foam.

"What are you going to tell me? How miserable you are? I know how miserable you are, but I can't do anything about it anymore. Whenever I'm positive and optimistic and try to find a little progress, you immediately tell me everything that's wrong and why nothing can improve." Susan lays her lean body against the socked door to seal it. She's moving fast in bra and panties and grabs a robe that's draped over the rod in her closet to cover up. I've promised to install a hook and haven't.

"What am I supposed to say? Am I supposed to lie? Every day there's a new problem on top of the old ones. My doctor's visit today was horrible. I told you what Abrams said. 'There was nothing good in the report.' You think I *want* to live this way?" I flick my index fingernail against the upside-down bottle to knock out the air bubbles filling the syringe. I can't break them down and have to start over, draining the B12 serum back through the port into the vial.

"I never said you're not in pain, and maybe I can't under-stand what it's like to be so sick, but what else can I do about it? You don't want to be cheered up. You're depressed. You refuse to talk to your doctor about Prozac." Susan tugs on a tangled silver necklace buried in her jewelry box. Silver's her color—it took me several pair of gold earrings to learn that. The necklace isn't coming loose, and she sits cross-legged on the floor with the jewelry box in her lap. The room is crowded. She lowers her head, and her brown hair rolls off her shoulders onto the raised lid. She shudders, upset, away from me.

A thud shakes the door, then a giggle. The boys are playing ball in the tin-can hallway between our bedrooms.

"Teddy, stop!" The Prozac remark launches me into the

stratosphere. "You think that's some kind of answer, another medication? Isn't this proof enough?" I yell from the bed and hurl a balled sterile wipe across the room at the mini-fridge. "I don't want another medication. I've already got two refrigerators filled with medical crap, and I'm only getting worse. All I'm doing is making the pharmaceutical industry rich. Of course I'm depressed. Who wouldn't be? Everything I had has gone to shit. You think some antidepressant with side effects that can kill an ox is going to heal my gut, or let me eat, or get me a job? That's not going to solve anything that I need solved. It's a pill when I need a meal. If it's so great, why don't *you* take Prozac?"

This is an absurdly juvenile attack, like saying, "You love Prozac so much, why don't you marry it?" But our fights have a way of leaving reason in the dust. What can I say for my outburst? I've eaten nothing but a plate of crazy for too long. I'm impossible to live with, and Susan's packing to leave. Nobody's frying me a steak to cut into with a cleaver.

Throwing the sterile wipe at the fridge jerked the needle from the B12 bottle. A shot of the premium juice drips on the leg of my warm-ups. The syringe is getting funky, and I'll need to open a fresh one. I dump the used needle in the sharps jug and bark in frustration. A little too loud.

"You can't do this to us. It's not fair to me; it's not fair to the kids. I have to leave." Susan unsocks the door and goes to the boys' bedroom to comfort them and pack their bags.

There's a lesson here that I have been incapable of absorbing: Solipsism is destructive. It has infected our marriage with an explosiveness that neither of us knows how to cure. I'm driving the hunger straight into her. Unfortunately, it's only after the fact that I seem to comprehend the damage. Susan is done with trying to hold up the walls. She can't understand why I keep taking them down to the studs. It's painful to look that close.

Life's undoing happens with no regard for your expectations. Our fight wasn't precipitated by anything especially new, yet it escalated to a crack of anger and hurt in a flash, as though these problems haven't been with us for a long time. One moment Susan was folding a cotton V-neck, in the next the kids were being emotionally scarred. One moment I was planning on tuna fish for lunch, in the next my guts exploded. There was a ticking bomb inside me masked by outward signs of stability. Expectations are window dressing. Sid concealing the jacket's bad stitching on the Bond's mannequin. Like the surprise perforation, the trauma of suffering has exposed an underlying weakness in our marriage, or in me, one that also may or may not heal. We need food.

Moonstruck ends with Dino crooning "That's Amore," and I shut off the TV. Outside, the windows in the courtyard apartments are dark, save for the spines of white emergency lights. I can tell by the shot of TPN left in the bag that the new day will break soon.

I think it's an hour earlier in Indiana. Their legislature has messed with daylight savings, and I can never remember what time Bernie and Marilyn are on. Whenever it is, Susan and the kids must be sound asleep in the McMansion. It's in a development named Royal Woods Hill, an honorific that invokes the nature that was cleared to build the houses. She's sleeping in the upstairs front bedroom with the putty-colored walls and the wedding pictures from all the generations displayed on Great-Grandmother Edith's Chippendale-style dresser. Susan actually called her "Grandmother." It sounded so foreign to me. Edith lived to ninety-eight. Bernie and Marilyn are barely adults in their photo, smiling big in the backseat of a wedding cab, the Kentucky summer heat flashed on their smooth foreheads. Susan's sister and brother-in-law still show baby fat plumping their cheeks in their reception-hall portrait. Ours is framed by inlaid wood, ornamental in a wedding-picture way, a contrast to the raw landscape composing the background.

We were married outdoors, on a rocky bluff overlooking the ocean on an island off the Maine coast. After days of rain and weather anxiety, the skies cleared in the afternoon, and the sun glinted yellow on the scalloped water. It's déclassé to wear heels or a tuxedo on shale cliffs, but we didn't stand on pretense; that was the spirit of the wedding. We chose the location because it was spectacular. The only clergy in the state of Maine who would marry us was a lesbian Unitarian minister with untamed curls and a husky voice that rung in the atmosphere. We got our marriage license from the part-time town clerk who also issued fishing licenses. It was all part of the fun. I can imagine what Sid would've said about photographing the ceremony: "This is a wedding? It looks like a picnic. What are you, a character?" But there's a bride dressed in a silk satin sheath column and long white gloves—elegant, poised, tall, radiant—she's beautiful.

I never thought our marriage would fail. Of course, there are no perfect couples or perfect people, and there are differences between Susan and me. In our habits, we can be like Felix and Oscar living together, but if anything, it seemed as though we'd grown more alike in thirteen years. Some of the prickly issues that used to vex us, like what to do about religion with our mutt children, were smoothed over by discovering the shared things we wanted from life and from each other. There have been inevitable strains and surprises to blow our newlywed dreams: My health episodes have infected many plans; my layoffs and the money squeeze are prevailing stresses; and parenting challenges any marriage. However, I felt that we were surviving the troubles with our wits intact, still seeing the world for its good and bad, still wanting happiness for our family, still calling each other "Ace."

For years, Susan and I have used that nickname affectionately. Susan tied the name on me from an anarchic gag in a Marx Brothers movie, and it's hung on like a favorite scarf. She made it official on a note affixed to the Golden Harvest refrigerator in our old apartment: "Turn the Crock-Pot down to simmer. Don't forget, Ace!" I liked the nickname so much, I stuck it on her, too. Ace has replaced both of our given names in conversation and e-mail. After all this time, Susan and Jon sound to us like somebody else's parents. Lately, Ace has disappeared. There's nothing loving being said between us, and I'm in a black hole that feels like it could collapse what we've built together.

Through the setbacks, we've tried to keep life stable for the boys: not selling our apartment to buy time with the money; keeping them in their bunk beds and not moving to a cheaper city without jobs or friends; enrolling them in baseball and basketball and tennis and swimming and chess and skiing; finding corner booths in diners for grilled-cheese sandwiches; and doing as much as we can to give them happy childhoods within our strapped means, sheltered from the struggle. I didn't know we had no money when I was growing up, and I don't imagine that Teddy and Finny do, either.

Now I'm worried about what will happen to us. I look strange and scary to them since coming home from the hospital, more patient than dad. My illness is harming them in ways I feel powerless to prevent, and it's tearing me up. Teddy wants to know if I'll coach his baseball team this month; Finny wants to know when I'll eat. They want certainty, and I can't provide it. My situation has the potential to make the boys feel unprotected and abandoned—no matter how many years I've schlepped them back and forth to school and how many meals I've made— to undo what's been done. I can't bank any parenting credit to cushion their fears in the here and now. Every kid's stomachache triggers worry. If things don't improve for Susan and me, what kind of lasting impact might there be? Would it harm the boys' ability to form and trust their own relationships as adults? Fear is a lousy legacy to leave your kids. Susan doesn't want to be married to me, the me that I've become, and I don't want to be married to her if I can't be honest. She tells me honesty isn't an exclusive goal, it needs to be balanced with sensitivity and forgiveness, and that my honesty is an excuse for selfishness. Until this latest trauma, the boys have lived in blissful ignorance, going unharmed through my unemployment and illness. But what would divorce do to them? What would it do to us?

I finish the nighttime Oreo pumping and complete the four-hour saline and octreotide drip while changing my dressing to fresh windowpanes. Our health insurance has maxed out on the allotted home-care visits, so I see no more of Nurse Patty or

Debbie, the West Indian with kind eyes and a headful of fusilli who bled me several times a week. She laughed like a crow at my pale St. Thomas kindergarten picture hanging above the dresser. I use the last of the gauze pads on the two-over-two bandage. I'll need to shop at the pharmacy for this evening's change. The insurance coverage has also run out for supplies, so it's up to me to restock.

I haven't been outside since Susan and the boys left, and I'm shaky on the pavement when I exit the apartment at noon.

The interminable winter has delayed spring. Bald buds canopy our block. A coveralled gardener is up a ladder at the brownstone of the media star whose son Teddy plays tennis with, planting geraniums and vines on the dozen window boxes that adorn the house. The only other sign of life on the block is the knife sharpener parked in his jalopy by the hydrant, ringing the bell to an empty sidewalk. The truck has the old sharpening blocks and wheels rigged on a small stage in the back like a traveling medicine show. Susan stopped using him after he ground a beveled edge into our Global knife. I wave a feeble hello. He looks me over curiously from the driver's seat.

By the time I reach the pharmacy, I'm fatigued from the two-block walk. Perspiration is pooling under the shirt layers I wear to keep from freezing. Inside the stale chain drugstore, I find the gauze pads quickly and am headed to a long checkout line when a commotion at the back breaks the din. I rubberneck and see a severely disabled guy by the hair products who looks to be losing a fight with his motorized wheelchair. An overmatched store clerk stands with him, trying to help, but is getting frustrated and angling to leave. The disabled man speaks loudly in a painful moan, laboring hard to be understood. It sounds more like an animal keening than human speech. I walk over.

Up close, the situation gets a little clearer and more complicated. His condition is very bad, advanced Parkinson's, I guess. He has minimal control of his twitchy movements and can't articulate intelligibly. With one clumsy hand, he's smacking a chair arm, pounding it like a dead car's dashboard, and I come to understand the cause of his anger. The mechanized chair has lost its power. Poor bugger. He's trying to spring himself up from the seat and is getting nowhere with the clerk. He points awkwardly at a men's hair-color product boxed on an unreachable shelf.

"Excuse me, do you want that box?" I ask.

He utters a relieved "yes" and rubs a comb of bent fingers over unruly gray hair and a spotty beard. A grimace and a few finger jabs explain the rest: He motored to the drugstore for hair color, and the chair quit. He would use the touch-pad display cabled to the chair to tap out language and communicate, but it draws power from the same source as the chair and is dark and dumb. The guy is stuck in the silent metal contraption and will be forced to spend eternity in this corner unless he finds another power source.

Aside from his crippling disability, he wears other unmistakable signs of oppressive hardship: bagged-at-the-joints soiled sweatpants and hoodie, corroded sneakers, grimy fingernails. He smells rank. The store's staff would rather not deal with this very unfortunate, unpleasant soul who can't just go away.

I plant the hair-color box in his jumpy hands, and in appreciation, he tilts a dark mouth of toothless pockets. A small victory in his cruel day. But now what? His chair is shot, and I can hear the store manager fretting at the security guard to have him removed. A wrinkled shopping bag is bunched in his lap. He pulls out a prescription bottle and taps a finger on the label. He lives two blocks south and three long avenues east of the store, toward Central Park.

"You need me to take you home?" I ask.

He tilts his mouth again.

"No problem, John," I say. "I read your name on the bottle. That's my name, too."

I push him to the register and charge the gauze and the hair color. "This one's on me," I say, and we exit the store onto a side-walk sparkled by the climbing sun.

John's chair feels heavy as a steamer trunk full of pig iron, and I strain to make excruciatingly slow progress on Broadway. Other than slinging Oreo in the backpack and lifting the TPN bags, I haven't exerted myself in so long that I've got comically little strength or stamina. What did I get myself into? I have doubts we'll make it to John's building, and I can't just leave the guy in the street. I heave us past a newsstand at a pace so slug-gish I can read the photo captions on the *Post*. Passersby shoot looks of dismal contempt at this creepier Ratso and Joe Buck.

John lives in a block-long penitentiary of bricks across from the park that I've passed a thousand times on my bike and never much regarded. The institutional 1960s complex is fronted by a circular driveway and a stationed doorman who doesn't budge to help me open the door and swing in the chair.

"Hello, there. I've got a passenger who needs to get home," I wheeze. "His wheelchair conked out on Broadway."

The doorman is strangely disinterested, to the point of inso-
lence, and I quickly get the sense that John is considered not
worth the time. It could be for any number of reasons: The staff
might be tired of the demands his needs place on them; today's
wheelchair tow may not be unique in his history of episodes;
John could have a sweet deal on his apartment, and the management would like to kick him out; or the doorman is just an
asshole. He pushes John's apartment keys at me across the security desk, and I'm left to shove the chair in the elevator for a
musty ride to the third floor.

I force the apartment key and unlock John's dead bolt, bump
the metal door open with my backside, and pull the busted
chair in off the hallway carpet. "Home, sweet Home," I reassure
John and myself.

John's apartment is a shit hole. Beyond the front door, there's
barely a path wide enough for me to squeeze the chair in. He's
pointing stiffly to a small clearing by the room's center window,
where a computer monitor sits atop an office-surplus cast-off
missing a wheel. The Collyer Brothers would have felt at home
in the three claustrophobic rooms cluttered to the corners with
newspapers, magazines, flyers, boxes, duct-tape rolls, plastic
bottles, faceless electronics, garbage bags—anything that's been
carried into the apartment. Things come here to die. The toaster
on the sticky kitchen counter is fractured in pieces. Take-out
packets of ketchup and mayo and a spoiled banana are the only
food in the putrid refrigerator. How does this guy even feed himself? I unpack the hair dye and set it down on a rusted, listing
TV tray where there should be a proper kitchen table. The apartment's windows are shut, and the stench of decay encroaches like

the piles of debris. You can never entirely imagine what goes on inside all the windows in New York. I can't see how John survives.

There's nowhere for me to sit—the lone couch is buried under a file cabinet missing a drawer. The bare walls offer no distraction from the debilitating neglect of the place. John two-finger-types on the keyboard, then motions for me to look at the monitor. Pushing his loaded chair up the long slope to this building drained me, and I bend at the waist to support myself against the desk, but it shakes nervously, so I stand. John is animated about what he's typed. I read it aloud so he knows I'm paying attention. "thank u 4 help," he's written.

"You're welcome," I say. "Listen, we sick guys have to stick together." I cringe inside and force a numb smile. Compared to John's, my situation is about as bad as a boil on my ass. He's written more, a lot more, and scrolls down, jittering a finger on the arrow key, for me to read.

"'Dear Mr. Mayor,'" I begin. I read the letter rolling on the dusty screen and then the next one to "Dear Mr. Senator," and the one to "Dear Mr. President." They are missives, dense, furious diatribes about the very real pain and helplessness in John's excruciating life. The concentrated energy and motor skill summoned to type page after page is a testament to John's will. Anger motivates him. He's trying to be heard, making the effort, like he did getting to the store for dye to color his mangy hair. His spirit is sound. But the letters to the men in power are laced with so much rage their explosive tone shatters John's legitimate gripes and escalates him from poor, unlucky soul to menacing crackpot. The hostility confuses whether John is appealing for help or threatening revenge, or both.

Wanting to take the sting out of the agitated air, I've resorted to the stagy inflections I used to read *The Cat in the Hat* when I wanted to relax the kids at bedtime. Given the plight in this hovel and the letter's dark temper, my reading is absurd and insulting—it's bullshit patronizing. I stop after the bomb to the White House and try to transition John with a silly pat on the back.

"John, we have to get your wheelchair running. Is there someone I can call about it?"

He sighs and points to a Post-it on the computer showing a Brooklyn phone number. I don't see a phone in the rubble, so I use my cell and reach a social-services office. The name on the Post-it is that of John's caseworker. She's busy, and I talk to someone else who takes down my message but doesn't seem terribly concerned.

"Someone will be there in three to six hours, and they will make an evaluation about the condition," the woman says in a dull voice. I can visualize the open pack of Newports fingered on the metal desk.

"He really needs his chair to be fixed. He can't get around, and I don't see a backup in the apartment."

"Who are you, sir?"

"Just someone helping out." I regard John with a cheery look, as though I'm getting somewhere.

"Three to six hours is standard response time. Someone will be there—" A noise in the background chokes her off. Maybe a loudspeaker or a fire bell.

"What happens if the chair can't be fixed by that person? He's got nothing else."

"The client is entitled to a temporary replacement. If necessary, that will be delivered in up to twenty-four hours."

My impulse is to force the issue with the bureaucrat, damn the pleasantries. I feel my back rising to the anger of John's letters. I know the situation stinks for both parties. I know the blasé woman on the phone works in a crummy office so overtaxed by demand that she's backing up someone else trying to perform mouth-to-mouth on a city full of Johns. I also know when it's essential to get a swamped doctor's attention.

I repeat to her all the information I've already reported, for no other reason than to delay hanging up and facing this cruel scene and the obligation that comes from having failed. John considers me. His mouth is twitched into a frustrated gash. The obvious question coats his oily face, and I share the curt update, presented in the lie of manufactured optimism. The truth is too hard.

Severe illness is terrifying. Aside from your own agony, your pitiless needs can starve people to fear. It can be too much for others to bear, scaring friends into strangers, and you end up alone in a living hell like this. You get so sick of being sick that it consumes you until there's nothing else but sickness, and you drive people away, like I've driven away Susan and the boys. They left on Friday. No hugs good-bye at the door. Susan carried the bags. I'm not sure when they're coming back.

John needs someone—the hair color was a calling card—and I want to get out of his apartment. It's a vision of a bleak future I don't want to see. I reattach the Post-it to the computer monitor, and he turns down his madman's grin. He knows exactly what's going on.

I shouldn't be so unnerved by John's grim existence. I used to know a lot of people in situations like his. In my twenties, I managed an arts program for people with disabilities. I didn't have a clue as to what I was doing and took the job because I needed money. There was a steep learning curve.

I worked with a painter, Claudia, who used a wheelchair and lived in subsidized housing on a cobblestone street near the river in the West Village. Claudia had strong, sharp features, a cut jawline, Northern Italian coloring, and hair that tumbled like Venus's over the shoulders of the batik tops she wore. Hers was clearly a remarkable face before survival became its dominant feature. She painted large canvases in acrylics and maneuvered her chair on a makeshift series of ramps and risers to reach the far surface areas. Claudia didn't have the resources of a Chuck Close to install hydraulics, and her studio apartment was entirely given over to the ramps and risers. It was like living in a skateboard park. The kitchen was crowded with Chock full o'Nuts coffee cans and the usual scavenged art supplies, but there was no refrigerator and no food in the painted cupboard. I could never figure out where she slept or ate. "Buy me dinner. I'm a starving artist," she said.

Claudia was a savvy lady, twenty years older than I was and a lifetime sharper. I liked her. She was direct as a headlamp, and I learned something whenever I shut up and listened. She told me which of the artists in the program were willing to tolerate me and my bureaucratic burden and which ones thought I was an empty suit and wanted to fry my nuts. "Kieran has a wicked sense of humor and would like you if you dropped the corporate act. Inez just hates your guts." She also let me know that leaning against her chair was an invasion of her personal space, like leaning on her body. I got the message.

She was the first real artist I knew. She introduced me to Claes Oldenburg, Merce Cunningham, and others in the neighborhood. On a few occasions, I went shopping with Claudia to Pearl Paint so my organization could foot the bill, pushing the wheelchair along Canal Street back to her apartment, her lap loaded with bags of paints and primers, tubes and jars the colors of root vegetables and tropical fruit. A canvas bolt and stretchers lay across the chair arms like a safety bar on a roller-coaster seat, and I'm guiding the racing wheels through packed sidewalks of leather-goods hawkers, years before curb cuts. At every corner, I pivot the chair wheels and grip the rubber handles tight to keep from dumping Claudia face-first into a westbound bus. It's humid July, and my strength is unraveling from the load.

When we cross the cobblestone intersections closer to her building, I lift the wheels to lessen the bumps and the pain shooting through her crushed spine. I'm talking nervously, idiotically, too much at every drop and jostle, trying to cover torture with politeness.

"Sorry about that. Whoops. Almost there."

In the gauntlet of the streets, I stop being the program manager, and Claudia stops being the artist. I'm not thinking about the canvas bolt she'll measure and cut and the new paintings that will stack farther out from the walls like plowed snow in the blizzard of her apartment. "Didn't see that one, sorry," I apologize after another jolt. Everything is an obstacle from the moment Claudia wakes up; just getting over the stones is a project. That's why there's no food in her kitchen. Shopping, cooking, serving—more obstacles. Her life feels so solitary and confined. She'll never get out of the chair.

Standing in John's brutal apartment, I'm reminded of Claudia and of the phone call I had before leaving this morning. A lawyer and I discussed filing for disability insurance because I can't eat, I'm sick, and I qualify. Her name is Claudia, too.

"The law defines you as disabled," she says in an incidental voice on the phone. It's disturbing to hear. I'm defined again by what I'm not—"dis"—and the hole in me is bigger than my gut. This Claudia is well informed and gives me a lot to think about, but I tell her not to pursue it and end the call awkwardly. I don't want to be on disability. I don't want to be disabled. And practically, disability doesn't pay nearly enough to live on or allow enough secondary income to do so. "Disabled" would be an admission that I've given up, that I've failed, that it's over. I'd be a charity case clinging to the margins, and that's all I'd ever be. Shit, I haven't achieved much as "able-bodied;" how could I even think of achieving anything as the Man Who Can't Eat?

I know what the other Claudia would say, the painter who gave it to me straight: "You're disabled. Take the money." I think of Claudia living in her chair, battling the clobbering streets. I think of her foodless kitchen and the currents of pain that twisted her noble face, that face cracked too young by the betrayal of her broken body. I remember it all, everything she faced. And I don't remember one of Claudia's paintings.

I run from the crumbling scene in John's apartment and turn the wrong way on the sidewalk.

I don't leave my phone number. I'm fleeing in terror, a moral failure, scared self-preservation. John's odor is on my coat collar. It's time to start the pump on the overnight fix, but I can't go home and tie up. I can't confront another eighteen-hour shift with Oreo and the pole after this.

I climb down the stairs of the subway station on the corner and get on the first train. My unlimited MetroCard is long expired, and I put the five dollars in my wallet on a new one. Riding the subway again is jarring. My bony ends have no cushion on the hard bench. If I shut my eyes, I'll go back to the nightmare of John's apartment, and I've brought nothing to read, so I stare at the panel ads for beer and seafood. Pink shrimp, brown beer, white teeth. A man and woman happy and happy and happy and happy on all the repeating panels lining the subway car. I stay on the train past Columbus Circle, past Times Square, past Penn Station. I'm headed south. I decide to get off at Franklin Street. The ride was for a quest. Pump time, my ass.

Out of the covered station, a funnel of traffic converges toward the Holland Tunnel at rush hour. I tramp the busy thoroughfare over to the quieter side streets. A painted sun is dropping west over the Hudson, rolling strips of mustard down the blocks. The buildings here are ancient, brick industrials from the days when things were actually made in Manhattan, and they're still as picture-perfect as a Hollywood back lot. They maintain the illusion that nothing changes, even if I don't remember the real estate office at the near corner or how long the storefront next to it has been vacant. My friend Milo lived in an artist's loft there above a bakery for years and paid three hundred a month. He slept on the floor for the radiant heat when the bakery oven fired up at three in the morning, warming on his air mattress like the bread crusts.

As it turns out, I am on a back lot. A movie is being shot on this preserved block. Dressing-room trailers and craft services trucks line both sides of the street. Folding tables of frosted pastries and sliced fruit. Pasta salad. An army of clipboard-carrying walkie-talkie operators commandeers the sidewalk, guarding the food. I detour south and walk in the middle of an empty street that frames a view of the river three blocks away. At the shoreline, a front-loader dumps landfill into the river, making Manhattan bigger.

I am approaching the mythic Chanterelle corner again, the big windows looking into the dining room where Susan and I will someday eat stuffed seafood sausage and celebrate the special occasion that's made us so happy.

This mission to the restaurant feels like a pilgrimage, like the journeys that people make to religious shrines. I've seen those journeys on television, the slow swarms under the influence, the masses of disabled following the path to salvation, to Lourdes Cathedral in France and the miraculous healing inside. "Walk by faith, not by sight."

One block to go.

"Lord, be the companion of my journey." If I can get to Chanterelle and stand at the window and see those honey walls, and watch the plates come out with the day's catch, and open my mouth at the sight of a bottle of red, and read that holy menu with the hand-drawn cover, if I can get to Chanterelle and feel all that, then I'll be able to dream again of eating there someday. The power of belief, in something—belief in Chanterelle, belief in brook trout sauté, belief in a special occasion—can save me. That's what I need. If I am able to believe, I can transform my mind and body. "Let me go to the house of the Lord," I say. I'm so close to the restaurant, I can practically taste the grilled sausage. Miracles can happen.

"Stop! Rolling, stop!"

I've misjudged the size of the movie shoot. As I turn the last corner to approach the glory of Chanterelle, I'm blocked by a clipboard woman who throws her body at me like a barricade across the sidewalk. "Stop, now!" She bayonets my pigeon chest, and I pitch back like a punching clown. Walkie-talkies and cells load her utility belt, and she rushes a unit to her assertive mouth. "Set. This is Two. Rolling? Uh-huh. Stand by."

Production trailers line this block, too, expandable cabins pushed over the sidewalk. I raise a hand to shield my eyes against towers of clamped lights glaring down white-hot, brighter than the sun.

"You can't walk here, sir. This area is closed. There are signs posted," the Clipboard lectures me, shaking an orange-and-black flyer officiously. She rattles into the handheld, "Two, standing by. Standing by for Standby. Standing by."

"Sorry, I thought I was clear of the shoot. I'm just trying to cross the street." It hurts to breathe. "I think you may have broken a rib."

"Quiet," she seethes, and buttons my mouth with a fingerless-gloved hand.

"Rolling. Speed. Action," a unit director calls down the staged block. An actor couple opens a silver doorway and walks toward us, their movement shadowed by a camera crew rolling on dolly tracks. Snowflakes float down from a raised jib, speck-ling the actors' thirties-style clothing and dusting the sidewalk. Arms locked, the two strut like a sharpie and his moll under a cocked fedora and a chapeau. They flap flirty gestures to each other, intimate on the street, playful and a little illicit, lovers in their own world. They share matching smiles, glittering like the set lights on the artificial snowflakes, and swing together out of the shot just short of me and the Clipboard standing at the end of the tracks. The director calls, "Cut!"

Close up, I recognize the actor in the camel overcoat. Susan and I met him at a holiday party. He was playing in a series Susan was hooked on. He was pleased, I thought, by the atten-tion. He lives in our neighborhood. I turn my face away. The actors walk back to the silver door for another take.

"Go! Now!" the Clipboard commands, and I obey, making a break for my honey-baked temple of cuisine just across the street. I dash from the set to that monument of devotion to the kitchen, singing the soundtrack to my scene: "Shout hallelujah, c'mon get happy, we're going to the promised land."

Chanterelle is closed.

Dark. Shut. Shuttered. An AVAILABLE RETAIL CONDOMINIUM sign is plastered across the front glass, and a metal scaffold wraps the elbow of the building. *This can't be.* The ruffled curtains are dropped shut over the tall windows. They hang like shrouds of petticoats. I drift from window to window, looking for an open-ing, so I can see the glory I came to know. At the locked front door, I find a slivered gap and look in through the glass.

The thriving golden altar of a room has been stripped nearly bare. The floor is an exposed concrete slab. The ceiling plaster is peeled down to the studs between the three spider chandeliers which have had their bulbs plucked. A single square table survives in the back, covered with empty white plates and soup bowls and champagne flutes and wineglasses loaded in dishwasher racks. The restaurant's steam-bent chairs are stacked against the dining room's long wall, where the pedestal moldings' cornices have been sheared off, exposing gouged faces of naked plaster. Near the front sits the writing desk that held the liturgical menus. They're gone. Four sheets of architectural paper have curled into scrolls on the oak top, plans for a rebirth that was begun but never finished. The place looks to have been left in a hurry, unexpectedly, like the dining room of the *Titanic*, a moment of time sunk into decay. I'm viewing the ghost of a remembered stage set, now struck for an unknown show. As with most vacant spaces, it looks smaller and less remarkable than in memory.

I'm confused about so much. I have to wonder: Did Chanterelle really exist? Is this empty room a casualty of the dismal economy, or did I just imagine the place all along?

What did I think I would do here? The food would kill me.

I'm standing at the window. Chanterelle closed before Susan and I made it inside. We waited too long for the special occasion.

There's nothing left.

Around the side of the building, a hard hat drooping an orange flag is the only person on this eerie street fenced in by barricades. The other storefronts are all boarded up or in transition.

I'm so hungry and weak from the long afternoon. My legs feel like they're about to go as numb as my gut, and I stumble into a slump against Chanterelle's curtained window. I don't know what to do with myself. I'm hours late to start the pump, but I can't go home this empty. There's nothing left there, either.

This doesn't make sense. I know Chanterelle existed. I read about it in Zagat every year. It had a CAPITAL LETTER listing and the highest ratings for food. I walked past this window every time I could, after all the meetings, and watched the food come out on the plates, and the waiters talking, and the people eating grilled sausages and beef carpaccio. The grilled sausages were cut into medallions and pinned across the plate. The curtains were raised, and the chandeliers were lit, and the walls were the color of honey.

I saw it.

It's hard for me to move from the window. I look in again, searching for the old sight, the one I came to see, but the room is empty. I don't know where to go.

"Action," the director's voice calls from the restricted set across the street. "Cut." The actors finish another take and start again at the silver door. "Action." I feel lousy and can't think straight. This is a dangerous place.

Up the fenced sidewalk comes a woman bundling two paper funnels of white roses in her arms. She angles tight to round the corner and crosses in front of me, eclipsing the sunset with a head the size of a honeydew. She sees me shaky against the window and stops and leans close. "Mister, you okay?" she asks. She's short and brown with parted hair bunned at the back, and I smell the sweetened coffee on her quick breath. It stinks and overwhelms the cut flowers pressed to my chest.

I love the smell of the coffee beans in the barrels and at the counter where I order Susan's Danish blend—the wood, the secret of the roast, like nothing else. In the store, I breathe deep and don't mind if there's a line ahead of me.

The woman opens her mouth again to say something—a brown and yellow hole. The coffee odor is nauseating, and she won't move away from me with her awful smell. I start to gag up spit and foul the tight air from my useless insides, and it smells like decay, like the garbage decomposing in John's apartment. It smells like death.

"You look very bad," she tells me, her eyes small and direct. The flowers poke under my chin. "You should lie down."

I don't say anything, and the woman walks away talking to herself, in the direction of the movie set.

Come on, God, I think, you've got to be kidding me. You're sending me my *flores para los muertos* with a bad coffee chaser? Here? It's a black joke, and I wish I could laugh. From desire to death on one street corner. Where can I possibly go from here?

But this corner is no place to die. I want something else. I push away from the closed restaurant.

Everything I have left in me is used up on the short walk to the Hudson. I've gone a long time without food. My feet feel like sandbags in the insulated rubber boots.

The pier at the end of this street juts far out, into river water that I can see swelling to the bay. I'm only a few miles downriver from our apartment, but the water is different here at the mouth of the harbor. In the boat traffic's churn, it somehow seems darker, older, as if there are more spirits rolled up in the current. And now the river looks so close. It is so close. *I've* never been so close. It wouldn't take much of a jump to go in. My pits go sweaty at the idea. People do it. Spalding Gray jumped in off the back of the Staten Island Ferry. I couldn't understand it at the time. They said he was in pain.

Quitting's not my style, but I'm running out of options. I hoped looking through the restaurant window would save me. I thought watching eggs in the hole again would help. Christ, that movie was just this morning. Will all the days be like this?

Living without food, without Chanterelle, without work, without money, without my family. I should just drop in the drink. Maybe this is the place. Cast myself upon the waters; I do know what disaster has come upon the land. The current can take me away. Past the Statue of Liberty and Ellis Island and Grandpa Jake and Grandma Jennie's ghosts, under the Verrazano, past Coney and the spirits of Nat's fruit store and the potato-chip chair, and my father calling games on the boardwalk.

The sun is larger at the water. It confounds the sky and bears down on me. My vision is fuzzing over into blindness. I'm weary. I haven't eaten since the bag emptied in the morning—no, it's been much longer, months, and the longer it goes, the worse I get. The sky is going orange, green, white. The sky is black. *"Are you a threat to yourself?" "Like I told you, Dr. Singh, I don't even have the strength."*

I can't lift another step, and my legs give out. I start falling headfirst in the street, tumbling forward, windmilling. My boot toe catches against the pavement. I trip over a curb and crash on a patch of sidewalk, flat on my belly and face. My arms twist under my chin, which is beginning to sting. The fall pulled up the windowpanes across my middle. I can feel the bandage hanging loose. I'm so tired.

My eyes close. The dark is peaceful, silent. I'm not connected to the grinding pump. I won't be waking to piss. I can sleep as long as I want. Susan and the boys are in the kitchen in Indiana, helping to get dinner ready, at the oval table rolling the napkins into the silver rings with the animal heads. I wonder what time it is there. I pass out and rest in peace.

I've forgotten what sleep feels like.

After a minute or an hour or a day or a month, I don't know, the angry horn of a passing car wakes me. I try to roll and pivot on my elbows. The driver blasts the horn again for good measure and tears off in a squeal.

My chin is sore from the fall. I rub a swollen hand across and feel crumbs of caked blood. My right shoulder and gut hurt, too, so I guess I hit the sidewalk hard. When I open my eyes, I can see clearer than before I blacked out. The sun is gone. The streetlamps on this block are lit. I guess the divine messenger with the coffee breath was right—I just needed to lie down.

The sidewalk under me is slate, buckled at the seams. I look around to focus, and I recognize where I've come to rest. It's a postage stamp of colonial row houses that have been standing so long, they've got 1/2 and A and B addresses on their paneled front doors. Ivy vines and redbrick walls. Six-over-six panes of wavy glass. White wood shutters peeled from winters at the water. Widow's-peak dormers and slate roofs necked with chimneys. I've been here before.

"The land under the dozen houses was planted for corn, wheat, barley, rye, and flax when New Amsterdam was the breadbasket of the colonies. In the next century beer was brewed on the property." I read that to Teddy out of a guidebook when he was three. Susan, he, and I led ourselves on a walking tour to shoot pictures for his scrapbook. At the river, I set down the guidebook and the lunch bag carrying Teddy's Goldfish and peanut-butter-and-jelly sandwich to snap a picture of him that's framed on the desk in our tiny entryway. We dressed him in above-the-knee shorts and a striped sailor's shirt, and his sandaled feet are turned in on their sides. His hands are tucked behind, curled to grip the pier railing, and he's smiling, thrilled and perfect. Juniper eyes on an angel's face. The three of us ate lunch at a café. We told Teddy that day he was going to have a brother.

I'm mesmerized by the old houses, and I wander around back to the courtyard, where I find swings, hammocks, gardens, a wooden arch, hoes and gloves, clay flower pots, flower boxes, bags of soil, wrought-iron patio chairs and café tables, picnic umbrellas, carved birdhouses, training-wheeled bikes, two hockey goals, and taped sticks. Signs of life. The three-story houses have porches to anchor the prospect of traditional backyard living. It's a bit of an illusion, as they exist in the well of a ghastly apartment complex with forty stories of die-cut terraces, but it feels like a prospect worth preserving.

Almost all the backyards have outdoor grills. I count four Webers, same as my beloved propane in Maine. One of the Webers is cooking in the vined plot where the houses' two wings intersect. The metal hood is up. A vapor of smoke is rising over the peaked roofline; the lid must have been just opened. The house's back screen door swings shut. Someone's getting a jump on spring. A platter of marinated chops rests uncovered on the grill's side prep shelf—four thick bone-ins sitting like sauna bathers in their juices.

No one is in the backyards. I'm drawn to the open grill and drop my face close. The damn thing smells like life to me. This is what I need. These coals are ready to go, but the fuel gauge shows only a drink of propane in the tank. Likely, it's been sitting unused since the last fall cookout. This guy's going to miss his hot fire and will have to cook the chops in the kitchen oven. That would be criminal.

There's a nice set of grill tools looped on the perimeter hooks, so I grab a pair of tongs and put the metal hands on the meat. The chops go on like the *Moonstruck* eggs with that beautiful sizzle, and I close the lid to seal the heat. The Weber thermometer reads 425°F, the sweet spot, and I figure five minutes per side. That will give the pork a nice braided char and leave a marble of tender middle. Presumably, that's the way these folks like their pork cooked.

I'm not wearing a watch, so when it seems about time, I raise the lid. A zeppelin of smoke and sound and smell releases from its hold and plies me with delight like I'm standing in wet swim trunks under the pines. I lift the first chop with the tongs, and it's perfect, a gorgeous tread of tire tracks rolled on the meat. After the flip, I may take the second side down to four minutes. These are really looking good. Another couple of ticks, and I'll have dinner ready.

It occurs to me that these months have been more nothing than just nothing by mouth. Other than tearing things apart—

my fingers crushing the fries and the Bundt cake—I haven't used my hands to *make* any food. Shooting up the TPN bag doesn't count. I haven't cooked, I haven't cut or chopped or spooned or served. My exile from food has been complete, tactile as well as taste. It feels good to hold the tongs in my right hand, grabbing the chops off the platter, squeezing them by the fat ends, satisfying the way a workout brings you back to yourself, like a runner's high, more than just physical. It feels good to make something. This is better than being in the river.

At the brick house, the absent griller knees open the screen door. He's holding a cocktail in one hand and a shaker of seasoning in the other. I startle him, and he jump-stops on the backyard stepping-stones. I didn't think ahead to this possibility. I'm on a mission—I hadn't considered trespassing. I'm a sight.

The griller regards me, unsure of my intentions, and pockets the shaker in his apron's front pouch. He's got a comfortable paunch and neatly cut hair and appears to be about my age. I'm so close to finishing.

"Just looking," I say.

CHAPTER 6

I'm back in the hospital.

I suppose I shouldn't be surprised, but again, I was trying to fool myself. Despite the sweating and pissing and all the nothing-to-be-done tortures from Oreo, I'd started to think that I was making progress. In small measures, believing in the vague signs that can mean something to a desperate patient.

My desire index was climbing. Even if I was delusional, my actions were those of a man who wanted out of this sewer. *Tell me what you crave, and I will tell you what you are.* What force other than outright desire could have fueled my pilgrimage to Chanterelle or driven me to commandeer the Weber behind the old house and grill a stranger's pork chops? That rush was a sign of recovery. I even talked my way into finishing the cooking. "Just two more minutes and these chops are going to be pure heaven. Look at that char, eh? Is that sea salt you've got in your apron pocket?" The guy was decent enough not to have me arrested.

Draining as that marathon day was, I came to believe it was a turning point. I felt something—devastation and then elation.

By the time I got off the subway back uptown and hooked up, I had faith that the NPO therapy was working, that my man-holes were closing, and I was healing. Next stop, Normaltown. However, as I should know about this chronic illness, catharsis doesn't stop the roller coaster. Coney Island would have been the more appropriate pilgrimage.

Susan and the boys came back from Indiana looking refreshed and bonded, as if they'd gone someplace exotic. Then we all woke the next morning with sore throats and fevers. Doc-tors' visits showed the three of them to have strep throat, and they started on an antibiotic. I took an IV version that gave me the runs, relentless dam breaks like after the surgery, and I had to stop. My fever got dicey, but I didn't worry because it was just strep and it would go away. A little sore throat was no match for me—I cooked a man's pork chops, dammit.

Our apartment became a decrepit sick ward. Susan, Teddy, and Finn were home from school with no one around to nurse them—my parents are in Greece, and Patty and the others are long gone. The house was a mess, and even boiling last-resort ramen noodles for the boys was a sweaty ordeal. Everything seemed to be in the shitter again. Susan was miserable and surely wondering why she left Royal Woods Hill for this black hole.

Today, thankfully, they all seem to have turned the corner and are well enough for school, but I woke from a short doze feeling a stab in my gut. It's different from the ache I got fall-ing down on the pavement. This hurts on the inside. I haven't used the bloody tank in months. It's been shut down like an old railway tunnel, and there's nothing going in, so what the hell is this?

Dr. Abrams is concerned and sends me to Dr. Kaplan's radiology lab on the East Side for a CT scan. Even though my gut has been paralyzed, Abrams tells me on the phone there still may be internal inflammation in the small intestine that's causing the pain and fever. I'm freezing when I get the order to go. I dress in long johns, insulated snow pants, fleece pullover, down parka, wool hat, earmuffs, Thinsulate gloves, SmartWool socks, packets of hand and toe warmers, and the furnace snow boots my parents gave me for Christmas that never made the ski trip to Matt and Ellen's. I last just to the corner of my block, fold over, and have to rest against the mail drop. Bundled for a blizzard on a cheery spring day, I must look bizarre to the dog walkers and nannies. I spend money on a cab to get me to Kaplan's.

Inside the radiologist's crowded waiting room, I keep the Unabomber look intact and shiver through a bracing aperitif of radioactive drink. It's an auspicious return to the bar. The bug juice is cold and clams my insides, forcing me into an agitated cricket rub to try to combat the chills. The act of swallowing something is ecstatic at first, a welcome surrender to temptation, but the gross flavor kills the thrill in a few gulps, and I switch to sipping. An old man in a houndstooth jacket and his West Indian nurse move two seats away from me. I'm drinking alone.

After several hours, the orange drink filters low enough in my gut, and I'm in a frigid exam room. Mercifully, the nurse allows me to wear my thermals for the CT scan. I've been radiated in this lab for years and get on well with the senior doctor; perhaps that buys me the extra TLC. Even so, when I lie on the CT machine—the long sled that slides through the big vanilla donut hole—I'm rigoring uncontrollably, like on Uncle Nat's potato-chip chair at warp speed, and Nurse Cathy ties me down with cotton blankets and restraints. She's kind, showing a gentle smile of polished teeth, and I try to make conversation. "Thank you so much, Nurse," I bang out through the shivers.

"It's not a problem." She pulls the blanket tie tighter across my shoulders. I'm shaking too much. "We've got to keep you still for the scan."

"Normally, I like this exam."

"You do?" She thinks I'm teasing.

"I'm serious. Not the drinking, that's god-awful. But I like lying on the sled and going through the donut hole. It's very peaceful. I actually look forward to it. A few times I've been so tired and empty from the prep that by the time the scan started, I fell asleep on the machine. I'm not a great sleeper, I've got trouble some nights, but I go right out on this baby. At one point I was thinking of putting a machine in my bedroom. It seems to relax me." My head is rattling on the sled, and the nurse presses her weight against my body to still me for the pictures.

"Hello, Jon," Dr. Kaplan says, presiding over me in his pressed white coat with stitched monogram. He's past seventy, but his hair is still wavy and full and his posture impeccable. Kaplan speaks in a strong voice, perpetually standing inside the control booth. "Dr. Abrams called me. He told me what's been going on. You feel lousy?"

"I do, Dr. K."

"Let's find out why."

Ordinarily, Kaplan talks to me at length about the novels he and his wife are reading in their book club. It's always an extensive list, carrying us through the slow passage of barium and the long looks on the table. Today he forgoes the casual spiel.

"Hold still and stop breathing," his miked voice instructs, booming from behind the glass.

I bear down to stop shaking for the pictures, trying to hold myself on the sled. The strain is giving me a colossal headache. The concave sled slides in and out of the whirring hole. The scanner spins around me like the deli slicer on the boys' Black Forest ham. An IV plugs my left arm to inject radioactive contrast for a more precise diagnosis. The contrast streams in blessedly warm and triggers the usual accompanying urge to pee. I know it lasts only about a minute. Then I start to sweat. I feel nauseated. This hasn't happened before in the donut hole.

"Nurse! I'm going to vomit."

Cathy opens the door and dashes to me with a bucket. Quickly, she unties the restraints holding me to the sled. I get the jitters lifting up, and I spew.

"Oh, shit," I groan. "All the exam juice—it came back up. What does that do to the test?"

"It should be okay."

I vomit again, and Dr. Kaplan leads me down a back stairway, away from the waiting-room patients and toward another exam room, where he wants to look at my gallbladder. Taking the stairs is agony. I'm wrapped in the blankets and rubbing maniacally to stop from freezing to death. Kaplan shoots ultrasound images and gets me a thermometer, then calls Dr. Abrams from the room and includes me in his broadcast conversation.

"Gary, I've examined Jon, and I don't see any evidence of perforation or blockage in the ileum. I can't tell about the status of the fistula. That will take a GI series. I've looked at the gall-bladder, and there is some thickening, likely a result of the NPO. But you should know, he looks terrible. He's shaking and vomiting, and he's got a temperature of 106. Yes. Sure, I'll put him on."

I wriggle an arm free from the blankets and take the phone.

"Hi, Jon," Dr. Abrams starts. His voice is deceptively calm and moves quickly to a decision. "The pictures are inconclusive, so my guess is that you have an infection. That would be consistent with pain and fever. I'm calling the hospital and admitting you. You've got to go there right now."

Come on, the hospital? Back to Mount Save Me. Just the sound of it is depressing. "Shut your cake hole," I want to tell my doctor, whose clipped phrasing blunts my ready-made objections. I thought the point of nothing by mouth was to keep me out of there. "Okay," I say.

It's a brilliant afternoon, cloudless swimming-pool sky, and the cab I'm taking back to my apartment to pack is halted by a traffic cop on Fifth Avenue. A parade is marching uptown and blocking the park transverse entrance to the West Side. We idle. The paraders roam the wide street in loose formations, decked out in bright swirls of costumes, splitting off their lines to blow horns at the crowd and mix with the spectators at the curb, more party than patriotism. Drummers play a heated beat faster and faster, urging the circle of dancers blocking the intersection into a frenzy that rouses cheers from the tourists hustling down the adjacent museum steps to take in the show. The parade is a box of crayons come to life, and my driver rolls down his window to flap a rhythm hand against the car door.

"You want to tell the cop this is a medical emergency?" I say after ten minutes of meter running, but the driver just smiles and taps his fingers.

A dozen or so acts sing and spin and revel in their annual moment until a break in the flow permits us through. We lurch in slowed traffic on the potholed transverse. I open my door and yak on the road.

When I arrive at the apartment, Susan and the boys are home from school and feeling better. Dr. Abrams has already called to make sure I don't go AWOL, so Susan knows. I pull my hospital things together and try to clamp the shakes when we sit Teddy and Finn on our bed.

"I'm so glad you bums are recovering. Were you all right in school?" I open the duffel bag strung with an Indianapolis airport tag and pack a flannel bathrobe.

"Yes, Dad," Teddy intones in an irritated voice. "What's going on?"

Teddy's long hair is in his eyes, and I reach to push it back. I want to see his baby face and connect with those searching eyes, but he'll have none of it and jerks his head away, grazing Finn, who pushes back. I'll have to settle for a squirmy hug good-bye at the door.

"Dr. Abrams wants me to go to the hospital to figure out why I have a fever and don't feel well. It's not strep throat, like you and Mom and Finny had."

"Teddy banged me with his head. Jerk!" Finn wails. They're fussing on the covers, and he kicks a bare foot, knocking over the IV pole standing bedside. It tumbles and smacks the wall.

"*He* banged *me*!" Teddy retaliates and gets in Finny's face for threatening emphasis. "Stupid baby!"

Maybe the hospital won't be so bad . . . The thought crosses my mind, then the guilt of leaving Susan to have all the fun pops the bubble.

"Guys, please," I intervene. "I need you to calm down so we can talk." Finn is best when he has something to do, and I enlist him to pack my toothbrush and two more pairs of thermal socks.

"Are you going to have surgery, like last time?" Teddy sprawls to the bed's edge, tipping a box of gauze to the floor. He's a long beanpole. I see that the hem of his go-to warm-up pants ends halfway down his stick legs.

"No. This is nothing big, and I'm sure I'll only be in the hospital for a few days. I just need to get the fever down, and the doctors can do a better job there." That's what the boys need to hear, and I hope there's some truth to it. I know I'm going to miss the start of Little League for both of them this weekend. I heard from Teddy's coach that he's scheduled to pitch. I remember our taxes are due to be filed. I can't spend too long on hospital time.

"Which hospital?" Finny asks.

"The one you made the model of," I say, zipping the toiletries bag he's finished packing for me. In the living room, Finn has taped together cardboard boxes he scavenged from the service hallway into a replica of the Mount Save Me medical complex, cutting out windows and connecting the buildings with a paper-towel-tube sky bridge. He's a resourceful kid, and adventure calls. He and Teddy are so close—despite their bunk beds, we often find them sleeping together—yet their impulses are wired so differently. Teddy is in his head; Finn is in his body. First and second children.

Teddy is sinking into the bed pillows, internalizing his wound, more like me. His face is a naked contradiction, beautiful and pained, more complicated than that of the boy in the striped sailor shirt in the picture. Teddy's wide jaw, my father-in-law's jawline, spreads his cheeks into open plains that leave him nowhere to tuck his emotions. His private conflicts surface like a map on his features, and he armors himself by hanging his chin and hunching his shoulders or lowering his dream-boat eyelashes. Someday, I imagine, he'll stand tall and show the world his sweet smile. The boys' contrasting personalities become vivid to me when I've been away from the business of daily parenting. I'm leaving again, and their expressions hit hard. I thread Teddy's long, grimy kid fingers with mine and pivot my thumb for a quick wrestle. His nails need trimming.

"The hospital with the big revolving door?" Finn asks, and wants in on the thumb wrestle.

"Right, honey."

The intercom buzzes, and Teddy jumps off the bed to answer. It's the doorman calling. Ruth, a school parent, is in the lobby with dinner. I finish packing, kiss Susan and the boys good-bye, and force myself to keep things light. It's better this way. Susan and I have not really spoken since she returned from Indy and got laid up with strep. We're either cooling off or cooling out, I don't know. I'll take myself to the hospital in a cab.

On the way out, I run into Ruth in the elevator, and she's surprised to hear where I'm headed. She's made a steaming dish of baked ziti and cheese with Italian spicy sausage; Parisian salad with feta, nuts, and dried cranberries; an Oreo berry cake; and carrot soup the color of the radioactive junk that I drank in Kaplan's waiting room. I take the elevator down and smell parsley. It opens in my nose and even makes the ride smell good.

In three hours, I'm back in the GI ward, shivering in a tiny room I share with a sleeping old dog. His wife sits by his bed, reading a thick hardcover and listening to a Mendelssohn concerto piped through the TV, which I'll happily take over the static of gunshots. My high fever has the doctors on edge, and they order blood cultures.

Over the course of a week, the cultures will grow the strains of a bacterial infection that formed in my intestine at the anastomosis, the emergency surgical fitting buckling my pipes. The infection seeped through holes in the compromised tissue and spread to my bloodstream, causing the fever and abdominal pain and infecting the PICC line. Immediately, the catheter is pulled out of my biceps and the TPN halted, since liquid nutrients can't be pumped safely if there is an infection in the bloodstream. Again I'm on nothing but an IV saline drip while the doctors try to determine what course to take. I've reached Dr. Eberhardt's three-month mark, but further surgery is still inadvisable due to my lousy condition. Alternatively, reinserting a replacement PICC line for a TPN infusion runs too high a risk of a more serious infection than my system may be able to fight. In other words, even the liquid food could finish me off. Food, either solid or intravenous, has become my body's enemy.

Meanwhile, my cravings have swelled like teenage hormones, and I'm starving for something to love. When I change my gown before bed, the scary sight in the small bathroom mirror of my skeletal body whittled down to kindling looks less like the comparatively robust Sid Vicious at the Chelsea and more like the old black-and-white postcard of a reptilian Sam Beckett I still use as a bookmark. Nothing to be done.

Nurse Sheila is my attending early one weekend morning, and I'm lifted a smidge from my gloom by her engaging manner and *Wayne's World* mullet. She has a trim build and a narrow, honest face, pleasant, and I can't help but wonder if her loved ones have ever recommended a more fashionable haircut. Where does she even find a barber to maintain that bilevel, falling on the shoulders of her scrubs like a raccoon cap?

"The last time I saw you, you told me about the celebrity wing on the other side of the atrium," I say, angling for the diversion of gossip until visiting hours. It's a slow and quiet Sunday, and from the window of my dim room all I can see is a plumber's rain forest of gray pipes and platforms. For once I have the window, but the scaffold consumes the view between me and the patients across the way in the premium seats. "How's life on the other side these days?" I ask.

"You mean at One Park?" Sheila asks as she tears a blood-pressure sleeve off my outstretched arm. I nod gamely. She squeaks away on iridescent running shoes, then returns quickly with a color marketing brochure for One Park in hand. I see in its glossy photographs how swanky a hospital cell can be: private rooms furnished with Regency-style dressers, three-hundred-thread-count reverse sateen sheets, and double-window views of the park. Robes as thick as pelts and salon products tucked in the breast pockets like silk squares. A tableclothed dining table plated with bone china and marvelous food. The brochure names the facility's culinary-trained chef and rhapsodizes about the freshest locally grown, organic produce; all-natural grass-fed American beef; Moroccan-spiced rack of lamb; jewel couscous; wild salmon wrapped in a Yukon-gold potato crust

served with oven-roasted asparagus and mango aioli; and com-
plimentary Belgian chocolates. Zelda Fitzgerald never had it
so good.

If I could, I would eat the brochure. The guy in the bed next
to me is in a coma, so he's not eating, either. There are no Avocado Gals bearing trays of wobbling Jell-O cubes or Florentine-
leather filet of beef. Apart from the drip, drip, drip of the saline
soup, these pictures in the pamphlet are as close as I've come
to food in this room. I thank Nurse Sheila and get up to take a
walk.

Hospitals are, for the most part, shamefully designed bunkers,
and Mount Save Me is no exception. Its location is a cat's cradle
of enviable real estate and criminal neglect. I have to wheel my
poles and monitors to the far side of the building to see out the
bank of perimeter windows.

Standing at the tinted glass, life-affirming views of the
luxuriant park, a Cole Porter chorus of apartment buildings,
breathtaking sunlight, and postcard-perfect midtown skyscrapers feed my fantasy of getting out. A very cruel tease. The
patients' rooms are wedged like pits into the enclosed core of
the tower, light-years from the humanizing circadian signs of
sky and sun and people moving to the rhythm of the day. This
place must have been designed by a bat. My gurney transports
allow perhaps a minute out of my typical day for a panorama of
the majestic world outside the window before we descend to the
bowels of the hospital. When I'm able, I free myself from the bed

rails and rise to the building's skin to sightsee a few minutes
more. The rest of the time is spent stewing in my room or on the
floor circling the nurses' station, shut off from the sky and sun.
It's like lockup without the yard.

Today my sister, Lisa, is running a 10K race in Central Park.
We've tried to map the right coordinates for me to stand at the
floor's corner window and see her wave to me midrace. I discovered the vista one day from my end of a chauffeured gurney ride.

By the time I get to the viewing stand, the race is in full trot.
There's a conga line of runners tracing the curves of the park
roads around the ball fields. Scanning the bubbling stream of
bodies for Lisa's red top and black pants, I discover the park
coming back to life, fringed with emerald-green buds, like tissue paper. Around the soup bowl of the reservoir, the lovely pink
cherry blossoms are beginning to paint a decorative border over
the water. It's a ten-minute walk from the boys' school to those
cherry trees, and this is the time of year I sometimes go there
after drop-off to commune with the blooms lining the jogging
loop. They thrive only briefly until spring wind or rain showers
the ground with pink and white confetti that gets stomped into
mulch.

Whenever I circle the reservoir's northern tip to the granite
fortress of the old pump house, I feel like I'm turning the pages of
a giant pop-up book. The flat, glittering water, the carpeted green
lawns, the silver schist cliffs and lookouts—they're Magic Marker
foregrounds for the soaring skyline that fills the background.
Even after fifteen years living here, I'm dazzled by the sight.

Increasingly, though, it feels out of reach.

Runners pass me in stride on the cinder jogging path, their

bodies moving fast. So many beautiful shapes: contours of mus-
cled legs and backs chiseled like the pump house blocks; long,
ropy skyscraper limbs; a blond ponytail swinging in time with
a girl's bouncy strides. She looks twenty-two and fresh as the
blossoms. The city in all its possibilities is exciting. The possibilities are what *makes* the city.

At the hospital window, the elevation provides a different
perspective. From sixteen floors up, Manhattan shrinks to a very
small place. I shift my head an inch or two in either direction,
and I see the water tower on our apartment building roof; I see
the castle turrets on the boys' school; I see the office buildings
where I worked; I see the tennis courts where I played twice
a week before the kids were born. The city's puzzle pieces fit
together—my life fits. It *should* work. Point-to-point-to-point-
to-point. One-two-three-four. The aerial logic of this map conjures the illusion of control, the fantasy of order prevailing over
lives spun into chaos. If only. In reality, I've become a spectator
in my hometown.

The runners keep coming without end; there must be ten
thousand. There are too many runners, too many red tops moving. They look like crumbs from up here. I can't find Lisa or her
wave.

I'm tired from standing on the hard floor and keeping my IV
raised and go back to my room.

There's a visitor fidgeting with a bag at the room's window.

"Cherry?"

"Hey," she says, startled into an abrupt turn. "The nurse
didn't know where you were. I was beginning to wonder when
you'd come back. I'm so glad to see you."

"I'm shocked to see you," I blurt, unable to hide my surprise. Cherry and I worked together for several years and hated each other. I've entered swinging a filling station's worth of lines and bags, so a hug would be deadly, and a handshake seems weird. She's pinned between the wall heater and the bed and looks uncomfortable. "Just let me get by you, and you can take the comfy chair."

I don't want to harp on it and make her feel self-conscious, but I never would've expected Cherry to visit.

We shared a boss, Gordon, a tenacious, bracingly successful businessman and blowhard who practiced the death-match model of management, pitting his employees against one another in order to boil the best results from their survival instincts. Cherry and I were assigned overlapping duties, and we followed Gordon's Machiavellian lead by spending the better part of our days in combat trying to destroy each other. It was ugly and, in retrospect, embarrassing. About five minutes after Gordon sold the business to a bunch of bean counters and became grossly wealthy, Cherry and I were cut loose and became enlightened ex-dupes. Since then we've enjoyed a civil truce. There's probably too much shameful history for us to ever be fully relaxed together, but there is such a thing as decency, and our conversations dance between the two.

"I'd offer you something, but I can't imagine you're in the mood for saline. I don't even have a pitcher of water to give you. Had to remove the temptation, you know. How on earth did you find me?" I ask, wriggling onto the bed.

Cherry sinks into the chair's collapsed cushion, disappearing by half in the bucket seat. She's a short woman of forty or so (some years she didn't age at the normal annual rate) whose weight swings are exaggerated on her compact body. She looks skinny, a little too skinny, in her inked-on jeans. Cherry survived breast cancer last year, an isolated tumor in a duct, and I hope she's still in remission. Her hair is shiny and bobbed at the shoulders and colored a more flattering brunette than the blond ruse she fashioned when we sat in adjoining offices poisoning the air. It swoops away from her face, which is pointy like a three-cornered hat. For about five minutes when we worked together, Cherry was married to a bizarre guy, a shifty type who looked like a warlock and slept in the park and disappeared one day with a good-bye text to her phone. I treated her like an unbalanced train wreck of a person after that, which was unfair. (There's an orderly in Radiology who looks like her vanished ex, but I think better of mentioning it.) She's more comfortable in her skin and easier to be around. In the old days, we wouldn't have lasted two minutes.

"Susan sent out an e-mail saying that you were back in the hospital but you were okay to see visitors. I think Lola got it and posted it on the alumni chat board. It's amazing we all still keep in touch." Cherry smiles hopefully through an uncertain silence.

"I suppose that says it all." My IV alarm beeps, and I shake out the snagged line. My veins are tapped out, and there's blood darkening the port. "Well, at least Gordon gave us a common enemy to loathe. Has he sent you any more pictures of his yacht?"

"Just an update from some race in the Caribbean. He asked about you." She pushes to straighten herself out of the hole in the busted seat.

"You're kidding. He did? Jesus, I must really be sick," I say. Cherry laughs, which is helpful. It makes me feel a little less pathetic. We see each other maybe once a year at a birthday party, and the nervous suspicion that can still twist a dialogue seems to be fading. If we're edgy, it's more likely with ourselves than each other.

"Susan's e-mail said you're still not eating. When do the doctors say you'll have food?"

"They're a little vague on that. Food doesn't seem to be their concern right now. I think I've passed the threshold from eating to existing." My remark makes the color rise on her tinted cheeks through the cover of a full face of makeup. I'm aware it's upsetting to see a bag of bones rattling in a hospital bed, even on someone whom you once detested. "Speaking of food, you look skinny. How are you feeling?"

"I'm good."

"Really? Everything's okay?"

"It is." She knocks on the chair arm for good measure.

"Cherry, you know I hope it is, but look who you're talking to. You don't have to pretend with me if you're sick. It's not like we're duking it out to see who can work later in the office anymore."

"I know that. I'm healthy. My second look was clean. I'm working out a lot and spending less time in bars." She smiles again to assure me. Cherry has a child's smile, evenly spaced small teeth that fit her face like a toy piano. It's not a smile that I always trusted, but I'm pleased to see it. She slides a silver and turquoise ring on and off of her left index finger.

"All right, then, I'm extremely happy to hear you're healthy. That's great news, though I don't like the sound of the less time in bars business. You do look exceptionally fit, like a warrior princess. Small but ferocious." Her mention of working out provokes my frustrated desire to leave this bed and exercise. When I stretch my legs, they jam the metal footboard holding my chart.

"Thank you."

"You'd whip my ass in hand-to-hand." Nurse Sheila checks in and flushes the blood in my line, then darts out. Buzzers sound down the hallway.

Cherry's expression freezes. "That's some mullet," she whispers after Sheila leaves.

"I think she sang backup for Whitesnake in the eighties. I haven't worked up the nerve to ask." The vein that Sheila shot up feels tight, like it's going to explode. "So, tell me what you're working on these days." I tread lightly. After we were laid off, Cherry went without health insurance when her COBRA ran out. I know she had to put her surgery and radiation bills on credit cards, and it has dented her. She can't afford to be choosy.

"I have some new work. It's for a start-up, so it's nothing like the money we used to make, and who knows if they'll last past Thursday, but it's fine for now. Want to hear about it?"

"Sure." I don't, really, but it might do me good to listen to the sounds of the outside world. Her language is gorpy businessspeak, a conveyor belt of jargon and abbreviations that requires a practiced level of concentration. "I turnkeyed best-of-breed ROI content-partner integration to ladder up a more top-of-mind brand identity." She was always better at spitting out the code than I, and at this distance, it might as well be whale talk to me. I take it in like programmed white noise and wait for her to finish. "I'm glad you're on your feet," I say, and mean it. "That must feel good."

"It does, and I'm enjoying it more now." Cherry is fishing in the pocket of her black gym bag as she talks. "How are Susan and the boys doing? You know, I signed up on that spreadsheet for a meal last week. Fried dumplings and sesame noodles and brownies. Of course, I didn't cook it."

"They told me all about that. That was so sweet of you. I heard that everyone loved the food." The last part is a friendly fib. The boys *did* love the brownies. "So many people have been feeding them, it's been incredible. I think the food is the one thing that's kept Susan from going over the edge."

"I bet things are hard."

"They are."

Cherry finds what she was looking for, a blue paper package that fits in her curled hand. "I brought you something I want you to have."

"Cherry, a present?"

"In a way, yes." She comes to the bed and hands me the gift. She must have perfumed herself after the gym. A licorice scent. "Open it."

Slowly, I raise my arms from their locked position, trying to keep the touchy IV happy. The blue paper comes undone with one tear, and I'm a little baffled by what I see.

"It's a chai," she explains after a beat.

"So it is." I'm holding a pocket-size circle of flattened smoked glass. Its topside curve bows in the center and shows the two Hebrew letters that form the word "chai," which I know translates as "living." The chai symbol in the middle is polished to transparency and opens a view into the core of the glass. The see-through letters catch light from the sickly fluorescent tube over my bed, and I can see maple-syrup swirls and air bubbles floating in a constellation inside the glass. "Cherry, this is so thoughtful. I didn't think you were religious."

"I'm not, really." She breathes up a giggle of admission. "Are you?" I'm sure she knows the answer, but things do change, I suppose. Here we are.

"No. I'm strictly a gastronomic Jew. I'm just in it for the food." The chai glass is smooth and cool, paper-weighty, and almost flexible pressed in my hand, like sea glass.

"A friend gave me this in the hospital when I had my surgery. She said, 'Keep it with you, and when you're well, give it to someone who needs it.' So, you need this now. I'm giving it to you. When you get healthy again, you'll be able to give it to someone else who needs it." She speaks with more surety and grace than I've known from—or allowed—her. This is a mission she's been living to complete.

"Cherry, I don't know what to say." I hold the glass up to view again, absorbing its meaning. "I'm truly touched." Every foul, mean-spirited, and treasonous thing I ever said and did to her seems utterly preposterous. She bends over the bedside, kisses me a peck on the cheek, and clasps my hand over the chai with hers. Her hand is warm. I'm floored by her kindness.

People often invoke that old saw about being sick: "You find out who your friends really are." While I am definitely aware of who has or who hasn't come to me in tough times, that's not necessarily a measure of their friendship. I have friends who haven't called or written since the emergency happened, and I still consider them friends. What you truly discover about people is what they're capable of. Cherry holding on to this life symbol, recognizing someone in need, an old adversary like me, and delivering it to heal—that's the astonishing part. I won't think of her the same way again.

I hold the stone like a prospector and squint to search the light that passes through the lettering.

"I actually went to a Seder on Thursday," she says, sitting down. "The first night of Passover, and friends in Brooklyn hosted. It was a crazy mishmash—I don't think the Israelites had sushi hors d'oeuvres before the ceremony. I brought the hard-boiled egg for the plate. Can you believe I had to buy a whole carton just to make one? I never have eggs. Oh, sorry, I shouldn't be talking about food. You must be so hungry." Cherry bites her lower lip in apology.

"That's okay, I don't mind hearing it. You know, talking about food is half the pleasure. I don't get to do it much. Where in Brooklyn?"

"Borough Park."

"Really? Are your friends Hasids?"

"No, hipsters."

"Same difference. Beards, black hats, bathing optional. If not for the shellfish, you'd be hard-pressed to tell the difference," I say, grinning for a rim shot. "We went to my great-aunt Letty and great-uncle Jerry Grubman's apartment in Borough Park for Passover when I was a kid. No hipsters then. God, it would go on so long."

"Was your family religious?"

"No. And the Seder food was dreadful, so I don't know what they were in it for."

"All that weird stuff, like the gefilte fish in the gross jelly? It's so freaky."

"Worse than that. It was just, I don't know, crazy. You think the hipsters' Seder was a mishmash? This was like *The Honey-mooners* with yarmulkes." I've been gripping the chai, and I can feel the pressure of a clog in the IV line. I try to keep still, but it's no fun. "We would drive in from New Jersey at the worst time, since our school wasn't closed for the holiday, through jammed tunnels and horrible traffic, and then we'd spend another hour looking for parking in Brooklyn. It felt like two days in the car, and we'd be famished. The Chips Ahoy my mother packed were long gone.

"Finally, we'd get to Letty and Jerry's apartment, and it did look like the Kramdens' place—a couple of rooms, nothing much on the walls, a fire escape—only it would be packed with about thirty people in a space fit for a coatrack. There were four tables squeezed into the living room and not enough chairs to go around, so people would stand up like at a bus station, or sit in shifts, and when the kitchen stove made the apartment hot, they'd be on the fire escape."

Cherry sits straight in the collapsed chair. An amused look widens her shaped brow. I usually feel that I've got nothing interesting to say to people from this bed, and I'm sure I'm boring her—a robot head kvetching about some poor Jews without chairs forty years ago—but a force takes me over. I haven't thought about those claustrophobic Passovers in decades, and suddenly, I'm recalling details and names and incidents. A spontaneous burst of energy opens the spout.

"Stop me if you've heard this one before." I ham it up. "Coming from the hinterlands in New Jersey, we were always the last to arrive. We'd get there well into what should have been mealtime, famished, as I said, but there would be no food on the table. Not a piece of matzo, nothing. Everybody would be standing around, or climbing out the window to the fire escape. It hadn't occurred to Letty and Jerry to start cooking before the guests arrived. They'd talk about the Seder food even though there wasn't any, while we were starving. Just like in this room."

I pause, stunned by the parallel I've inadvertently drawn, then cackle a sharp laugh. It must sound odd, like an inmate loose on the grounds, because Cherry clenches her mouth in an unsure smile. I'm out of practice.

"There was only one comfortable chair in the place, a burgundy recliner," I continue. "And this fat guy who I only saw at Passover Seder, some Great-Uncle Jack, would camp out on the chair for the night. Everybody wanted the chair, and I think he showed up the day before and claimed it just so he'd have a place to sit. Some years he'd eat in the chair and fall asleep, snoring with his mouth open, blowing crumbs down his shirt." I punch up the picture with a decent impression of phlegmatic Jack, gathering my wits to continue the shtick. The labored breathing of the guy in the other bed makes it a chorus.

"Letty was my grandpa Sid's sister, and Sid had no patience for Jerry—thought he was an unworthy know-it-all. Jerry *was* sort of a minister without portfolio, and the fact that dinner hadn't been started made Sid so crazy, the tension froze the room. Even as a kid, I could feel it. Sid would barge into the kitchen and start pulling out pans and turning on the stove, heating water, anything to make his point—meanwhile, he couldn't even boil the egg. One year there were still cardboard boxes from the previous Passover under the table in the living room and no space to put your legs, so Sid threw the boxes out the window. That went over well with Jerry."

Cherry's laughing. It's a throaty laugh, and I think it's real, which gives me license to keep going with this burlesque. "What did you finally eat?" she asks.

"That's just it. I don't remember eating anything. I remember the ritual food around the Seder plate—the egg, the parsley, the charoset, the gefilte in the gross jelly, the choking matzo, and that blistering horseradish that cleared people's sinuses, my relatives would actually honk—but I don't know that we ever ate a meal. The service took so damn long, we wouldn't start driving back to New Jersey until after midnight."

"It's true," Cherry agrees enthusiastically. "The service can take forever. In the Seder I went to, we weren't sure what parts were okay to edit, and it went so long."

"Well, you know, there was no express lane out of the desert. Those Jews had a long list of gripes, and God was a patient listener. Like you, here. But the reason our Seders took longer was because of Jerry's song."

"What's that?" She drums two fingers on the hollow of her neck and tucks a wing of hair behind an ear.

"The traditional service alone wasn't good enough for Jerry. Among his many unrecognized talents, Jerry fashioned himself an interpreter of popular songs, and he prepared one for the occasion. It was more of an homage than an original. Some Jew tunesmith had appropriated the melody of that traditional Hebrew hymn 'My Darling Clementine,' and the highlights from the Passover narrative in the Haggadah, and woven them together for twelve nutty verses. Jerry typed up lyric sheets and photocopied them on slick gray paper. He worked for the phone company and waited one night for the office guys to go home so he could use their primitive copier. We'd all have to raise these stapled sheets year after year and follow Jerry's plodding, nasal singing of this song of cultural dissonance. Naturally, Jerry gave himself a credit on the cover page: 'Compiled and Edited by Jerome Grubman.' What kind of person would claim credit for copying and stapling?"

Cherry looks genuinely amused. I may have earned a new degree of sympathy. I'm having fun telling jokes, thinking about something other than being sick.

"Please, would you sing a little? Please," she requests in a pleading giggle.

It is amazing what the mind is capable of and, it appears, the heart, too. After a lifetime of putting it out of my head—the grubby scene in the stifling apartment, and the animal relatives snoring in the velour chair or unbuckling their pants and moaning on the floor, and the disgusting gelatinous pool under the fish brick on the scary ritual plate—it all comes back like the sunrise, and I'm singing Uncle Jerry's version of "My Darling Clementine" to a woman I once shunned like a Passover plague:

"Said the father to his children, 'At the Seder you will dine. You will eat your fill of matzo, you will drink four cups of wine.' Now, this father had no daughters, and his sons they numbered four. One was wise and one was wicked, one was simple and a bore."

It's probably a good thing my roommate is already in a coma. I make it to the fourth absurd verse before I get dry from singing and reel out a string of hacks. Whatever comes loose in my mouth tastes awful, and I could really use something cold. Maybe an ice pick. Cherry's triangle face freezes in that helpless look I've seen on other visitors.

"I wish I could get you something to drink," she flusters. "You've got to finish singing the song."

Choking on coughs, I spasm for a minute until it passes, then settle back into the pillow. My hand is clammy from holding the chai, and I place the damp stone on the cluttered bedside table.

"It must be Jerry's ghost come back to smite me. That's what I get for disparaging the Tony Bennett of Borough Park. Sid should have thrown him out the window when he had the chance." The hacking comes back. I feel like I'm turning crimson.

"You all right?"

"Never better," I wheeze. "My system's just not used to having a good time." Hack, hack, hack, hack.

"I bet. But you need something. Really, you can't have *anything*?" Cherry hesitantly pulls a vitaminwater bottle from her unzipped bag.

"Really." I wave off the water, which is berry blue and looks heavenly. The coughing settles down.

"What's it like?"

"Nothing by mouth?"

"Yes."

"Emptiness. I have to say, though, I've met people who've been NPO for years, or who will be for the rest of their lives, so I've got no business complaining. I don't know how they handle eternity."

"I can't understand how you can live without eating." She drops the water bottle back in the bag.

"That's what I hear the most. Everyone assumes you're hungry all the time, and I am, but there's something more than food that's gone." I'm back to talking about being sick, which is not as much fun as singing the Passover song. At this level of emotional intimacy, Cherry and I are still strangers, but as is often the case, our guards fall away. It's easier to be honest, and hospitals have a way of breeding confessions. She starts.

"I know. Since my cancer, things are different."

"How so?"

"I was never sick a day in my life. I'd never even spent a night in the hospital. I didn't know what to pack when I went in for surgery. Afterward, I felt bad all over, everything hurt. I guess I imagined those pains would come on slowly someday when I got old, but they came on all of a sudden."

"How do you feel now?"

"Better," she says, and smoothes the sitting wrinkles on her dark jeans. "But I'm still tired. I fall asleep at ten thirty, which is not me, but I can't stay awake. And my memory is shot. Remember how I used to go in front of a client and just talk out of my head? I can't do that now. With this project I'm working on, I've got to take copious notes and keep them with me when I present. I'm different."

"But you just told me all about the strategy for your new client, and I didn't see any notes."

When we were waging a misguided ego war, neither of us would have been willing to admit the smallest failing. She *is* different.

"It's not the same." Cherry's a rapid talker, fitting in as many words as her little-kid mouth can hold, but here she takes an unusual pause. She's sliding the ring on her index finger again, and I remember: She started wearing it after her humiliating divorce. It was a gift to herself she picked out on a business trip we took to Utah. An overpriced tourist storefront. Too many wind chimes. At the time, I thought of the ring as another needy attention-grabber. "Do you feel vulnerable?" she asks.

"I feel mortal. I didn't before." It's the truth, and it's frightening to say. I haven't said it until now.

"Me, too."

When Cherry leaves, I pick up the chai again and roll it between my fingers. I'm spent from the laughs and the weight of our admissions. As I told her, despite my years of living with illness, I had never felt my own mortality. I'd never even bothered to believe in it. Living had me wrapped up enough. Maybe the nature of the emergency brought on the change; maybe it's because I can't put anything in my mouth to heal myself; maybe my worries for Susan and the boys are the reason. Now it's with me.

I'm bleeding into my line, and I rest the chai. Cherry's gift is remarkable.

———

Another week passes in the hospital bed. I'm seeing a lot of a new doctor, an infectious-disease specialist, a personable Bugs 'n' Drugs guy who hobbles in a leg cast and crutches he took home from a Colorado ski slope. He has good humor about his accident, and it buys him a measure of empathy. He's more concerned about the state of my infection than he is my gut, and I've heard he and Abrams in the hallway discussing the need to do something else.

The rest of me may be nearing life support, but my hearing is still strong. Sonar ears are both a blessing and a curse in a noise factory like the hospital. Any doctor's murmur that you can pick up from the hallway chatter is gold, it's a line in to something meaningful after too many twenty-thousand-dollar days of "I really can't say." More than once, I've called the nurse for a forgotten order that I'd heard the doctor give outside my room. There is no patient vigilance without hearing. The downside, of course, is being tortured by the noise of an annoying roommate, as I was by the TV junkie with the stale jokes and the endless call list. For every one or two of those boobs, you might be lucky enough to get a roommate like J.P., whose company I truly enjoyed. He left another message on my cell phone yesterday. I should call him, but I don't want to unless I've got good news.

Listening, or eavesdropping, in hospital living, also becomes the best form of entertainment. Over the course of visits and conversations, you can piece together the lives of the families on the other side of the curtain. Getting involved in their stories keeps you engaged in life, even if it's someone else's. Sometimes the issues are so crazy they can make you feel less stressed by comparison. Sometimes the situations can parallel your own or lead you to a new understanding.

From what I've overheard, the guy in the coma next to me will be moving out tomorrow to a hospice near his home in New

Haven. The family's been in the room steadily, and their conversations have sunk from optimism to loss. This is painful for the survivors.

His wife, Barbara, has an indomitable will. She's in her early eighties, will soon become a widow after fifty-six years of marriage, and stays composed despite the added burdens of two pending knee replacements and a needy daughter my age, who turns every moment of real grief into an occasion to make herself the center of attention. Barbara sits in the unforgiving chair by her husband's bed and maintains serenity in a devastating time.

One day at lunchtime, I relieve her from the vigil and listen to the difficult daughter tell me her life story. She lives in Miami and runs an online company that sells designer clothes for dogs. She's single, with a married sister who's been in and is reasonable like Barbara and whom she clearly resents, playing a nasty game of sibling favorites over the comatose body of the father.

There's a preppy granddaughter who's come down from college, an Ivy League winter-carnival type with raw skier's lips and the myopia of youth—talking and talking, her infinite thoughts unfiltered and unaware, she radiates earnest excitement about everything she's discovering that no one else has ever known. Her boundless ego works on me, too, and I'm drawn in to her naive prattle. It's not narcissism when you're young. So different from the problems of her diamond-dog-collar aunt.

Barbara walks slowly into the room tonight, back from a visit to her orthopedist, dressed in cocoa-brown slacks, matching sensible shoes, and a cable-knit cardigan sweater. She doesn't slum in sweats even on these exhausting days.

"Thank you for the directions," she says to me, standing between the two beds, her hands resting in the cardigan's pockets. She's good-humored, like my mother, but without the nervous energy. "The bus worked out perfectly."

"I hope it wasn't too difficult a walk."

"I managed fine."

"Are you certain about the knee surgery?"

"Yes. I was surprised to see the X-rays. There's more damage than I imagined. The doctor recommends operating soon, and I trust what he had to say." She sits stiffly in the hard chair and flattens her palms against the sides, bracing herself through a pause. "I don't mean to be forward, but we'll be leaving for the hospice early in the morning, and I want to say good-bye. All the logistics have been worked out, and it's time for my husband to move on."

"Barbara, I'm so sorry. I can't imagine how hard this is. You've been bearing it so admirably." I'd get up out of bed to comfort her if I thought I could make it to the chair without the slapstick. Sitting under the covers for this conversation seems so callous, but I doubt lurching at her, clutching the clumsy IV pole, would bring her peace.

"Well, thank you. We'd hoped there would be an answer in the hospital, but leukemia is tough business. The pneumonia came on before treatment could even start. Fortunately, Arthur was himself until the end. He'd have hated to be diminished. He worked in his office until two weeks ago."

"What was his profession?"

"Arthur's an architect," she gently corrects me into the remaining present tense. "He's an old-fashioned kind of architect, a one-man practice. Houses, libraries, churches, vineyards. He loves it."

"That's wonderful." In one gracious statement, the inert body in the bed has been reanimated into a person. Loyal until the end.

"It is, and I'm happy he's been able to work after the diagnosis. It's who he is." Barbara halts after the testimonial, either for Arthur's due recognition or for her composure. She switches the subject to the dog-collar daughter, so I presume it's the latter. "Denise said she talked to you about her business. Thank you for being such a good listener."

"It was my pleasure." We both play this small charade. A Schubert quartet is drifting softly through Arthur's TV. It's late, but it seems Barbara wants to keep talking. I go on. "I never knew there was a fashion industry for dogs. My kids want a dog, but I'm allergic, so that's been the convenient excuse. Our apartment is too small, and my wife and I know they'd never walk it."

"What do you do?" She completes a difficult push-up from the chair and goes to Arthur's bed to straighten the unmoved cotton blanket on his still body. All of the day's movements — the covers that don't need straightening, the orthopedist visit, the doorstop book she checks in her handbag, our conversation — are useful diversions.

"Oh, nothing so prominent as your husband. When I was younger, I thought of being an architect, and I still read a bit about it. I worshipped Frank Lloyd Wright. Too many jobs to name, and I haven't worked in a while. I never imagined things would end up this way. Sometimes I think if I'd written the disco hit 'Der Kommissar,' I would have made a greater contribution to the world."

"What's that?"

"Just a silly old joke."

"Oh."

"I envy people like Arthur, who have that kind of fulfillment, that purpose. And your granddaughter—her life in front of her. Everyone should get a chance, and I'm afraid I didn't make the most of mine when I had it. Frankly, I was too dumb to know. I lived in a kind of fantasy about what my real priorities should have been. When I had the energy to fight being sick, when I was cocky and fearless, I spent too much of it screwing around. Now, with my career vaporized, my health what it is, my marriage and parenting challenging, it feels like my time has passed, and I don't know what to do about it."

Barbara examines the heart-rate monitor and wipes Arthur's silent mouth with a tissue. I raise my bed a notch to see her around the curtain.

"I'm sorry, Barbara, you were being friendly, and you've got so much to deal with, and I'm whining about my nothing-ness."

"That's not it." She quarter-turns and looks at me, stopping her speech abruptly. Backlit from Arthur's overhead, the net-work of pins sectioning her red hair exposes it as gray at the parts. Her voice rises by the subtlest measure and hushes my blabber. "I don't know all the details and difficulties of your life, and I've heard enough of the conversations with your doc-tors to know what's real. You're sick. But I also know what I've witnessed in this room. The people who've been with you. Your family. Your friends. Jon, you have people in your life who care about you. That's everything."

Barbara's been listening.

Before breakfast the next morning, she calmly instructs the orderlies who wheel her lifeless husband from his side of the room down the windows-on-the-world corridor into the van that takes them to the hospice. Arthur has been driven away in his bed, so the room is half empty. No cleanup is necessary, since he never did anything but sleep, and Barbara picked up the few loose ends. It doesn't feel like another roommate will be coming.

At seven A.M., Dr. Abrams strides across the bare floor and has no need to pull the curtain before he sits for our morning talk. He opens the three-ring binder holding my chart and reads a summary of the doctors' circular opinions: Due to the incidence of infection, a good intravenous option doesn't exist, and the final measure left to propose will likely fail. I've been subsisting in the hospital on saline and potent antibiotics to attack the infection and stop the fever, but they've also brought back the shits.

Dr. Abrams unbuttons a checked blazer that contrasts with his sleek complexion, compresses in the chair he pulls to the side of the bed, and breaks down the situation. There's disagreement among the doctors, and his remarks are divided by pauses bracketing contradictions.

"I believe that surgery is becoming the only option, but it's still too soon, given your present condition. The disease has returned and is more advanced. The infection shows that. But I don't want to start on anti-inflammatory medication now to address the disease. It could interfere with post-surgical healing in the gut and closing the fistula, and you've got enough to deal with on the antibiotic. Your hemoglobin and protein levels have dropped again, but you can't go back to TPN with active infection. However, you can't live on saline. We've got to get you nutrition, even if it's just to get you healthy enough for surgery."

He comes to a qualified stop, and I can't imagine where this report is going. Dr. Abrams brings his pen cap to his mouth and chews, a habit that often accompanies his internal deliberations.

"You couldn't come up with a better prognosis?" I say. "You're describing a turkey being stuffed for Thanksgiving slaughter."

Grimacing at the cheap analogy, he doesn't respond directly, hesitates, and glances down at the chart. He bites hard on the pen like a Popsicle stick and rolls it absently in his mouth before speaking.

"I'm going to start you on food."

"How?"

"Liquids first, then softs, then solids. We'll see how you do."

"Meaning what?"

"Diarrhea, nausea, pain, fever. If there's a problem, I'll have to convince Dr. Eberhardt we can't wait any longer for surgery. Hopefully, you'll improve."

"'Hopefully, you'll improve'? Gary, that doesn't exactly inspire me with confidence."

"We've got nothing left."

Nothing by mouth.

PART
THREE

CHAPTER 7

"The Empanada Lady is here. Can I get one?"

"I want one, too. Dad, please. Do you have your wallet with you?"

The deep-fried aroma of oiled meat and cheese pockets drifting through Riverside Park overpowers everything in its wake, even the scent of the lush pink blossoms. For me, empanadas are the true harbinger of spring. You can't eat the blossoms.

I haven't bathed in this Latin perfume since last year, and man, have I missed it. The Empanada Lady has an actual name, Ana, and sells snack food besides empanadas, but the incomparable taste and value of her filled-crescent delicacies has branded her eponymous to us. From spring through fall, she stands under the green-and-white umbrella on her rolling metal cart, dangerously in view of our apartment building, baiting us to salivate like wild dogs on roadkill. Even Teddy is crazy for them. How much more proof can you get?

I fork over four dollars so the boys can indulge their crispy ritual—cheese for Teddy, beef for Finn, naturally. I'm spoiling them a little, allowing the treat this close to dinnertime. With any luck, the empanadas will fill them up and I'll catch a break from cooking, but I know the snacks are just a warm-up. It would take half a dozen for a meal, a deadly option worth remembering.

I picked up the boys after school today for the first time since I got sick, and the weather is so glorious that I'm keeping us out longer than I should. They've got homework, and I've got to start the fish, but it's rejuvenating to be outside, worth injecting a pocket of joy into their lives on this delicious detour from responsibility. They're not used to my being around.

I'm sitting on a bench on the tree-lined promenade where the Empanada Lady parks her aluminum kitchen on wheels. Finn runs to me across the busy path, a carnivore in ecstasy, and nearly gets plowed by a speeding tandem bike. "Look out!" a biker warns. The hot vegetable oil has clouded Finn's judgment. He's sheared off a crimped empanada end with his checkerboard teeth, and the glistening crumbled beef jiggles in my face as he bursts with the big news.

"Dad, the Empanada Lady has chicken empanadas now! She told me they're brand-new. Do you want me to get you one?" Brown juice bubbles sputter from his mouth like water boiling over a pot. I reach for the mess with a paper napkin. Finn rams another hunk into his mouth before I can wipe. Two more thrilled bites, and his empanada will be history.

"Chicken? That *is* exciting," I say. A new flavor? This short gal in the apron has my number. I smell the goods on Finny's hot breath. "It sounds great, sweetie. Thanks for letting me know. I think today, though, just you guys will have the treat. I'll wait until Mom's here to get one."

Finny skips away and tells the Empanada Lady I won't be having one. I do want to chomp into that golden-brown crust and ravage the entire beef, cheese—and now chicken!—booty in her magic cart. I would even pinch the uneaten end from Finny's filthy hands for a bite if I could. The fact is, I can't. I have been eating for a few weeks, but it isn't going well. Actually, it's lousy. I can't taste anything I eat, and food makes me sick. I didn't think "Hopefully, you'll improve" would mean this.

As prescribed, I started on liquids in the hospital, followed by soft foods, then the trophy tray of solids. As soon as Nurse Sheila pulled down the NPO sign from my door, I was granted human status again, just like that. It inspired me with happiness, and visions of Entenmann's Rich Frosted Donuts danced in my head. Yes, I'd survived the starvation months and anticipated a digestive surrender of biblical proportions: Bring me this day my daily empanada. Huzzah!

I should have been tipped off by Dr. Abrams's bedside pessimism, but I wanted to believe, and the dammed cravings broke and flooded my senses like spring rains. The moment the NPO sign came off, I relived tasting the first sips of apple juice, the first spoonfuls of vanilla yogurt, the first bites into a dinner roll, all the firsts that some Avocado Gal would deliver to my room. They were revelations in my mind, and my mouth was poised to follow. Based on all the past fast-breaking, I imagined sweet and salty and savory and rich and tart and spicy awakening a garden of dormant taste buds and filling my mouth. Starting with the hospital's overzapped penne and rancid cheese sauce, rubbery green beans, cherry Jell-O, and generic ginger ale would be no hardship. Bring it on!

The food has not been the cream of my fantasies. The absence of flavor on my bristleless tongue stayed with me during the tasteless hospital meals and has yet to check out. My tongue is dumb without taste buds, the cells atrophied from neglect, a piece of cardboard flapping in my mouth. It's a bizarre paradox. Though I've resumed the mechanics of eating, the flavor cravings that both plagued and motivated me during the nothing-by-mouth months go unsatisfied. As an experiment, really a shock treatment, I've heaped dishes with vivid peppers and saffron, but even those molten spices have failed to raise the dead.

My stomach also remains entirely paralyzed. The induced gastrointestinal coma of TPN and octreotide has left an even more absurd legacy: Despite the fact that I'm eating, I have no feelings of digestion or satiation. I'm literally going through the motions. Equally maddening, the slightest cold and heat ache my forgotten teeth, so the soy milk, apple juice, ginger ale, beer, tea, and ice water I want are out, unless I sit them to reach a less painful room temperature. The entire eating process is anesthetized from tongue to gut. It's remarkable. I am an empty vessel into which the last hope for healing is being spooned, only to pass unnoticed and flood out as unstoppable diarrhea. I can eat, but I can't experience it. I'm a spectator in my own body. My gut is a phantom displaced from the rest of me, quartered like Oreo the cow's.

"Dad, she has chicken!" Not even the Empanada Lady's magic meat can break the glass on my stomach. A soccer game on the adjacent field just finished, and there's a line forming at her cart. She'll sell out the Gatorade, too. I see the boys in a conniving huddle, trolling in their spring shorts. Teddy is per-

suading Finn to ask me again about the chicken and whether he and his brother can have a second round of pastries.

Time to go home and cook dinner. Susan likes the tilapia poached. Teddy will hate it. I hope Finny has a few bites. As for me, I'm going out later to eat. My first dinner date since coming off NPO.

The tilapia goes off as expected. I make scrambled eggs to compensate for the leftovers on Teddy's plate. He asks for three desserts.

After I help get the boys to bed, my friend Mark treats me to what is supposed to be a celebratory dinner. He's been a great pal these past months, rustling time from his excessively busy life to hand-deliver shopping bags of books to my hospital room, even coming by with his wife, Jessica, one Saturday night. Forfeiting babysitting time on their movie-date night for a hospital visit—that's the ultimate sacrifice. He and I planned to celebrate my eventual discharge with a post-NPO meal at a favorite neighborhood bistro. During my starvation, the lively restaurant with the mosaic tile floor shone in my fantasy firmament. I make good on my mooning by ordering from memory a roasted-beet-and-goat-cheese salad and the house special, steak au poivre vert. Surely, the peppercorn crust or the garlic pommes frites will reanimate my lifeless mouth. Aiding the cause of my gastronomic therapy, Mark orders a plate of escargot soaked in pools of garlic-herb butter sauce to share.

To beef up in public, I've dressed in three layers of shirts, a turtleneck sweater, and a tweed jacket. Wearing my wardrobe like a refugee. I babble like a speed freak over the pungent courses set on the white tablecloth. You'd think there was caffeine in the food. Since being sprung from Mount Save Me, I dominate conversations as if I'm cashing out months of banked silence and getting paid by the word. It's too much. Everything in the busy dining room—the chopped beet quarters reddening my plate, the butter-yellow walls, the sapphire light spraying the bar mirror—fires a synapse in my convoluted head. Our escargot arrives, and I'm off to the races:

"Susan and I were eating dinner on our honeymoon in Paris, and I was so obsessed with fishing out every last bit of escargot that I went back like a frog through the dozen cleaned shells on my plate, and on the last shell, I pushed the fork too hard and dumped the entire mess on my jacket and tie. The oil soaked through my shirtfront. I sobbed to our waiter, and he brought us a flourless chocolate torte on the house. It was so delicious. They used to make a great flourless chocolate torte at Balthazar, too, downtown. Did you ever have it?" I rattle these tangents openmouthed, chewing and breathing on the words and snails.

Mark spears the last of his half of the escargot and looks longingly at his cell phone. Removing his rimless glasses, he rakes back his fine, dark hair and swivels in search of the waiter. He wears the Happening Guy uniform smartly: dark blazer, crisp white shirt, flared jeans. I've got to shut my mouth. Mark is a terrific friend, but he doesn't need a fool stealing his time, and tonight he's paying for the privilege. I don't think I've allowed space for him to say more than "What are you having?" Jessica and he have two kids, and he has a high-profile job that owns him. He's also a brilliant guy. Mark earned his place in a white-shoe business on sheer talent and drive—his father worked in an oil refinery—and I'd benefit from handing over the wheel for thirty seconds. What a show I'm giving him tonight. I can't stop the talking cure. I start talking about talking.

"I once acted in this obscure Pirandello play, *The Man with the Flower in His Mouth*. It's a two-character play set in a bistro, like this. My character is dying, he has cancer of the mouth, and he collars another diner and talks at him nonstop. He's terminal. His wife can't take his grief anymore, she's left him, and the only people he has to talk to are strangers. Talking is his only means of staying alive. He believes if he stops talking, he'll die. I had to deliver his monologue nonstop for an hour. Non sequiturs. Desperate. Afraid to stop."

My verbal diarrhea is pouring out of a compound fracture. Presently returned to the outside world of this café table and the social contract of a menu, I'm dislocated from common sense. A displaced-persons camp of one. Between soliloquies, I polish off my portion of the escargot, and the goat-cheese salad, and the peppercorn steak, and I don't taste any of it. I don't feel any of the food inside me. I look down at my empty plates and the used forks and knives. Though the meal has run the entire course from mouth to stomach, I have no sense that I've eaten. Mark finishes his meal a little after me and rests both hands agreeably on his belly. My only physical awareness of the food comes when I excuse myself to get sick in the restaurant's tiny bathroom. The shits have been relentless since I resumed eating, and I'm empty. I hate bathrooms like this, one toilet and someone knocking on the door to get in. It's frustrating, so soon after all that craved food, the immediate slug. I clean up and let in the door-knocker. He looks away when we pass. Back to the table. My incessant talking is another symptom, another sign of trying to fill up, a patch I'm abusing to cover the hole.

"You okay?" Mark asks. He opens his eyes in a general way, inquiring without overtly intruding on my bathroom business.

"Clean as a whistle." Our individual pots of herbal tea and coffee have arrived. I nudge my cup to the center of the swept table. The plain hot water seems more than I can handle.

"Ahhch. Let me get the check, and we can go." Mark motions for the waiter, who's stepping down a ladder and carrying wine bottles. The restaurant is running a popular special tonight, and the dark bottles are being pulled from the beehive rack like blue jeans.

"Finish your coffee first. I'm in no rush," I say. I should have lied about the shits; Mark is disappointed. What a waste this meal has been. Not the grand boys' night out I'd dreamed of. I also need to stay by the bathroom a little longer, just in case.

"Did you taste anything this time?" Mark pours dark coffee into his blue-handled cup. The aroma is lush.

"Not really."

"You're kidding. You ate everything so vigorously, I thought you were back." Mark flourishes that hope with an elastic chuckle, one of a few East Texas grace notes that still pluck his seamless speech.

I step on the wrong claw foot and jiggle the table. A finger of water spills over the teacup. "I've been thinking about this restaurant and this food for so long. You know, since that night in the hospital. But the flavor is all in my mind."

"What do your doctors say?" Mark scrolls through text messages he's received during dinner, and his penetrating eyes hold

on a long one. The waiter appears and takes his credit card. I
feel rotten about flushing the money.

"It could be temporary. And the meds could be causing the
runs. My gastro thinks I'm kidding myself and that I'll need
more surgery. I was hoping food would be the cure."

A couple I know from Finn's class comes through the restaurant's cigar-box entry and idles at the bar stools, waiting for
a table, out for fun on a school night. If I felt better, I'd wave
Larry and Charlotte over to join us for a drink. Larry should be
properly thanked for taking the boys to school when I was in
the hospital. I look down instead, avoiding eye contact. I'm still
not myself.

"I've gotten to this place I idealized only to miss what I'm
putting in my mouth. It's the sensual equivalent of terminal
foreplay with a blow-up doll," I say, trying for a laugh. Mark's
concerned expression doesn't change. If my sense of humor has
gone, people are really going to be done with me.

"Are you mad at your doctors or at God?" he asks. Mark
has come through a gauntlet of dysfunctional-family pain and
knows the difference. Despite a herd of surviving siblings, he
manages the issues in Texas and elsewhere mostly alone.

Fingering the rim of my tepid cup, I'm beginning to register the value of his time, implicit in his compact observations,
and I come to a point. "Mark, let me ask you something. You're
a smart, successful guy. You're a winner. How am I going to get
through this?"

He offers the full attention of his bright, sturdy face. We're
the same age, yet he looks a decade younger in the restaurant's
half-light. I don't imagine he has prepared for my particular

desperate question—after all, this dinner was supposed to be a celebration—but he draws a ready answer from his estimable wisdom well. As he speaks, it strikes me: That's why he's so successful. He's able to meet challenges head-on with intelligence rather than close them off out of fear. He's got courage.

"You're going to have to find meaning in this experience." Mark's voice is sincere. It resonates with his experience and pierces the distortion of the noisy room. His long fingers are splayed on the table like he's planting for a push-up. "That's the only way. If you get better and you just go back to where you were as though none of this ever happened, you will be cheating yourself out of something that's vital to living your life."

He finishes his coffee and signs the bill.

I wrap myself in an overcoat and scarf and we say good night at Mark's apartment building. Window lights glow white and yellow in the sky and the street life is winding down when I walk home. The dogs are out making last calls on the sidewalks. The early-spring tulips have gone to green stalks. Mark is working late tonight, preparing for a meeting with the president. Amazing.

His advice to me is right, more profound than "think positive," but, in my state, no less abstract. Wise as it is, I don't feel that I've got the working equipment needed to find the answers. Unfortunately, I'm still digging in the pathology of the past, wanting to return to where I was before my gut exploded, wanting my health, my weight, my strength, my appetite, my taste— wanting all of it back. How can I improve if my circumstances don't? If my gut doesn't heal, if I can't taste what's in my mouth, if I can't eat like a normal human being, what meaning could I possibly find that would make my life feel vital?

The following day, I've got a scheduled doubleheader of doctor appointments. I see Dr. Abrams first, in his office on the ground floor of a brick pre-war. The exam is an exercise in studied skepticism. He looks unmoved by the unclosed belly hole and silently records in the dog-eared file my description of the steak au poivre nondinner and the longer ladder of complaints. The next patient murmurs to a nurse through the wall of the adjoining room. This must be the bottom of professional punishment, writing the same crabby sentences over and over again from visit to visit. How many times can you write the word "evacuate" in a file without wanting to flee?

I pull on fleece-lined jeans and a turtleneck sweater, and we move to his desk for him to scribble out more prescriptions. I've come to the doctor for answers to questions that have persisted for nearly half a year. Going through the rote of gut reporting and vitals, or even calling him Gary, isn't sparking a breakthrough.

"Levaquin. Five hundred milligrams, once a day."

As he tears sheets from the pad, again I peel back the sequence of events from the incident that happened months ago, parsing shit for clues of what led to my undoing. I'm speaking into the atmosphere. "I had a good day on that Thursday before the rupture. I even swam an extra twenty laps. I ate chicken for dinner."

Dr. Abrams looks up from the desk and stops my history expedition. "Jon, you want to know what caused this to happen." He slows to enunciate precisely. I've gotten his attention, and I ready myself for an explanation, for clarity. He gives the pen a chew and continues. "You want to understand why so that you can prevent it from happening again. I can appreciate that.

But my honest answer to you is I don't know." He hands off the written prescriptions. His face is stretched in resignation, like it's drawn on a balloon.

I sit in the chair facing the desk cluttered by files and pictures of Dr. Abrams's two kids and say nothing. "I don't know"? That's the prognosis? How am I supposed to find hope, let alone meaning, in "I don't know"? He's a doctor; he's *supposed* to know. Every time I sit on the toilet, I worry I won't come up whole. I can't live this way. I want answers, man! Turns out, I'm mad at God *and* my doctors.

I carry my existential ache to the second appointment, with Dr. Rothschild, the hematologist. Rothschild and Abrams: old blood and guts. Rothschild's office is in Mount Save Me. The voices and footsteps echoing in the hospital's cavernous atrium are ominous, and I'm revisited by dread. Before this year's episodes, I'd walked this building routinely dozens of times for office visits and tests. Now it's a foreboding place that bears no resemblance to Finn's cheery cardboard model. It's a place where I can again be tied to a bed and sliced in half.

Three vials of my blood are bottled and documented by the West Indian nurse in the hematology lab. While the samples are being studied, I sit in the lab's small waiting room, a space that's whimsically stocked with mini–ginger ale cans and saltine packs in wicker baskets riding on end tables, like the hospital's version of a talk-show greenroom. Everybody in the narrow chairs grabs the free snacks—the chemo patients, the bone-marrow transplants, the head-and-neck people. Today I don't.

Rothschild is fired up when he enters the cold exam room. He has an old-time doctor's disposition, interested in the whole patient, as much psychologist as blood man, and he's concerned and agitated by the figure he sees curved on the table. I've been his patient for only two years, since the blood clots first struck, but his approach to medicine has intensified the relationship, which can make for either comforting or disturbing discussions, depending on the test results. Blood is another essential food my body has rejected.

"We'll discuss your blood in a minute. I've got the lab results." He sits bent on the rolling chair in the corner and opens my chart on the desk. Rothschild's shoulders hunch in what my parents would call "a rabbinical stoop." This has the effect of inching him even closer for conversation. He rolls to the exam table. The chair wheels rattle on the tile floor. "But first, let's talk. You were depressed when I saw you in the hospital. Are you still depressed?"

"I'm happy to be out of the hospital."

"That doesn't answer the question."

"I don't know. I still feel horrible."

"What's wrong?" The doctor writes down our conversation on the chart in a careful hand, concentrating on his notes through thick glasses. The guy really should be charging by the fifty-minute hour.

"You know what's wrong," I tell him. "The new me. My gut isn't working. I'm finally eating, but I can't keep anything in, and I can't taste anything."

"What does Dr. Abrams have to say about this?" Rothschild was Abrams's medical school professor, and he doesn't hesitate to play instructor and check up on his student.

"I just saw him before I came to you. He said, 'I don't know.'"

I sit cross-legged on the slab table in boxers. My arms are wrapped tight to stay warm. The paper hospital gown is folded on the table. I never wear the useless body-sized bib, but I'm under an arctic vent, and our chat is beginning to chill me.

"He's being honest with you. Living with chronic illness is living with uncertainty. That's the hardest part." Rothschild stops writing to deliver that conclusion, looking straight at me through his lenses. He speaks bluntly, with candor that corroborates his famous-doctor status and likely unnerves his residents. He hammers the oral-exam questions, expecting thoughtful responses. His bushy mustache is also old-school and trimmed with gray. Facially, Rothschild resembles the funny physician in a book my boys used to enjoy, a cartoon picture that contrasts with his clinical probing.

"I've heard something to that effect," I say, too sarcastically for this earnest conversation, and the doctor comes back fast.

"Doctors are just people who went to medical school. You should know that by now." *I know, you want God, go to a temple.* Rothschild pulls down the skin under my eyes with his fingertips, shines his flashlight, then sticks a depressor on my tongue, talking while he looks. "I talked to your father about you at the hospital. He's worried, too." The AC vent blows, and I wriggle my crossed arms and ankles. "How're you doing with your wife?"

"We're talking."

"How's your sex life?"

"Infrequent."

"Why?" Rothschild asks with a canary-in-his-mouth New York–inflected lilt at the end of the word—both, it seems, as a lead to what he thinks is an important topic and to send me a message. I've heard this tone before and recognize its implications.

"I think Susan's nervous with me physically. I think she's afraid I'm going to bust. I suppose I can understand why. I've kept my shirt on during sex, which is hard to miss even with the lights off. As you can see, the dressing on my gut is still the size of a picture window, and I don't want her to see it." My hands point to the sides of the bandage. Rothschild nods and moves closer in the chair. "Or I can just blame everything on the kids."

"Are you embarrassed by the wound?" he asks and feels my joints while we talk.

"It's not my handsomest feature."

"What's your level of sexual interest?"

"Overwrought."

"How's the sex itself?"

"Good but cautious. We've had sex a few times since I came home."

"Are you worried about getting hurt?"

"I'm too horny for worry."

"Are you working?"

"No."

The desk phone rings loud as an alarm and abruptly halts our rapid exchange. Rothschild wheels to the phone and speaks harshly to some unfortunate nurse on the other end. "Yes, yes. He'll have to wait. I need a minute."

Rothschild stands up from the chair and comes to the table. "Lie down." He probes my abdomen as he speaks, in a more expansive voice than on the phone. "I had quadruple bypass when I was forty-nine. That was twenty-two years ago. Did you know that?"

"No." My head is tipped back. Rothschild's voice is coming down from the ceiling, blowing on me with the draft. He's out of my sight.

"The statistics indicated that it was unlikely I would ever work again. In those days, quadruple bypass was a big deal. It's still a big deal, but then it could be permanently devastating to the body, if you even lived." He lifts my window dressing and looks into the trap. "My cardiologist told me I may not be able to resume my practice and my teaching. After I got out of the hospital, I was home for six weeks, and I felt terrible. The surgery left me in tremendous pain.

"Eventually, the pain subsided, but I was still miserable. I was depressed, and I saw where things were headed—no practice, no purpose, nothing good to say to my wife, no life. I couldn't handle that. I knew that if things continued that way, I'd be dead in six months. I realized there was only one way out." The doctor presses my legs, checking for inflammation at the areas where the blood clots formed. My limbs are as skinny as matchsticks and hurt under his thumbs.

"When patients are hit with this kind of trauma—what happened to me, what happened to you—you can do one of two things. You can settle and do nothing, or you can move forward. If you do nothing, you'll withdraw into yourself, and you'll be finished.

"You're sick. You're always going to have illness. Just as I still have the DNA that gave me the heart condition. But I made a choice to move forward." Dr. Rothschild is poking around my pelvis at the surgical area. The pain I feel from his pressure is not the familiar bloated distress of inflammation but what feels like the opposite, an ache of emptiness, like pieces of me are missing. His hand could go right through me.

"My wife lives with cancer. It impairs her breathing. In April it was our fiftieth wedding anniversary. It's been a dream of hers to go to Machu Picchu. The site is at eight thousand feet, and the altitude could have severely compromised her ability to breathe, but she was determined to see the ruins."

"Jesus. What did you do?" I ask.

"Certainly, we went. She breathed, and she walked in the Andes, and it was spectacular."

"That's fantastic."

The doctor's hands are at my throat, checking the glands. He drops from there to my pulse and takes a moment before speaking. "You have a choice to make. You wanted certainty from Dr. Abrams, and you can't have that. That's your lot. But if you move forward, you can live."

I leave the hospital and walk across the park to pick up the boys. In the community garden opposite the school, I sit on a bench by the daylilies Finn's class planted. He showed me yesterday afternoon the spot where he dug the soil. I have a few minutes before the classes get dismissed in the playground.

I appreciate Dr. Rothschild's point. I tread in the past because it offers certainty, but I'll never recover by withdrawing into history. Since the surgery, my withdrawal has only compounded the deeper issues I face. Nothing by mouth eliminated food, and it contributed to my isolation. I withdrew into a hole I'm stuck in. But my inability to move out of it is about something missing in me besides the gut. It all makes sense.

What I can't figure out is, move forward to what? And how? I

have no energy; I may be in for more surgery; and I have no opportunity for work. The career I had is gone. Whatever's next will have
to be different from what I've done before, that's certain.

My final project before the ax fell crystallized just how bleak
and pointless the economy and my career had become. I was
responsible for telling a prospective client what words and
images they could use to motivate increased sales of saturated
fats, high-fructose corn syrup, refined sugar, hydrogenated oils,
and empty calories to poison the public and pollute the world's
landfills with Styrofoam plates and cups and plastic bottles and
forks. I laughed out loud when my new boss assigned me the
pitch. That may have been a mistake. But given that I'd eliminated those very same toxic ingredients from my own family's
diets, as well as my continued interest in living on the planet
without having to wear a hazmat suit to bed, I felt that selling
these corporate jokers the creative ammunition to commit mass
murder was nothing short of personal betrayal. No different
than pushing cigarettes to pregnant teenagers. As swan songs
go, this was a funeral march. However, as Upton Sinclair wrote,
"It is difficult to get a man to understand something when his
salary depends on his not understanding it." Not my finest hour.
I was a fool to be in this kind of regrettable situation yet again.

When Gordon, the opportunistic loony I'd worked for, cashed
out, he sold the agency to a rack of faceless suits at a holding
company called InterCommUniversal. The name sounded to me
like they made loudspeakers. Everyone else in my group was laid
off, and I was covering multiple jobs. The new head of the office
was a real prick, a smart and slippery guy named Roger, who'd
been transferred from London to fire everybody. He flashed a

senator's transparent smile and silently walked the office's bar-
ren squares. The company paid to ship his fifteen-hundred-bottle
wine collection to his new cellar in New York. He showed me the
packing list one day in his office. He was ordering new furniture,
and he held it up for me to read. After joking about customs, he
summarized the pitch opportunity. It was up to me to save the
business for Roger's bottles and ol' ICU.

I sat for the prospective client's product-briefing meeting at
their suburban campus headquarters, feeling like a man hired
to build coffins during a plague. Everything about it offered the
specter of death and disease under the surface. The dark-paneled
conference room was built like a coffin, airless and oppressive,
and the expensive art collection dressing up the walls and land-
scaped grounds was a kind of sick representation of man's limit-
less capacity for self-destruction. A lot of deadly fast food and
soda had to be sold to buy all those Cézannes. Without question,
the painted apples were the healthiest food in the whole place.

The conversations in the conference room and private offices
were funereal, hushed, either in deference to the adjoining
golf course or the incriminating nature of the words themselves. Everyone I met—the scientists, the executives, the sales
force—told me something I didn't want to hear about products
I wouldn't want anyone to consume. The word that kept coming
up was not "delicious" or "tasty" or "nutritious" or even "ingredients" but "efficiencies," spread across the campus like a new
kind of dessert topping. The obsession with market share and
margins outstripped everything else, and there was no interest
in other topics like, say, food. My questions at the meetings were
worthless. It was my job to make the company's customers feel

good and forget about the silent bombs being brewed and deep-
fried. It was sinful bullshit.

There's been a lot of information equating high-fructose corn
syrup, lab-flavored sodas, and other food-like products with the
perpetuated health dangers of the country's tobacco scourge.
Three packs of cigarettes a day is the oral antecedent to fifty gal-
lons of soda a year. The analogy is even more frightening since
some of the Big Food producers like my prospective client are
owned by cigarette companies, so selling death in every swallow
simply honors their corporate heritage. Building unhealthy bodies one empty calorie at a time. To hear them talk, you'd think
they never got the memo about two thirds of Americans being
overweight and one third obese, and the correlation between diet
and the critical rise of heart disease, diabetes, cancer, Alzheim-
er's, and other killers. I was in the belly of the beast. They wanted
help killing the opposition before the situation got too serious.

On a shameful winter night, in the name of research, Susan
and I took the boys for dinner to one of the client's chain restaurants to sample the goods and enable me to lie with the benefit of
experience. We were a nuclear family loading up on an American
pastime and the country's signature export. I encouraged the kids
to eat lethal food off of environmentally criminal tableware after
having forsworn both—a bit of a conflict. They loved it. Teddy ate
everything on his tray and refilled at the fountain. Even now the
boys ask for it. "Gross" was the word Susan used the next morning to describe how she felt. I could have used a week of detox.

Like a man thirsting in a desert, I swallowed the corporate
swill hard and came up with a swell plan to promote global
genocide. The facts disappeared. For weeks I came home from

the office, a stooge working solo in the greater efficiencies of corporate restructuring, and continued through the night on the living room couch after everyone went to sleep. It was work better done in the dark.

Near the presentation date, I started feeling odd pains in both legs, steady and intense. I'd wake up on the couch in agony. The pain began around my ankles and eventually rose through my thighs. The night before the presentation to the client, it got so excruciating, I literally crawled into an ER and was diagnosed with bilateral deep vein thrombosis, or blood clots in both legs. Perhaps a side effect of the Crohn's disease that was active, perhaps a divine act of moral vengeance. Either way, it was an alarming discovery. The doctors were stunned and concerned. However, I was committed for the morning to sing the sweetened gospel in the corporate pleasure palace. So I signed medical waivers and passed a crash course in shooting up anticoagulants, left the hospital at dawn on hands and knees, and made it to my meeting in the conference room walled by the oil portraits of French apples and dead white men.

It went well. The people in the room liked my proposal, I thought. The marketing chief didn't ask any questions but showed a hint of emotion about the concept, which had nothing to do with food or drink. Fitting. They never served any of their products in the meetings.

On the car ride back to the city, I got a phone call from Roger. "Congratulations on the presentation. They seem interested. Brilliant. They'd be such a big fish. Fingers crossed." His voice had the slick smile in it. He was pleased, sitting on the new furniture, an expensive modernist update on Gordon's schlock.

Before I could ask which of the fifteen hundred bottles he'd be opening that evening, he spoke again. "Glad I've got you still in the car. There's no need returning to the office. You've been let go. Tough business, that. Your severance package will be delivered to your home this afternoon. Sorry."

A week later, the client bought my idea. I watched it run for about a year.

Tough business, that.

It was my third and last layoff in the grim first decade of this century, and I was no longer shocked at getting canned. I was angry. Not with the mercenaries at ICU. I'd experienced enough ruthlessness and sheer stupidity to know the state of employer loyalty. But angry with myself.

I see now it was a consequence of my own bad choices, made repeatedly, knowing too well the likely outcome but hoping for a different result. Like eating the fast food and being surprised by feeling gross. I had no confidence in my company's leadership or faith in their preposterous plans, but I stayed anyway. Much of it was driven by our unyielding need for affordable family health insurance. That has had an outsize impact on all of Susan's and my career decisions. When we've been between jobs and had to pay for insurance on our own, the premium has cost nearly two thousand dollars a month, not including medications. My blood-thinning injections ran fifteen hundred a batch. Insurance drives everything else.

Insurance aside, my wrongheaded choices were a matter of more functional denial, the patient's alter ego. In the aftermath of the emergency, it has become clear to me that my health problems and career problems are linked. Pimping for deadly food should have told me that when I was in the conference room with the Cézannes.

Willful ignorance—about diet, about career, about priorities—is what has gotten me into the holes of illness and unemployment. Unfortunately, I'm late to the window. I've been down this hole for so long, I can't see the way out. I know the changes I want, but the climb to reach them seems impossible where I am. To make Dr. Rothschild's prescribed move forward, I'd need to have something real, something promising to hang on to and pull me out. I don't know what's in front of me.

Ms. Jordan has brought Finny's class to the playground. He doesn't see me waving yet. I wonder if he ever told her about the chocolate-chip pancakes. He's trying to hustle a playdate, I can tell, bending his head down to his shorter friends. I hope I don't have to wait too long for Teddy—I've got to get to the bathroom. Food isn't doing me any good, even though the cravings still hound me. As real as the pockets in the Empanada Lady's cart.

———

The diner on Third Avenue is crowded, a crash of conversation, plates, and smells saturating the narrow restaurant. It's a friendly place, and I grab the last open stool at the curve of the counter, in the sight line of glass platters housing a glinting apricot Danish and glazed donuts. Cantaloupe and grapefruit halves arc in a metal bin like the roof of the Sydney Opera House; mini-boxes of cereal and tea and a tavern's share of green and brown beer bottles line the shelves behind the counter; every available inch consumed by food as product and decor.

I'm here under doctor's orders. It's the tail end of the school year, and I've spent most of the day in Dr. Kaplan's radiology lab for a crucial small-bowel exam. The pictures will determine the status of the mystery fistula and disease, images that will challenge or corroborate Dr. Abrams's judgment and tell me how I should feel. My usually reliable patient's intuition is sidelined by the paralysis that numbs me from tongue to gut, so everything seems to be in the doctor's hands. Thankfully, the cups of barium are less vulgar than the last time, and our table talk is enlivened by Kaplan's running literary commentary. He inserts citations between shutter orders delivered in his announcer's volume: "Turn to your left side. Turn back to your right. Stop breathing. Hold it. Breathe. I've never been able to get into Richard Ford."

Kaplan shoots dozens of pictures through the day and gives me a full table workout. At two o'clock he instructs me to go have something to eat, then return for a final round of pictures. Most doctors would have stopped the exam by now. I appreciate his extended effort to provide conclusion. So far, the pictures are mixed.

Miraculously, it appears from the cloudy forms made clearer by the doctor's voiceover, the fistula has healed. The NPO/TPN approach provided time for my body to regenerate cells and close the spout. Where I felt dead, there was life. To be certain, Kaplan will check again after I eat, but I'm exhilarated by the news. This could—in my mind, *should*—mean I have the chance to be normal again, to eat, to gain back the weight and strength, to bury the agony of deprivation, to live. I can cruise the supermarket aisles and talk up the Yankees with Eduardo the cheese monger and eat green olives out of the tub if I want. I can withstand an eight-pound plate of corned-beef hash this summer. I can rejoin my family.

On the other hand, the X-rays also show significant Crohn's disease around the area of the surgery. Pockets of inflammation and stricturing are larger in number and size than before the eruption, and I am now living with the pronounced symptoms of active illness. The images definitely show something troubling for the future, but the specifics and implications of that something are impossible to know.

Uncertainty fills the plate before me. "Living with illness is living with uncertainty"—Dr. Rothschild's pronouncement from a few weeks ago has again proved prescient. By now I should know that raising the shield of certainty is illusory, no more real than the fiction of immortality I used to peddle to myself. Learning to live with uncertainty may be the approach I need in order to survive, but it's difficult to embrace. Most of the time, I still clutch to willful ignorance, my own worst enemy. Acceptance will require ditching the delusion that has seen me through decades.

I tell Dr. Kaplan I'll be eating at the trusty diner around the corner on Third Avenue. Over the years, I've designated the place as my end-of-procedure Bacchanalian destination to break the barium fast. The doctor regards me with an approving smile and recommends for dessert a bakery one block farther east. He's been shooting me with radioactive juice since college and has yet to steer me wrong, so I make a mental note.

It's been a longtime mission of mine to keep alive the city's remaining coffee shops. Call it a common man's gourmandise, but the appeal of good, cheap food and the atmosphere of spinning stools and patrons—that's luxury to me. It transcends class or taste. I moved from Washington when I could no longer stand the lack of a good diner.

In his diary, Richard Burton, a man urged by unrivaled cravings, writes of the pleasures of American short-order cooking he discovered at one of my West Side favorites, the Excelsior. Burton ate there in the early sixties during his *Camelot* Broadway run and was hooked by the instantaneous wonders of the griddle. Good for hangovers, good for the soul. The Excelsior was a charming dump I habituated for years, though I never managed to pry any Burton tales from the stony owner, who sat behind the cha-chinging register fortressed by cigar boxes. A warning glare was all my Burton questions ever drew.

Tragically, the Excelsior closed a few years ago, a victim of Manhattan's real estate obscenity. In its place is an expensive, shiny brass restaurant. Perhaps it's better that Burton isn't around to see it.

The loss of the Excelsior, the Munson, the Cheyenne, the Empire, and their aluminum-skinned cousins costs New York its character. Without these hash houses anchoring city blocks, we're just Indianapolis with taller buildings.

Today my hallowed post-barium diner is also a personal test site. The counter man, Kit, takes my order. He hangs reading glasses from the V of an open-collared shirt and speaks like a logician. I don't need to consult the dense menu. It's an ambitious spread, from pancakes to clams casino—an omnivore's menu, as if to say everything is possible here. And it is. In three minutes, the oval plate is out from the deliciously noisy kitchen, handed through the open top half of a Dutch door and set down in front of me. Fried egg and bacon on wheat toast, my stalwart companion, has never failed to satisfy. After scratching on dead-tongue curry and saffron and steak au poivre, I'm rolling the dice on a safer bet.

Once more unto the breach. I chomp into the crisped wheat toast sandwiching layers of fried egg and bacon curls, chewing to exorcise the ghost of the barium chalk coating my mouth.

What's this?

There is a trace of flavor in the bite. I tumble the mix around my mouth and feel a little of something that's been missing for months—the patchy return of baby taste buds on my tongue. I examine them in the blade of my butter knife. Kit, standing with arms folded at the hacked end of the counter, freezes his gaze on me. The buds are only partially formed, shot through like old sandpaper, but what I lack in taste is slaked by the sensation of the sandwich's texture on my tongue. The combination of crusty toast and crunchy bacon congealed by the precisely-cooked egg commingles in my mouth like a deep-tissue massage. I am deliriously happy. I slow to savor the sandwich, sipping orange juice like a baby, smiling at Kit, who's bowed to the *Post*, and disturbing the poor guy sitting next to me, absorbed in his Kindle, to announce that this sandwich is the best thing that's ever happened to me.

"Oh, yeah," he says, indulging me with a sideways glance. "You should try the meat loaf."

There should be no stopping me. I want to order another, and the clams casino, and work my way through the dessert cases shining on the counter. Then I'd come back for dinner and start on the specials. However, remembering Dr. Kaplan's recommendation, I leave the Danish and donuts caged and head to the bakery.

Just stepping inside the cozy barn-doored bakery with its glass cases displaying ruffled round cakes rising high as soufflés, their icings scalloped and braided in chocolate, vanilla, and pink, I know Kaplan got it right. This place is a dessert junkie's crack den.

Two older women in loopy conversation share a wedge of carrot cake and a brownie at a demi café table by the window. Overwhelmed by the choice of sugar highs, I go with a house special chalked on the menu board, a red velvet cupcake that measures the diameter of a sunflower. It's handed to me on an undersize white plate. I knife the mound in two and take it to a table to stop myself from inhaling it in a single gluttonous gulp. That was my preferred method as a kid, practically swallowing waxy Hostess cupcakes whole.

I hold the spongy red cake by my fingertips, mounted like a mammoth cut diamond. The cherry-colored base is cool and moist to the touch and is topped by waves of elegant cream-cheese frosting, combed into swirls that look oddly like my rutted intestinal loops. In the first bite, I can tell the cupcake justifies its chalkboard billing. The cream-cheese topping is rich and avoids the treacly sweetness of icing. Its density is consistent through each invigorating chew and adds appreciable heft without matting the airy red bottom. It's a delicate balancing act. The baker's dusting of red velvet crumbs on the center-frosted peak, rather than the mistake of an insipid cherry or candy, is a deft touch.

I scrape bits of stuck cake off the wrapper with my front teeth and have to restrain myself from eating the paper. I want to call Susan and tell her about this, and the fried-egg sandwich, and Kaplan's picture showing one hole closed, but she's in school. There's still no feeling in my gut, so the cupcake pleasure ends at the back of my throat. Until that point, it's pure bliss.

CHAPTER 8

It's Labor Day, and we're stretching summer to the end with one final footloose day at the beach. We've been away from the city the past two months, healing, repairing, playing, and eating in the great outdoors. As has become our cash-strapped annual custom, we freeloaded all summer. Maine, Martha's Vineyard, Nantucket, Royal Woods Hill—top-drawer freeloading. Gracious invitations made the sponging possible, invitations that were especially welcome in light of the cudgel of medical bills that have continued to pound us deeper into a financial hole. Until I find work, we're wrecked. My résumés and phone calls have resumed their steady flight into the ether and we're living on the fumes. However, I'll amend my prior statement about being unemployed. The only benefit to being unemployed is being unemployed in the summer *and* having friends with beach houses. Pity has its rewards.

Today we've fled close to home, to Jones Beach, just over the Long Island border an hour from the city. The train and bus were packed with people like us, playing a last hand in the sun before school and work kick in tomorrow. It's our first trip to Jones Beach this season, and I'm happy we've made it. There's a natural closure to the summer calendar today, and the season wouldn't be complete without a visit.

At a lip of stained, crusted sand by the water, I unroll two blankets and sink the umbrella, an awning-striped model Jones has rented since the swampy island was dredged into beach and opened for business in 1929. Made of heavy wood, metal, and canvas, the umbrella was hell to carry on my shoulder from the bathhouse, but it will hold up to the worst. I've never seen anything like them. A pounding tropical storm earlier in the weekend blew up the surf and swallowed the shoreline, pushing back our crumbling bluff like a cuticle edging the sea. We're just past the no-lifeguard flags, near the gay and topless beaches, where the sand is less crowded. I've packed two rounds of lunch and snacks to hold us, and I park the chilled bags in the umbrella's angled shade.

The summer escape has taken us refreshingly far from our regular lives to a series of safe houses free from worry. Clean beds, warm air, kitchens full of food. I also escaped further surgery. After the final mixed pictures at Kaplan's, I saw my regular surgeon, Dr. Meat Hands, and he determined no immediate need to operate:

"There's lasting damage from the surgery. Frankly, the surgeon didn't do you any favors. I would have done it differently." He raised the X-rays to the window light. I bent to look up from the table, my still-unclosed wound bared for the exam. "But the fistula has closed, so let's see how you do for now. You could be good for a while. If you feel lousy, you'll tell me."

Dr. Eberhardt is generally a reassuring guy, calmly certain and decisive, and this was not entirely what I wanted to hear. His dark, magnified eyes fell a little into their lids as he dispensed the vague prognosis. Maybe he was just tired. He'd been cutting since early morning. However, I was in no rush for another operation, so I took the gift of uncertainty and left.

Seeing Thompson Lake again reconnected me to what had died when I was nothing by mouth. With little besides the weather to concern us, meals and swimming have been the center of our summer days. I commandeered the grill practically every night and smoked my head in the smells trailing into the evergreens over the deck. Miraculously, gratefully, delectably, I could taste the briny Katz's dogs my father drove up from Manhattan. I could taste the fresh July strawberries the four of us picked in buckets at Goss's farm; and the Stars and Stripes cake at Bob and Marta's holiday cookout; and the August sugar and gold corn; and the tart wild blueberries in the low bushes by the beach; and the coffee brandy in the Maine martini; and the French-vanilla sundae at One Cow ice cream in the field off Route 26. My taste buds roared back. The summer has been a delirious tent revival of eating. The shits stopped when I quit the meds, and some subdued traces of hunger and satiation have returned. Although my gut sensations are still mostly numbed, eating is becoming a pleasure again.

I haven't yet circled the kitchen-calendar dates for the debuts of Beaujolais Nouveau and red D'Anjou pears. That's too far away. But I can't get enough of the food this summer.

Devouring lobster and beer and ice cream sundaes, I rapidly gained back half of the forty pounds I'd lost, then stopped. The doctors are not sure why. I'm a glutton in a greyhound's body again, with a new wrinkle: My gut looks scary in a bathing suit. When the skin finally closed, and the windowpane dressing came off, the surgical hole healed in an agitated way. My gut hurts when I touch it, like something's wrong. Apparently, the wound's gap was too wide for a smooth reconnection of muscle and flesh, and the skin clenched in two camel humps on opposing shores of the Thompson Lake scar that spreads purple down my middle. The effect of the humps, paradoxically, is to create the illusion of a pot-belly, a half hitch of incongruous knots bulging my pipe-cleaner trunk. It's absurd, and I am a walking contradiction, like before.

Despite the pain and ugliness, though, I feel human. I've exercised and played lots of ball with the boys. Teddy's gotten stronger. On the tennis court, he whips crosscourt forehands that freeze me on my heels.

Summer has been good for Susan and me. We've made love, grilled clams together, read on the beach. We've enjoyed each other. Better health has encouraged me out of being a cretin. This time to repair our marriage and enjoy a vacation has been a godsend, and we're both sorry it will end today. We don't talk about the past or the future right now. Maybe it's a fragile healing. I suppose the hostilities that divided us still exist in potential. But my feelings for Susan have enabled me to get past most of the issues that troubled me. Apparently, the hit to her optimism wasn't lethal. She's moving things forward one day at a time, wanting to keep all of us together. My relief has helped her, too. She's working at it.

Rebuilding our home began, for me, by tasting the fried-egg sandwich and red velvet cupcake after Kaplan's pictures. Returning to my normal functions—taking the kids to and from school, grocery shopping, cooking, housecleaning, laundry, even dealing with the onerous medical bills—was the foundation of my restoration to the structure of parent and husband. Eating made life possible again.

It would be nobler to be able to say, "I learned to live without food. I accepted deprivation and survived, a stronger and better person." The truth is, I didn't. Nothing by mouth is a fate I hope won't return for another course. I was weak in the face of suffering and awful to the people around me. If hardship tests your character, I learned that my will to live triumphed, but I can't say the same about my dignity. I'll have to leave stoicism for the heroes and ascetics.

Unpacking the beach bags, I stake our turf and settle in to enjoy the finale of this therapeutic summer. I inhale a peanut-butter sandwich and pass the others, trying to keep the boys' food out of the sand.

Uncharacteristically, Susan sprints to the ocean and motions for the three of us to follow. She cuts a diagonal path to the boundary inside the lifeguard zone and crashes into the water. I'm surprised. Typically, Susan doesn't even look at the water before opening her chair, organizing her reading, reapplying sunblock, brushing the kids' feet off the blanket, and eating. The beach always enlarges her appetite. She's also skittish about waves, and the swells rolling in and breaking at the storm gullies are larger than I would swim in with the boys. The surf is the highest I've seen this summer. Susan's usual reluctance is a product of poor vision and her landlocked Indiana childhood. She sometimes tethers to me in the waves. At heart, she's a swimming-pool gal, and summer at the beach is another marital compromise.

I'm confused by her sudden fearlessness. Who knows? Maybe all the time at the beach this summer helped conquer her apprehension of the water. Or enduring the months when I was MIA settled the doubts she had about herself, and she's showing the kids she can do it without me. Our traumatic experience was a chance for her to find meaning, too. Or maybe she's just happy. It's hard not to overthink things when you're putting pieces back together. She looks happy and sexy, waving at us in her bikini. On this final glorious day at the beach, before she has to return to the regimen of school and face the grim repercussions of brutal budget cuts, anything can happen. I put the sandwiches back in the cooler.

The destructive storm that moved out to sea churns a strong undertow. I hold the boys by the shoulders in a slope of shallow water. The current is too strong for them to make it out to where Susan is standing, so we jump around in the foam. A propeller plane flies low in the clear sky, towing a banner advertising the local dance club. Finn reads its inappropriate innuendo with an inflected smirk, and I congratulate him on his fine pronunciation of "hot sauc-e-licious booty-full." He curls his wet hands over mine and demands to be swung round and fly over the water like a superhero.

"Teddy, it's Kadima zero hour," I say. "I'm going to swing Finn a little. Why don't you go grab the paddles from the blanket, and we'll play." We've been playing the paddle game all summer, keeping a running tally of consecutive hits and challenging our record of fifty-seven. The plastic handle has come unglued on one of the paddles, and the top layer has sheared off of the other.

I swing Finn by the arms, high enough for full-body extension above the ripples bound for shore. He screams and busts out a droll guttural laugh. Teddy's too big to be swung anymore, and Finny's just about over the limit, he's grown so much this summer. I'd like to keep him aloft forever. The gusty sea breeze is blowing the hair off his face, and his rubber cheeks are dimpling in a soaring smile. We spin four, five, six times. When my strength and balance give out, Finn flipper-kicks the water to launch back into flight. "Dad, more! Lift me higher! Don't stop!" The splashes slick his smooth sack-of-flour belly, and he looks like a baby again.

I'm trying hard to keep this going. Finny's heavy body is sailing on such centrifugal force, it feels like he's the one doing the pulling. My feet are corkscrewing and clouding the water with sand and shells and stones, and I'm getting dizzy from the spins. On the fourteenth or fifteenth turn, I catch sight of Susan and, over Finn's irate objections, set him down in the foam.

Susan is standing in a bad spot. She's caught in a no-man's-land too far from the shore to sprint back before the incoming waves break on her. A knife of whitecaps is angling to her position, and I know she can't see them clearly. This is dangerous. In an instant of sickening realization, terror washes over me. "Dive! Dive under, Ace, dive!" I scream, but she can't hear me over the crashing. She stands rigid and turns her back to the rushing sea instead of diving under the crest. The boys and I watch the accident happen in helpless slow motion. The lead wave slams her at the neck and skips her like a stone. The second wave is higher than the first and blows her out of sight. The kids are frightened, and my phony reassurances do nothing to help. The waves rumble on like drums and knock us back. Susan has disappeared beneath the waterline. We run deeper in the ocean, and the kids call into the surf, "Mom, Mom! Dad, where is she?" Teddy's mouth trembles.

Twenty yards from us, Susan surfaces near the shore. She's swamped and weaves out of the water on unsteady legs. Her hair is matted over her eyes. A gash is splitting her back between the shoulder blades and pooling bright red. My stomach seizes at the sight. She limps up the bluff to our blanket and collapses on her front.

I grab the football by my feet and throw the boys a long pass down the beach to distract them away from us, then move to the blanket to figure out what to do. I unpack the cooler for paper napkins and water to clean Susan's wounds. The surge dragged her on the ocean bottom, and her scrapes are ground raw. She's shaking.

"My God, honey, how bad is it?" I ask, folding the napkins into a compress. She doesn't answer. "What happened?"

"You were supposed to come with me. I waved for you." Her voice is distraught, ground raw, too.

"What? But I was with the boys. They couldn't go out too deep, and it looked like you wanted to get right in. Finny wanted to fly. Teddy was getting Kadima. I don't understand."

"I thought you didn't want to help me."

Both hands are pancaked under Susan's turned face. Sand clumps and pebbles litter her hair. Her body quivers in short breaths of pain and humiliation. It hurts all over.

The first-aid station is at the East Bathhouse by the umbrella rental, a distance from where we're camped. I'll need to take Teddy and Finn with me, and they won't like it. I glance up and see them losing the football in the tide.

"Why would you think that? I just had to stay with the boys. Ace, even I think this surf is dangerous today. Why did you run in?" My tone comes out sharp and makes her feel worse.

Susan's blood soaks the napkins, and I use them all. Her back got smacked worst, and her buttocks and thighs are inflamed red and will bruise. I drain the water bottle on a beach-towel corner and hold it to a shredded shoulder, kneeling over her. Tears are streaming down her cheeks.

"It felt like you left me," she says, and her voice breaks in anguish. "You were gone. I couldn't see the wave. I didn't know what to do." She moans and spits up a shot of seawater. "I can't teach the boys to bodysurf. I can't throw a football. I can't catch. I can't play ball with them. I suck at Kadima."

The sun is beating on her, and I tilt the heavy umbrella in the sand for cover. Her breakdown floods the cramped space between us. I'm shocked. It's been a summer of healing, I thought, a carefree vacation.

"But I *have* been playing with the boys all summer. I *have* been teaching them to bodysurf. I *have* been throwing the football. I've been a camp counselor since we left the city. I'm fine." Teddy is cautiously timing the waves, sprinting to chase down the football before the water takes it. Finn is calling to him, saying something I can't make out. My attention is there and here.

"What if you can't next summer?" she blurts out. "The whole time you were sick, I wanted to think, *If I just act like everything will get better, it will*. But it doesn't. How many times can I look at danger and sadness and assume things will work out? I don't trust in my optimism anymore. I got so tired going it alone." Susan winces and tightens her mouth to suppress a yell as my hand grazes a scrape that's opening to bleed. "I can't believe I got knocked over. I feel like a sucker. It feels like life sucks. And I hate feeling this way."

Susan buries her head away from me. The towel I press on her wounds jumps with each spasm. Her bent arms goose-pimple in the shade, and I drape them in dry T-shirts from the beach bag. I grab the freezer pack and four cold greengage plums from the insulated lunch bag, roll them in Finny's Spider-Man towel, and lay the compress down the frayed ridge of Susan's spine. I'm out of supplies.

"I'm going for first aid. I'll take the boys."

She says nothing, and I step away from the umbrella. I don't understand what happened. I replay it in my head as I walk fast to the bathhouse with Teddy and Finn on hot sand: Susan runs across the beach into the rough water. I'm on shore with the boys. We've traded places. I've got them by the shoulders in the foam. She waves to us and smiles, and that looks like an invitation, not a request. It was a misunderstanding, a communication glitch. I didn't know what she wanted.

The beach is crowded behind the lifeguard tower. The boys are kicking up sand, yelping because of the heat. I can't carry both boys. They're going to have to tough this out. We make a run for it.

I missed the signal. I see it now.

"What if you can't next summer?" That's what she says to me. But what if *she* can't next summer? She thinks about it but can't say it. We could both go under. Teddy, Finny—we can't.

When the boys and I reach the boardwalk, I cool our burning feet in an outdoor shower. There's a jet of pressure out of the tap, and I get us soaked all over, still thinking of Susan's tears, her confession, the fears.

I took Dr. Rothschild's advice. I moved forward. Since I started eating again, I've acted to put the deprivation behind. An unfortunate, isolated incident. I've been acting alone.

Moving forward, I thought, put the troubles in a dimmed past. I hoped my psychotic hysteria would fade into a half-memory of regrettable bellyaching. I know the people who bore the brunt of my chronic complaining have a right to think: *Don't you know how impossible you were? Don't you know what you put us through? You made life miserable. We can't just forget that.* Mea culpa. I'm a terrible patient.

Susan's breakdown exposes a more enduring problem, one that I can't change alone by deciding to move forward. This year has been a nerve pressed raw on her, pressing against the years of other episodes. My presumption that everyone around me is progressing at the same pace of recovery is myopic. And callous. It presumes that I was the only one who was torn apart. Her outburst following my "I'm fine" tells me how much I've missed. Healing happens at different speeds for patients and families, and moving forward is not as simple as a page turn for Susan, Teddy, and Finn. Healing also happens in different degrees and not always completely. I thought I was aware of the damage wrought from living with a starving man. Playing camp counselor isn't enough to erase their lingering dread. People do disappear beneath the waterline.

The teenage first-aid coordinator stocks us with gauze and tape and alcohol wipes. Teddy is silently nervous, and Finn compensates by asking a barrage of questions. He suggests we buy Susan a lemon Popsicle, but the line at the food concession is frustratingly long, so we hurry back to the blanket. The boys run ahead, and I see Susan roll on her hip.

I remove the fruit compress from Susan's back. The blood has thickened over her chewed skin. As I swab her back, she flinches. I tear strips of tape and spread the gauze over the abrasions. "Don't worry, honey. I'm a professional." Teddy sinks into a sand chair, and I enlist Finn as an assistant, stacking the pieces of surgical tape on his hairless forearm. I assemble a long bandage sectioned like frames of film and gently press it secure on the more severe wounds. Our hands stay on her back and hold the dressing in place while she pulls on her shirt.

What happened to our Labor Day celebration? We leave the beach battered and confused and hungry, having eaten little of the food. The greengages were supposed to be a surprise treat. After searching all summer, I finally found the tart stone fruit at a farmers' market yesterday. They're back in the cooler, coated with grit from Susan's wound.

The crowded bus ride from the bathhouse stop to the rail-road station starts in jerks of forlorn holiday traffic, and the beach chairs knock Susan's shins. She's sitting across the aisle from me. Teddy is crunched in a rear-wheel seat, loaded down with pails and towels. His long feet, tipping over the ends of his open-toed slides, are sunned like seasoned figs. My good-bye-to-the-beach small talk goes nowhere; he tunes me out, thumb-ing the day's catch of rocks and seashells. Finny's warm body slumps on my lap. He's already squirming and head-bobbing for sleep. The back of his head is sticky, the summer-blond hair pressed in the mold of his sunhat. He's worn out, and I don't know how I'll carry him onto the train with the rest of our load. If he wakes up, he'll be a cranky hothead.

Susan's head tilts back on the glass. Her straw brim is pulled low.

"Ace, how are you feeling?" I ask.

Through her T-shirt, she scratches the back of her right shoulder, which is scabbed and itching badly. "I'm fine." She shuts her eyes. "I'm sorry I ruined our day."

"It's okay," I say. "But you really do suck at bodysurfing."

Susan looks at me and laughs. "At least I don't suck at eating. So you suck worse."

Traffic stops the bus on the crest of one of the graceful bridges that stud the drive and connect the archipelago of beaches to the mainland. I see the Art Deco bathhouse flapping orange and black under rippling flags in the sun. The ocean stretches at the horizon like a licorice whip. It doesn't look treacherous from here.

Over my shoulder, in the bayside shoal by the bridge channel, a reef of party boats is roped together at their bow railings. Anchor chains drop from the boat hulls into the shallow water and pull tight against the prevailing current. The largest, *Dom's Gift,* looks to be the buffet boat. A suntanned man in a cabana shirt chases down paper plates flying in the wind. Our bus crawls off the drive to the parkway, stopped cold with cars coming back from the Hamptons.

Awareness is a window of many angles. Susan and the boys also suffered from deprivation. I lost the pleasure and necessity of food, but Susan lost a husband, the boys a father, and their feelings of abandonment, I see, have not been fully healed by my stellar Kadima play. Being both mother and father, and her fear of losing again, pulled Susan under, and the boys felt it. There's an anxiety living near the surface that I've ignored—the lasting impact of my uncertain health. They live with uncertainty, too.

I've brought fear into Susan's life.

Despite my efforts to protect the boys from the distress, they've been exposed, and it's painful to know that I've brought fear into their lives.

The boys' claims of stomachaches and food intolerance sound louder and more frequent since my bout with nothing by mouth. After a bathroom episode in Maine, Teddy worried aloud to Susan about becoming sick with Crohn's disease. Presently, there's no medical reason for him to worry, as I assured him. But my condition hasn't gone peacefully into remission for the family. I thought being shrouded by the past was only *my* problem and didn't hang the same burden on my sunny wife and fortunate kids. Maybe all the steroids I've taken have swelled my self-absorption as well as my joints.

I do think a lot about what Mark said to me after my phantom dinner in the bistro: "You're going to have to find meaning in this experience." It's been more fun to eat the lobster rolls at Red's and forget about the harder search. I know it isn't ever far from me. There are reminders and blunt strikes, like what happened in the water.

I've been carrying Cherry's chai stone on all of our summer trips. It's a strange thing for me, since I've never been religious and I'm not normally superstitious. I wouldn't have expected it, but the chai has provided me with a sense of comfort. The symbol itself is almost superfluous—it could just as well be a devil's tail polished on the amber stone. I carry it, knowing what it meant to Cherry when she was sick and how courageous it was for her to pass it on to me. It makes me consider what I'm capable of. Leaving the chai behind in the apartment didn't seem right, and I've kept it in my pocket or on the bedside all summer. I'm holding on to it now.

The calendar moves on tomorrow, but the past comes along. The summer hasn't buried the past; it can't.

The bus pulls into the gritty station lot, and the herd races up concrete stairs to the elevated platform for an arriving train back to the city. A few miles from the beach, the long, steady measures of the ocean sounds have turned to screeching metal wheels and car horns bleating on the choked expressway beneath the tracks.

Finny bangs awake in a foul mood. He refuses to get off me and walk.

CHAPTER 9

On Sunday mornings in the fall, I look ridiculous. Dressed in my "Sunday best," a cardinal-red baseball shirt and hat looped with WEST SIDE LITTLE LEAGUE logos, I'm assistant-coaching Teddy's fall-ball baseball team. When registration opened in June, I asked Teddy if he wanted me to coach—lately, he's mortified if I so much as hum in public—and I got the go-ahead to check the "Coach" box on the form. I missed Teddy's pitching tryout and the entire spring season when I was sick, so marking the box seemed a hopeful commitment, an act of faith that I'd be well enough to cross over to the field side of the fence and throw a ball. Here I am. In past seasons, I've elected to stand at the fence by the team bench, knobbing my hands on the chain link like a zoo monkey, frozen in the enforced everyone's-a-winner posture of modern Little League. Another unreal abstraction. We're not supposed to keep score, but the boys all do.

The uniform sags on my still-skinny frame, and I cut a daffy figure, like a talking dried tomato. We're near the end of the season, and I've enjoyed coaching. The team has won about half its games, which helps keep everybody motivated through the slow innings when the ball doesn't leave the infield. I like being engaged with the boys, working out the drills, goofing around a little at practice and rooting for their success on game days. The kids who are spoiled pains or poor sports make themselves known right away, and I don't hesitate to get them in line before the other boys despise them. Mostly, it works. One anxious boy, Trevor, small with a helmet of blond surfer's hair scissored around dark, uneasy eyes, takes everything so hard. He cries after strikeouts. I sometimes amp up his esteem between at bats. I'm working against channeling my own Little League coach, a spooky four-hundred-pounder named Tommy Del Guidice, who was a butcher in our rundown supermarket with the sloshy meat. Coach "D" wore his bloodied butcher's smock to practice and was so round that he couldn't bend over to field ground balls.

Teddy is pitching the last two innings today, and he's bringing heat. He's coordinated, and his long, bony throwing arm whips at the release point and snaps the ball, firing the pitch at the batter fast and into a tricky drop as it crosses the plate. He's had a rifle arm since he was two. Teddy's all limbs on the mound, and his mop of chestnut hair blows wild from his cap. He looks like he should be pitching for *The Bad News Bears,* waiting for Tatum O'Neal to show. He faces three batters and sails through a ten-pitch inning, striking out the side to close the game.

Our field abuts the Hudson, wedged in a Riverside Park plot between a funnel of bike paths, basketball courts, a kayak launch, and the strutted West Side Highway. The flow of bikers and runners passing the baseball diamond is so heavy that Teddy has a bleacher of new fans cheering him when he whiffs the last batter. I love it. The team high-fives and runs to our picnic table for the after-game snack. Today is my turn to bring food. The strawberries, apple slices, grapes, and granola bars are going over well, judging by the rush of hands in the Tupperware. Trevor's mom says to me, "Such a healthy snack today. You've raised the bar."

I make light of it, but frankly, the after-game snack is an issue that vexes me weekly. Despite e-mails from the league director, despite the parents' general awareness of nutrition, despite the attention and care they otherwise appear to give their kids, the snacks typically are the same sugary ones I ate when fatso Tommy D coached me, as though nothing has evolved since the era when I thought Twinkies were food. I made a personal appeal to the parents at the team bench before the season opener, but Dunkin' Donuts and Fritos and orange soda load the table every week. As I collected the kids' medical release forms at the first game, a happy dad told me, "Snack is a chance to eat a bag of Cheetos, or something Ethan doesn't normally get to eat, which makes it all the more special." Disodium phosphate and monosodium glutamate are just a party waiting to happen. Why not hand out Marlboros while you're at it?

I don't get it. I even proposed that we eliminate team snack and leave it to the individual parents to feed their own kids, but that was voted down because "the kids like it." They like not bathing, too, but the parents don't cotton to that. I understand allowing your kid the well-timed guilty pleasure. We all do it. I do it. Susan and I take the kids to Katz's on occasion and follow the pastrami fix by loading up at Economy Candy down the street. Once in a while won't kill them, and it's fun. Unfortunately, weekly snack is a missed opportunity to encourage healthy eating for these athletes in training. Camaraderie doesn't have to be confused with junk food.

That said, the snack is a conundrum for me. I police against Teddy mainlining high-fructose corn syrup, saturated fats, and sugar, but I don't want him feeling excluded from the shared experience with his teammates, like some poor Jehovah's Witness kid who's banned from trick-or-treating. It reminds me of skipping greasy Friday-night buffalo wings with my coworkers, afraid of getting sick. I know how it feels.

Our Tupperwares are cleaned bare. Teddy and I pack up the baseball gear and walk to an outdoor café on the river esplanade. I'm treating him to a post-game meal. We take two open seats at a balcony table overlooking the marina of new-money sloops and the last decrepit houseboats that never leave the dock. At the game, I contained my full measure of pride when Teddy was fanning batters, and now I wash him with praise like he's the second coming of Sandy Koufax. We both get sloppy on the excitement and can't get the words out fast enough.

"You were smoking, baby," I beam. "Strike, strike, strike. I think we're going to have to get Cooper a pad for the catcher's mitt."

"Ten pitches, Dad. Ten pitches! Nine strikes, one ball! I've never done that before."

"Beautiful, babe. You were fantastic. Bend your knee, push off your back leg, keep the release point close to your head, snap your wrist, and you're unhittable. Lights out, Reiner."

"I struck out Julian on three pitches. He kills the ball. Did you see that?"

A mash of hot dog bites and bun churns in Teddy's open mouth with every word. I've let him order an ice-blue Gatorade, relaxing my high-fructose corn syrup prohibition, and he's sprouting a Smurf mustache. I tense, watching him scarf the suspect hot dog and chug the chemicals in a can, but there's nothing on the café menu that meets my code. We've finished the fruit and granola and purified water in the sport bag. I could take him home for a healthy lunch, but I want him to have this time, eating in the fun place above the boats, celebrating his triumph, smiling to teammates at the other tables. This is the good stuff.

"Dad, can I get another hot dog and another bag of chips?"

The boy does need calories. I'll have to let my judgment go for now. It's a blissful moment, and we're in it together. I know, like all moments, it will pass. We'll get home, and the atmosphere will be rushed by the inevitable Sunday-night clock and maybe a fuss over dinner and showers and bedtime. Perfection is an unreasonable expectation. This moment, though, does feel perfect. Who wouldn't want to ride it forever?

"Sure, honey. I'll flag the waitress," I say. I look around the café, then see a familiar figure approaching. "Well, hello, Coach Greg."

Our team's head coach strides through the columned dining room and stops at the table. Greg is a charismatic guy, effusive, still carrying his college pitcher's sure, athletic body. As far as I know, he's the last creative director working in New York. He wears his cap backward, a look that flashes attention on his prominent smile. With an easy flourish, Greg takes a blue ballpoint from his sport pants pocket, clicks the pen with his thumb, and writes the date, "Teddy," and "10" on a baseball squeezed in his glove hand. "Here you go, Teddy, the game ball. Ten pitches. Almost perfect."

Teddy takes the signed ball like a comet in his bony fingers and inspects the inscriptions. He beams and bends his head shyly. "Thank you, Coach Greg."

"You deserve it. That was an amazing performance. I've got you penciled in to start next week. Let's see if you can get down to nine."

I get up from my seat and show the coach my fatherly appreciation. I'm so happy for Teddy. I'm so happy to be part of it. I may look like a dried tomato, but Greg and I can share a man-to-man pride over my son. It's incredible. Greg leaves on a strong handshake, and Teddy's in heaven.

"Dad, the game ball. This is so awesome."

"Let me see that." Reading Greg's inscription out loud, I glow and raise Teddy's Soft Strike in my throwing hand. It's more forgiving than the hardball I got for pitching in a Little League all-star game. Brighter, too. The dirty Rawlings is still shelved in my old bedroom at my parents' house. "Wow. Wait till you show this to Mom and Finn. Where can we put it?"

Teddy grips the ball in a two-seamer, and a proud smile opens his broad, sweet face. Gatorade dribbles to the end of his chin. It's the same handsome expression he has on the league portrait I carry in my wallet. His floppy hair covers an eye and curls over the gripped bat resting on his shoulder. Susan's face. I carry Susan's Little League picture on me, as well as Finn's. She's about Teddy's age in her snapshot, dressed in a green-and-white State Farm Insurance jersey and patched bell-bottom jeans.

The waitress serves Teddy's second hot dog on a plain bun. The dreamboat eyelashes flutter, and he drums the table hard. For once, I don't shush him; that juice has to go somewhere. We finish our post-game meal and walk home along the river, bobbing on the flow of people. The sky is so clear, we can see the Little Red Lighthouse under the bridge, miles away. Teddy snaps the game ball in his pitching hand, throwing imaginary strikes, getting the pitch count down to nine.

A few days before Thanksgiving, I meet an old friend, Valerie, and show her the kids' baseball pictures across the diner booth where we're having breakfast. She's got two girls, so she looks the pictures over for as long as required. She doesn't volunteer to show me hers.

Valerie and I were young sweethearts. She's visiting New York on a girlfriends' getaway and has split off from their morning of shopping to see me. We've communicated periodically over the years but haven't seen each other in nearly ten. Though she heard I was sick, she likely doesn't know what to expect. I'm wearing two undershirts and a cabled turtleneck sweater to layer heft on my bones. I made sure to stand straight and smile when we met.

Valerie is skinny, too, by choice, I presume. When I put my arms around her in the hotel lobby, she held back, rigid and lifeless, like planed timber. I'm happy she contacted me but am unnerved by her lack of enthusiasm. Her girlfriends, who look shockingly like middle-aged ladies, were together by the elevators, so perhaps it was all too public, like a school dance. Or maybe the sight of me just caused Valerie to recoil.

She's a different person, certainly, than the nineteen-year-old I dated. A Nashville housewife, she's married to a health insurance executive, and their oldest daughter will start college next year. Still attractive and expensively dressed, she's gone startlingly blond and wears heavy makeup that hoods her pretty, slight face in the diner's white light. I don't see that she really needs all the paint. I'm most surprised by her slow, sluggish Tennessee Waltz of a drawl, as overcooked as the liner thickening her long eyelashes. Her three-syllable vowels are a twangy stretch for an Italian girl from Rhode Island. This is not the excitable, eccentric, sensual, dewy brunette with the animated cat eyes who laughed so loud we got shushed in movie theaters. If she's decided to recast herself as a country-club stiff, to bury the vibrant spirit that was her charm, it's an unfortunate move. Seeing her this way is disorienting. Of course, I'm one to talk. She probably thinks I look like a push broom.

Valerie's hotel restaurant charges thirty dollars for eggs, so I suggested this diner. Unfortunately, we're lodged right at the mouth of a frenzied kitchen, and I can barely hear myself speak over the collision of plates in and out of the metal sink. The place would be all right if it weren't as loud as a working junkyard.

"What can I do? What can I do-oo-oo?" Valerie repeats in that odd Dogpatch corn.

"You're doing it. I'm so happy to see you. We're having breakfast. Hey, I think that table just opened by the window. Shall we move?"

Valerie brings both hands up to the table from her suede purse and lays them awkwardly on mine. Her Mediterranean skin has begun to spot beneath the knuckles, souvenirs of the island vacations I've seen in Christmas cards. She wears two jeweled rings, a glittering platinum wedding set, and a Cartier watch. Less funky and more solid than the bangles I remember rattling in her sudden, demonstrative flings. She studied to be a sculptor, but in her tepid hold I don't feel the old strength hewed from tons of rock and clay. Her face is set sympathetically when she speaks. "Do you need any money?"

"I guess the diner was a tip-off, eh?" I say, brushing aside her well-meaning but uncomfortable question. "Don't worry, sweetie, even this close to the sink, they can't force us to wash dishes."

She won't be deterred. "Just tell me if you need money. How much do you need? My husband negotiates with hospitals. I know what those places do to people."

Valerie removes her laying-of-hands in order for the waiter to pour a dark cup of homebrew. He's hurrying to race back and smash some cutlery in the noisy kitchen and spills a gusher on her breakfast plate. The creases on Valerie's caked eyelids tighten. I grab napkins to wipe quickly and unnoticed, as if I'm going after a mess on Finn's mouth. Perhaps I should have sprung for the thirty-dollar eggs.

"Well, that's true. My bills are definitely keeping the hospital's floors waxed, and truth be told, we could use a bigger apartment." At the coveted table by the window, four rotund Broadway-bag tourists are being seated. Valerie and I will have to stay put in janitorial supply—maybe fitting, given the direction of the conversation. Who doesn't hate talking about money, especially if you don't have any? "We're okay," I tell her. "I'm lucky. I married a working girl who hasn't thrown me out on my bony ass."

Valerie covers my hands again with jewels and pulls her mouth down oppressively. Nothing I say is shaking off the cloak of doom. I try something else.

"I know that look. The pout: 1982. You're Valerie. Now I know who you are."

"I don't pout."

"Of course you do. Remember the creepy antique store in town? You dragged me there with Janet Wagner. You both wanted the same ring, and she got to the ghoulish clerk first. It was copper-colored, carved around the edges in little filigrees. You used that same pout on Janet. She kept the ring. I can't believe you're still mad about that."

This act goes nowhere. Affection, teasing, nostalgia, plates shattering—Valerie is unmoved. She's also not eating her coffee-washed eggs. I can tell she's waiting for me to start, to see if I can eat. Understandably, I get this royal hesitation from my dining companions. People actually want to see me eat. They pay good money for it, like a freak show. *Play Fascination. What a sensation.*

"What can I do?" she offers, even more emphatically this time, pronouncing it "deau-eauw."

"Tell me about you. I've told you everything about me, and I'm running out of material. If you don't ante up, I'll wind up talking about what I ate for dinner last night. Tell me more about your girls. Where is Campbell applying to college? Tell me about Mike. At least show me your pictures."

She shudders through a mild response, her striped blazer hardly moving, and doesn't change her solemn expression. "They're fine. He's fine. What you see is what you get with Mike. We're all good. Just tell me you're fine."

"I *am* fine. Look at me," I say, working my fork through the plate and into my mouth, chomping like a hack prop comic. "I can eat eggs. I can eat potatoes. I can eat bacon. I can drink orange juice. If I had a watermelon and a hammer, first I'd Gallagher it, then I'd eat it. I can talk in English. I can breathe. The whole megillah." I've stuffed my face to the verge of drooling, but I used all the extra napkins on the coffee spill. I'm talking crazy with my mouth full, and I'm bombing.

Valerie insists on grief. She cares, and I can't be angry with her for that. Our tortured conversation, though, spells out the patient's dilemma.

When you're sick, you can't get enough sympathy. What people offer is never sufficient acknowledgment of your misery. I stamped Susan guilty on the nights when she went home to the kids after work rather than giving up her dwindling sanity to grieve at my hospital bed. I wanted recognition of my suffering. When weary companions try to pull back from the abyss, steering the conversation topic away from your fascinating latest blood-pressure report, you demand that they know how sick you are. "Then the doctor wouldn't answer my question!" you shout, wrenching the attention back into the well of obsession.

After the patient's recovery, sympathy is as welcome as genital warts. It sounds like pity, and pity is the last thing you want to hear. Pity is a reminder that you were sick, and a sorry con-

firmation that people still think of you as sick. In the hospital, I
would have eaten up Valerie's "What can I do?" as if I were Judy
Garland. Now that I'm better, pity is degrading. I see it in the
other person's sad scrutiny of my body or in a fumble over a
menu. The stigma of illness intimidates other people, confuses
their sincerity with sorrow. I've been guilty of it, too. Apologiz-
ing to Claudia the painter behind her wheelchair on the cobble-
stones, scared by her pain, trying to help, frightened into being
a bumbling fool.

Hearing pity from Valerie magnifies my shame. Sure, it's
been ages since we were lovers, and any sexual tension between
us flamed out many Christmas cards ago. But in our teenage
history, sexuality defined us. Our bodies existed to urge each
other. That erotic vision is not the body she sees on the bench
seat, sputtering eggs. Time marches on, I understand. However,
her dead man's hug in the lobby, her grave mouth, her coldness
to the past, is a reflection on me. That's how she sees me. I take
it personally.

The patient's dilemma—I'm ungrateful no matter what. You
can't win. I hate being defined by illness. I still think I'm the guy
getting it on with her in her parents' backyard. *Tell me what you
crave, and I will tell you what you are.*

I'm also not telling my gal Val the whole truth. A new pain
has been squeezing my lower right gut around the area of the
rupture and surgery. It's not sharp; it's bearable but steady. It
has ached for several months, and yesterday Dr. Abrams scheduled a CT enterography for me at Kaplan's. Who would want to
talk about that over breakfast in this confusing booth?

"That Susan must be a real babe." Our talk jumps strangely,

skipping the natural transitions of comfortable conversation. Valerie's leap is awkward, but I'm happy to field the lob away from poverty and illness.

"She is. She's fantastic." Valerie has met Susan, and I'm not sure if she remembers. Bragging about my wife to an old girlfriend seems too much.

Valerie bundles loose eggs and sausage on her plate and spoons them onto mine when I speak.

"I'm not stealing breakfast on your meal plan today," I say, returning the charity provisions, as if I'm giving Teddy my extras to nudge him to eat. "What do you do for Thanksgiving?" I ask. "Do your parents come down to Nashville?"

"No. They stay local with my brother's wife's family. They have a humongous house at the beach." "Hu-mon-gous" comes out plunked with notes of envy or entitlement or both, I'm not sure, and I nod agreeably. Valerie ignores her food and fishes a lipstick from her purse. She's finished with the meal.

"Mine are coming down from Maine. If I make it through the holiday, I figure I'm good for another year." I've got an outrageous appetite this morning, but it would look too sorry for me to eat off her plate. That fat, juicy sausage—it's just sitting there. The thing must be two inches around. I can't believe she's not eating it.

"You know, I always think of your family on Thanksgiving. We were together when you got sick." More grave talk out of her mouth.

The waiter bumps the table and clears her plate. *Oh my God, she's not going to eat that sausage. Unbelievable. There it goes.* I hold him off mine. I still have three crumbs to inhale.

"We'll always have the emergency room," I say wistfully. Among the lowlights of our relationship was the rush to the hospital when I was first diagnosed with Crohn's disease. I'd been sick for about two years with a gut full of inconclusive tests. Thanksgiving has always been particularly memorable for me, for both good and bad reasons. "Do you remember where we were before the hospital? Bloomingdale's."

"What are you talking about?" She dabs the lipstick for a touch-up and blots on a paper napkin. The shade is a fruity coral. An odd choice for New York in November, I think, like an accent mark on the disorienting morning. The color isn't right.

"That day. You were so appalled by me going around without an overcoat that you took me shopping. You'd grown tired of my maroon Members Only jacket. I can't imagine why. It's still a classic look. I was going to England for the semester, and you insisted I get a new coat."

"I don't remember any of this." Valerie finally laughs a little, in a catch I recognize, but it resolves down into a subdued southern-parlor chuckle.

"The Friday after Thanksgiving. You drove us to the mall. We were futzing in the store, and you insisted I try on an overcoat you loved. It looked like a pimp's bathrobe. It was off-white, cream-colored, with wide lapels and a thick sash belt tied in the front. The kind of coat George Hamilton would have worn, or Sugar Ray Robinson. I had to wrap it around me twice."

"You're lying. I would never pick out an off-white coat," she objects. "That's just tacky."

The past is a welcome goose to the bereaved present and makes for easier talk, at least for me. The tourists at the window table have jump-started lunch and ordered four plates of creamy cheesecake, and I'm hungry for dessert. I doubt Valerie wants more food. I can smell fat sausages cooking in the kitchen. I hear the sizzle.

"Well, it may be tacky, but it's true." The waiter grabs my plate, and I ask for water refills. Valerie opens a silver compact and examines her coral mouth, shearing a corner clump with a thumbnail. "I modeled the coat in a three-way mirror and thought I looked laughable. We started debating it, how absurd it was, and I got an attack. Pain and nausea. Worse than I'd had previously. At first I thought it was just my grandmother's dry turkey revolting, but the sickness wouldn't stop, so we had to leave the store. Clearly, the prospect of having to wear that pimp coat made me ill. You drove me to the hospital, and I got sick on the way. That was when I met with my first gastro, Joel Miller. He told me the news in his office. 'Crohn's disease.' It meant nothing to me. I remember thinking, Okay, so I'll take some pills, and it will go away. I have a date for the movies tonight. What a child. It never occurred to me that I might not be able to go to the movies. I think we were planning to see *Gandhi*. Do you remember? Nothing Miller could have said would've made an impact. I was invincible.

"So you see, Val, you really shouldn't have made me wear that coat. Look what it did to me. That's exactly how Cortés wiped out the Aztecs."

"You're making this whole thing up." She's blanked on the trip down memory lane. "I only bought you the nicest things. A Fred Perry tennis sweater."

Finally, something we both know is true.

"I grant you, the sweater was posh," I say, "I took it to England with me and pretended to be a prep. I could probably fit in it again. But you don't remember the white coat? God, I'll never forget it."

"I remember the sweater. And the wristwatch and so many other things." The act of remembering brings traces of forgotten movement to Valerie's expression. The arched brows push against her smooth forehead.

"That was my first Thanksgiving in the hospital. I spent the weekend in a room with a devout codger who listened to sermons on a transistor radio. It was my first time nothing by mouth. Then I came back for Christmas and New Year's. I did that for years. Always at the holidays." I finish my water and sip Valerie's and look for the sloppy waiter. It's cheesecake time.

"That's what you get for being a bad Jew." Valerie laughs at her joke, and I enjoy it. Coming from her Bible Belt mouth, the words drip with even more pointed conviction. Much better than the pity.

"Point, Mrs. Williams."

The nostalgia is a nice hook in to more lively conversation, but I realize I'm talking about being sick again. I stop the medical tour for my uneasy breakfast companion, who has excused herself to "freshen up."

Those weeks of first diagnosis and treatment were such a surreal time. The details sometimes come back to me this time of year if I've got reason to worry. The timing of the new pain in my gut is in line with history.

Miller discharged me after the holiday and sent me to a specialist in the city, a famous guy who'd worked with Dr. Crohn. I thought Dr. Goldstein was a hundred then, but remarkably, he died just recently. He shared an office with Kaplan, my radiologist, on Park Avenue. Ground floor. My father took me to the appointment and had to pay on the spot by check. He must have been sweating the bill. He kept running out of the waiting room to plug the parking meter.

A freezing, clear day. I had to stand naked and sick against the exam table and hear the sidewalk chatter outside the window. The heels on the pavement. I didn't know what I was supposed to do, where to look, when to speak. I was a novice patient, self-conscious, a kid. Goldstein pressed every square inch of me like an appraiser, his firm hands and bald head moving in and out, up and down, probing, confusing, asking questions I stumbled over, all new to me.

"You definitely have Crohn's disease," he said decisively, as if announcing an election winner. He pointed to a framed picture on the wall of a serious-looking man sitting at a desk, then pointed through the open doorway to a large wooden desk in his office. "That was Dr. Crohn. That was his desk. He trained me in this office." Unschooled as I was, I could at least understand the reason behind Dr. Goldstein's certain judgment. He was present at the creation.

After I dressed and sat in the paneled office, facing him across the historic desk, he wrote prescriptions for drugs I'd never heard of, couldn't pronounce, never imagined. I took them in the pocket of my Members Only, bewildered, and thought I should shake his hand. He ended the visit with a bold statement that I'm sure he believed: "A cure for Crohn's will be discovered in the next twenty years. I'm certain of it."

I was twenty years old. Fuzzy math.

The waiter drops our bill on the table in a coffee puddle. Valerie has returned, and I snatch it from her hand. She's barely eaten her food. She's barely spoken, and my memory jag is unwinding. No cheesecake. I don't think I'll ever see Valerie again.

I walk her to meet her girlfriends at a cosmetics emporium where they're buying the same bottles I presume are sold in Nashville. It's a mild, bright day, and Fifth Avenue is heating up with tourists. I knot our arms at the elbow and lead her across the busy corners, trying to nudge one last image of vigor before we say good-bye. I hug her outside the store, away from explanations, and her embrace is as lethargic as the morning's.

"I can't tell what's different about you," she drawls, too lifeless for a real good-bye. It's a curious thing to say, coming from someone determined to forget who she was.

"I don't know. I guess I am different. I didn't think it showed," I say, reaching to hold open the shop's glass door for her. The store's strong perfume blows out to the sidewalk. "I thought I knew where I was going, but that turns out to have been wrong. Things have changed. They've forced me to begin to deal with what's been going on, not just this year but for a long time. It's been illuminating."

Valerie's head tilts to her dropped shoulder, the way she stands crooked in our old pictures. I wonder if she'd acknowledge it. Explaining myself to her sounds confusing, it seems. I'm just starting to say these things to myself, to straighten out the curlicues.

"People have been lovely," I continue. "Susan and I wouldn't have survived without them, and I treasure them, more than before. They're the most important part of my life. I understand that, now. That's different, I suppose. But there are also choices I have to make. Expecting that my old life will just resume won't work, and life wasn't working then, anyway. It's time to move forward. I'm trying to figure things out."

Valerie and I part on a quick good-bye. She goes into the store, and I cut across the crowded sidewalk, heading to the subway home. The weather is so invigorating. The sun shines white and yellow on the skyscrapers and fires them up like rocket ships. That picture-book skyline, closer than at the reservoir. It seems foolish to go back to the apartment.

On Thanksgiving Day, I eat light. Playing it safe, I go easy on the portions and quit at three thin cuts of turkey, not nearly enough of my sister's bread-crumb stuffing with cognac-soaked raisins, a half dozen of Susan's sautéed French beans, and one glass of the Beaujolais Nouveau I brought. I splurged and went for two nine-dollar bottles the day the fruity wine debuted.

My parents are hosting the holiday this year in New Jersey. Susan is too busy at work to cook, and our apartment won't fit everyone comfortably, since we don't have a fire escape like Jerry Grubman and my sister has brought a stranger to the table.

Lisa's been working and living in London this year, and she has a new boyfriend there, a banker with a ruggedly handsome face and the letter-perfect British name of Simon Clarke. Actually, he's an ex-banker, laid off a year ago, a status that squares him in my eyes. Today is the first time we're meeting him, so he's

on display. What pressure. He's a foreign curiosity in our parents' house, exposed to the twin stresses of introducing himself
on their home turf and decoding holiday rituals that are bound
like bark to a family history he doesn't yet know. "I'm sorry.
There must be a joke in there I've missed," he says, soft-spoken.
I pity the poor immigrant.

He's handling things admirably. Through the afternoon, he
gamely endures the hazing hurled at him, even encouraging
Finn's cheeky pan-British music-hall roast: "'Ello, Simon, me
mate. I'm all sixes and sevens." Finn's the only one in the dining
room not self-conscious about making a best impression. Simon
jabs back at our separation by a common language, spoons a
helping of stuffing, and loosens the knot around the narrow
table. Unlike Lisa's past boyfriends who came on Thanksgiving,
Simon is an adult, at a baggage station in his life that enables
him to navigate this alien place.

His alert presence in the spindle-back chair beside my sister's is having an unexpected go at my nerves. Not about their
compatibility—Lisa's radiant smile makes honeymoon blossoms seem inevitable—but his being here has me scrutinizing
our celebration of the holiday. Frankly, he must think we're a
pretty dull bunch. This improvised scene can't be the grand ceremony Americans claim as nourishment for the national soul.

A few days ago, my parents drove down from Maine to open
the place, but the seat cushions still carry the residual musk
of bedsheet covers. I'm becoming aware how much this house
works against the pleasure of cherished customs. Since retiring,
my folks live here only a few months a year, proudly invest-
ing most of their energy in the Maine house, so this is not so

much a living home as a convenient seasonal shelter. It's spotless; my mother still commands the vacuum. But the kitchen is minimally stocked—one stick of butter, short on spices, just the minimum—a condition that makes for limited cooking on this day that crowns gluttony as king. It doesn't beat with the nerve-center pulse of thriving Thanksgiving kitchens, even the manic clashes in Sid and Marly's tiny one.

The house's guest bedrooms are comic period exceptions, sagging shrines to Lisa's and my adolescence. Little has been updated in the carpeted rooms since the Adam Ant poster went up on her door. On its skin, this is very much the ranch house of my childhood, a relic that hadn't troubled me before but today, under a stranger's inspection, appears to lack the vitality that the holiday is owed. I right a shelf of slanted yearbooks and straighten my mushroom-hairstyle graduation picture, but they're suspect, worn with a deep inertia, like sweat socks used for door locks.

"We used to roast chestnuts," I say to Simon, pouring out my drink-it-now red. Lisa caps a hand over her glass, and I spill a few drops on her. Oops. They've brought two expensive bottles from some exclusive vineyard they visited in France.

My father has been interrogating Simon about his family, his education, the British elections, but I think we should talk about Thanksgiving, or the one he doesn't know. "There were twenty, twenty-five people at the table," I say. "So my grandfather and I would fill four pans with nuts."

Lisa turns from the buffet on the credenza, where she's doing the unthinkable—refilling Simon's bone-china plate; this must be love—to encourage the softer conversation. "Oh, the chestnuts. Simon, that was the only time my grandfather would set foot in the kitchen. He didn't have to. My insane grandmother would serve him before he even knew he was hungry. She basically killed him. Fed him to death."

"Now, Lisa," my mother scolds gently from the kitchen, where she's fetching more apple cider for my father. "That's unfair to say about your grandmother. Calling her insane."

Lisa looks at Simon pointedly, cutting the politeness in the dining room, and Susan busts a laugh, anticipating my sister's follow-up dig. We're both pleased to see Lisa being herself with Simon. It wasn't that way in the other relationships.

"She was crazy," my sister clarifies. "Couldn't relax for a minute. Worried about everything. He was a peach just to put up with her. But the chestnuts, right. I don't think I ever ate them. Weren't they dry? I forgot about them." She sets the food down for Simon and makes fun of her own sudden domesticity. "Here are your seconds, *sweetie*."

For a long while, we've drifted from the rituals that so vividly embodied my childhood Thanksgivings. Since Sid and I last roasted chestnuts in the dented tin pans, the extended family has splintered, and the traditions, such as they were—the moaning on the carpet; the screaming electric knife on the rye bread; even the greasy noodle stuffing cooked inside the turkey (amazing we didn't get salmonella)—have evaporated. Though the customs were loony, my grandparents became enduring chiefs, and no one has taken up the title, as though we buried the holiday with them. Thanksgiving has become a nonevent for us. A pleasant day, the start of a welcome long weekend, but not really different than an ordinary get-together, except for the hazing this year. Simon may have been baffled by the bizarre cultural schizophrenia on Sid and Marly's table pads, but not bored.

It hits me that Teddy and Finn have never experienced a Thanksgiving with any sense of ritual or family tradition or occasion, even the weird occasion I knew, and are absorbing the holiday like displaced cubs. It would be fun for them to roast chestnuts or do *something* to get involved with the holiday and their family. Presently, they've slipped from the dinner table to my bedroom to watch junk TV and pick at a pile of old *Sports Illustrated*s. I hear Teddy thudding my Little League game ball on the floor.

I wish Susan and I had the room to host. I'm sure my mother wouldn't mind handing over the cooking and cleaning, and I want more from the day.

If I want the boys to taste the ingredients of ritual while I can eat, I better come up with something besides buying the wine they can't drink or failing to cook any of the courses. I could resurrect Sid's chestnuts, but it feels like they belonged to him.

I did start one Thanksgiving tradition with the boys. Every year I take them to see the Macy's balloons on the blocks bordering the Museum of Natural History, as I did yesterday after school. Another one of my on-the-cheap thrills. We get through the security at three o'clock, before the crowds clog the square, and the kids run close to the zeppelin-sized Spider-Man and Big Bird to watch them inflate from flat skins on the street to soaring bodies and heads. This time of year in New York is glorious, and touring the balloons is one of my cherished things to do. However, I'm beginning to wonder if I'm the only one enjoy-ing it. I brought four of Finny's classmates with us. They were wild with the excitement of one another's company but raced through the lineup, and Teddy claimed to be too old and bored for the inflatables.

After finishing the balloon loop, I planned to take the boys for dinner to a favorite pizza place, where they stand by the coal oven and watch the crumbled sausage cook on our pie in the orange pit. But the balloon watchers overwhelmed the neigh-borhood, and there was an hour wait for a table. The other kid-friendly restaurants were packed, the sky turned murky and started to rain, and I had to feed the boys, who let me know they were starving. They wound up chewing on bready sandwiches in an oily, depressing Subway and fighting over soda. The night was a bust.

"I always looked forward to Thanksgiving. Now I dread it," Susan said this morning. I was standing at the sink, washing maple syrup off the breakfast dishes, while she seasoned the beans to take to New Jersey. "The fall is my favorite season. The weather's perfect and energetic. I get to wear fall clothes. It's not too hot anymore to bake. Then there were all the years you got sick at Thanksgiving when the weather changed. I worry from now till the spring."

I don't like what's become of Thanksgiving. My health has complicated the day. Here we are again this Thursday, and I've got a pain in my gut, another warning sign for the season. There's no denying what Susan said, but like so much else, it sounds more real out in the open, something serious to acknowl-edge. It's true, hospitals have been a second home for my adult

Thanksgivings, a tradition of a different sort. We have to turn this day into something else.

I'm hungry at the dinner table, not touching the dishes still sitting warm on the dining room credenza, afraid that indulging will land me in the ER. Simon's good table manners have cleaned his plate again. He must think I hate the food. In the culture of American eating, I'm back to outsider status, going skimpy on Thanksgiving, denying my Food-Self. Maybe that's why I'm having such a hard time finding the rhythm of the day and allowing myself to enjoy whatever happens on its own. I'm disconnected but not letting go. How can I make a tradition? I want to pass down something special about the day to the boys.

One of the boys has already established an occasion on his own, and it has nothing to do with the meal. The year Finn was born, he was delivered with epidural peace, like a slow-cooked bird, on Thanksgiving Day in a mostly empty maternity ward. (Teddy was born in a non-Epiduralized white-hot riot of pain on a Cinco de Mayo. There is something to this.) In a delicious irony, it was yet another Thanksgiving in the hospital for me, but an ecstatic one shared with a buoyant wife and a meaty new baby. Becoming a Thanksgiving patient was Susan's ultimate act of empathy. I left the hospital at dawn and ate breakfast in the Strand diner (RIP). In the evening, I brought Susan a Tupperware of leftovers from my sister's dinner, and she tore through the turkey and trimmings and craved another round.

Perhaps that's the trouble with trying to make a tradition, trying to force it, to replicate what I had in a house and with people my kids never knew. Finn had his own design on the day and that's outshone the others.

I call the boys to the table. Before dessert, my mother leads a ragged rendition of "Happy Birthday" to Susan and Finny and lights two candles plunked in the pecan pie Susan baked. Susan's birthday was yesterday, and Finn's will hit when his grandparents drive back to Maine. They blow out the candles, and my mother carries the birthday-holiday pie back to the kitchen to slice. The pie is a mishmash of customs. We should have a real birthday cake.

"The chestnuts were . . ." I start, but Simon is looking jet-lagged, and Teddy and Finn have disappeared again. How can I possibly make them know what those lousy nuts meant?

Simon gets up and dutifully helps clear the dishes. He plates the pie, which looks tasty enough but doesn't make magic in the kitchen air. I find the boys in my old bedroom, vacantly absorbed by a cartoon, and announce the imminent dessert to lure them back before time runs out. The day is getting late, and we'll have to hurry out the door soon after eating. It doesn't seem enough, like there should be another course. I haven't hit on it yet.

The chestnuts were . . . a mess, I think. It was all a mess. The meal that didn't go together, the wax paper on the grapefruit, the pickles and the sweet potatoes. The chestnuts were horrible. Nothing was more of a mess than Sid's chestnuts. Nothing was messier than those Thanksgivings. Somehow, though, in the middle of all that mess, it was special. A ritual that brought us together, free to moan on the floor or roast bad chestnuts. *That's something.*

I've been struggling to make order out of this day. To create the customs that will give it meaning. To forget the mess of ill-ness and hospitals that Thanksgiving has become for me. The meaning will have to come out of the mess. It will have to come out of disorder, out of chaos. It will come another way. It will come on its own. I will have to let it go. Something meaningful can happen in a mess. We had a baby who decided to come out on Thanksgiving.

To loosen up the mood before we go, I pull the boys away from the table and down on the carpet, unbuckle my pants, and moan like I'm reincarnating Sid and Marly's living room. "Aaaagggghhhhhh! Ooohhhhhhggg!" Finny does me one better and pulls his corduroy pants all the way off, and Teddy bends like a limbo dancer to puff out his concave belly. We're impostors, unworthy imitators of the original. I'm still hungry, Finn barely touched any dishes besides the turkey, and Teddy left his meat cold on the plate.

Anticipating as much, my mother baked a kugel, and the boys eat a few hunks of Jewish noodle pudding before we go. Just like the pilgrims.

CHAPTER 10

"Miso soup is so important for anybody, and especially for you. Have you been making the miso?"

Marcia Berry sits alertly on my living room couch. She's a whole-foods counselor, a macrobiotic practitioner and eater, and this is our third meeting since I started on a macrobiotic diet. Our kids went to preschool together. She contacted me during the holidays, offering help.

Marcia's face is a kept secret. She's fifty-seven and blessed with the smooth skin and energy of a woman twenty years younger. When she smiles, her heart-shaped face radiates and puckers at the cheeks like the Grinch's. A pair of rose-pink cat glasses accentuate the sense that she knows something. Marcia's cheery confidence is almost daunting.

Today she wears a purple blazer embroidered with flowers and stems, simple blue slacks and pumps, a crisp white blouse fastened by silver and turquoise studs, a beaded silver necklace, and silver earrings dangling a mysterious fish. She's determined to get down to business, but I stand to adjust the drapes and diffuse a blinding winter sun shining on her rosy glasses. I'm stalling.

"Are you sure I can't get you something to drink? Water? Tea? It's no trouble."

"Nothing to drink for me. I'm fine."

Marcia came to macrobiotics shaken by a health crisis. Wanting to have a baby, she was diagnosed with fibroid tumors. She talked to doctors, who all recommended surgery, though one discussed dietary therapy as a possible treatment. Intrigued, she educated herself, became a believer, healed, and stayed healthy.

Marcia's had several lives. She was a hippie from working-class West Texas, took off to New York and San Francisco, lived on a sailboat. When she got sick, she was working in corporate communications for a global oil company. She resigned and became a professional nutritional coach. She's also a belly dancer. I ask about her travels, partly because I'm curious and, presently, to steer her off of teasing out my macro cooking status.

Marcia has prepared for me a thick binder explaining the principles of macrobiotic nutrition, its benefits for the body, and dozens of recipes, meal planners, and food recommendations. The clearly written guidebook is intended to change my life, personalizing Marcia's basic macrobiotic treatment plan to the needs and challenges of my particular intestinal condition and lifestyle. It's a macrobiotic bible with pull-out pages.

"So," she says emphatically, "have you been making miso and gotten the three enzymes to take with every meal?"

In contrast to the rigid menus, Marcia speaks with beatific sunshine. Her expression positively glows as she elaborates. Most impressively, she's living proof of her earned wisdom's power to heal. Last week, when she fell hard on a cracked side-walk, chipping a front tooth and spraining her wrist, she carried on as if it were the smallest trouble and healed in about four minutes. Marcia leads by example. She's provided me with the information to follow and the tools to find my own nutritional nirvana. She sought me out, concerned about the harmful state of my eating and believing that I can be healed. Salvation couldn't be more available to me.

So why do I wish she'd go?

"The miso?" she asks.

"Well, no," I confess, and sink into the love seat adjacent to her. A disappointing admission, it doesn't warp Marcia's effervescent smile.

"Okay. Why not?" She fingers a pen from her blazer pocket and notates my status report on the coffee table between us.

"Laziness. I can't get myself to integrate all the new shopping and cooking." I open the binder on the table and turn menu pages, but I can't fake my way through the question. "Intimidation. It requires a commitment to advance planning that seems impossible while I'm responsible for everyone's daily meals. Last visit, I said I thought Susan and I were about half into a daily diet. Susan thinks that's a wildly generous estimate, but it feels like we're still at the same place. I haven't made any progress."

"Just remember, you are changing your habits for life," Marcia encourages me, smiling broadly, her cheeks Grinching. I can't tell which is the chipped tooth. "Taking it slow and easy is fine. You have to bend so you don't break, so you don't get discouraged. There are some things, though—the miso and the enzymes, for instance—that are essential. They will make a huge difference, and you're not giving your body as good a chance without them. Let's start with what you had for breakfast this morning."

Marcia turns down another offer of refreshments. I wonder if she doesn't trust the kitchen. We covered storage and filters in the previous session.

"Brown rice with chopped walnuts, carrots, leftover lentils from last night, an Umeboshi plum, a shoyu pickle, twig tea," I tell her. "Oats and pickles. Breakfast for a Hebrew horse."

"How did you cook the leftover lentils?"

"Don't make me say it." I sigh and drop my head in my hands. "Microwave."

"That's a no-no," Marcia admonishes with the slightest tongue click, and writes the horrible word on my chart.

"I know-know." Microwaves, those miracle hearths of modern convenience, create heat from polarized friction in a way that excites the molecules of the food in the positive-and-negative-particle image of its maker. The energy in the food aligns to the molecular pattern of the microwave. Essentially, my lentils were forced to learn the language of their captor. I swallowed a corrupt translation.

"And no miso, no enzymes?"

I shake my head, and Marcia writes out the sad miso-less state of affairs in flowing script. "How are you and Susan feeling?"

"Susan says she notices a difference. She's got more energy. She sleeps through the night and doesn't pass out when she gets home from school. I'm about the same, except hungrier."

Susan, always interested in the health benefits of food, has joined me on the macrobiotic journey. All her years reading the food and science sections in the paper have prepared her for this moment. The diet gives structure to her New Year's resolution to eat more whole grains and vegetables. She's also in it to help me change, and I'm not holding up my end.

"You need to start on mochi. That will help fill you up." Marcia almost sings "mochi," as if she's calling her daughter's name in the playground. It sounds good out of her mouth, but something tells me "mochi" is not Chinese for "chocolate-covered." "How did the breakfast taste?"

"That's the funny thing. I liked it. I like eating brown rice. I like the flavor of what we've added to our diets—the grains, the vegetables, the beans—I like them all, even the Umeboshi plum. I tolerate them, and I enjoy eating them. The problem is missing what I've given up."

"What do you miss?"

"Everything."

Marcia's smile is tireless. She can humor me without mocking and will outlast my whining. "What about everything? The taste?"

"Entirely. And I feel like I'm loading up on appetizers, waiting for the main course. Like I'm at a cheap reception. I never get full. I'm hungry, and then I want to start binging on the food I know will fill me up. I've lost twelve pounds."

"This is normal. Your body will adjust to the changed diet, and over time its capacity for absorption will increase, so the food you're eating will be broken down more completely and you'll gain weight and nutrients."

I'm struggling with the diet. As anyone familiar with macrobiotics knows (I was contentedly ignorant), macrobiotics is based on the Chinese philosophy of yin and yang, two opposing yet complementary forces of nature that are present within all people. According to the pushmi-pullyu belief, the body's internal, lower, back, and left regions are more yang, or contracted, while the external, upper, front, and right regions are more yin, or expanded. The body's right side is charged by yin, upward energy, and the left side is charged by yang, downward energy. Foods are categorized into yin and yang according to their tastes, properties, and effects on the body. As it pertains to digestion, the intestinal tract is mostly yang. The goal is for the intestines to have a slightly alkaline balance of enzymes in order to maximize the absorption of nutrients and the elimination of waste. Certain foods and their preparation promote a healthy yin and yang, others destroy it. And if you believe in astrology, I'm a Gemini—yin and yang plotted in the stars. Yet I'm resisting.

"Have you read the 'Twelve Strategies for Conquering Food Cravings' sheet?" she asks.

"Yes." I exhale and recall a particularly ludicrous recommendation. "When I think I want to eat ice cream, drink some carrot juice. That's a hot one." *Tell me what you crave, and I will tell you something else.*

At our first meeting in my apartment, Marcia got through the initial truths briskly. Holding her silvery head erect, she told me, "You will be replacing animal proteins in your diet with plant proteins. Animal foods have properties that form acids and toxins as they metabolize in your system. When you eat sugars, fruit, meat, dairy, the intestines become acidic. Good bacteria are overtaken by hostile bacteria; they build up and cause inflammation. You were born with a genetic predisposition for Crohn's. If you'd grown up in a macrobiotic home, you probably would not have experienced the disease."

The last point was both illuminating and worrisome. Marcia built something close to a proof that I've never heard from my doctors, and it makes me more concerned about Teddy and Finn's dietary crapshoot. Now I have the responsibility of knowing. Susan and I already walk a vigilant nutrition patrol, and the boys often resist. If they complain about the small portions of grains and vegetables currently on their dinner plates, how do we force-feed them a fuller macrobiotic diet that they will literally spit into the garbage, without turning the table into a battlefield and hardening our relationship? Or how many different dinners can we make every night?

At the same time, Marcia gave me an awakened appreciation for the boys' resistance. They don't want to be told what they can and can't eat. Neither do I.

Whole grains and vegetables are the foundation of the macrobiotic diet, which, conceptually, is designed to enable personal balance within the larger natural order of life. "Macrobiotic" is rooted in the Greek words "large" and "life," though I'd hardly call chopping carrots three times a day "living large." In a macrobiotic world, it could be said, everything that tastes good is bad for you. After eliminating the entire categories of bread, meat, dairy, baked goods, dessert, sweets, and a lot of fruit, I can eat anything I want. I am allowed a slice of sourdough once a week, steamed.

Everything and everyone in this world is a product of a particular place and time, and macrobiotics is no exception. Macrobiotics also encourages the practice of eating food from your own climate and season, so it reflects an Eastern philosophical and agricultural orientation. Regrettably, there's an inherent discrimination against the tropics. All of the juicy tropical fruit that would confuse the Buddha is off the map, even the produce historically considered medicinal. Fruit is full of fructose and very expansive, swelling the intestines, loosening them, and never giving them the chance to strengthen. A banana—nature's perfect food presented in its own case, bearer of potassium, beloved by monkeys and babies—is too viscous for healthy digestion. That seems utterly crackpot, the menu of a vengeful God. Uncle Nat would have had nothing in the store on Mermaid Avenue. Could the banana ban be accounted for, truthfully, by the fact that they weren't grown in ancient China?

Marcia's winnowing of the broader macro diet for my narrow condition is squeezed by other nutritional counterintuitions, restrictions on staples such as peanut butter, soy milk, and yogurt, also viscous. Viscosity causes mucus to clog the intestines like poor motor oil in a combustion engine. Tuna, another high-protein basic, is afflicted by a particularly gruesome pathogen, the Grateful Dead–cover-band-sounding burnt-tuna syndrome. In its struggle to escape being hooked into the fishing boat, the tuna fights so hard it starts to heat up and cook itself in its own scales. Apparently, for decades, I've been eating self-immolation in a can.

On the margins, Marcia's recommended diet makes even Spartan veganism look as sumptuous as the Viennese tables at the weddings Sid photographed. Tomatoes—meaty, tasty, vitamin C–rich tomatoes, so dynamic that the federal government labeled them a fruit—which I buy locally grown and eat almost daily, are prohibited. They're nightshades, and nightshades are acidic.

Intellectually, it's smart stuff, and I've been a rapt student in the sessions Marcia has led. But, as with the TPN pump, I'm having trouble reconciling the theoretical and the practical. Yin and yang is a brilliant concept, matched partners dancing across the body. Fred and Ginger in the stomach. However, it's systematically eliminating the food I crave and enjoy. I'm a pleasure seeker. Yin and yang may be the right rhythm for my gut, but its claim on my soul feels like another oppressive tyranny. It's inhuman. Paging Nurse Patty.

When it comes to the food I love and live on, I'm back to being nothing by mouth, only now the NPO is self-imposed. This is not the gluttonous future I envisioned when I rhapsodized over the red velvet cupcake. How strange to come all the way back from dead taste buds to being able to savor a Katz's hot pastrami on club only to be told that one sandwich and a pickle have a sodium count of 4,500 milligrams, way above the limit. Sodium overdose can raise blood pressure and other nasties.

Food knowledge doesn't come naturally to me, since I grew up in a kitchen where my Cap'n Crunch habit went unquestioned. The dried apricots that made me sick were the healthiest food I ate. My belated culinary education progressed from a starting point of zero to providing the four of us with, I thought, a healthy, largely organic, well-balanced diet. I wouldn't kill us with Pop-Tarts. But my knowledge is mostly limited to a Western diet and palate. I can no more identify a bok choy leaf than I can Chinese characters. Just schooling myself to the current level was a major achievement, like learning how to operate a stick shift and drive on the wrong side of the road. Understanding macrobiotics will be like having to fly a spaceship. None of this is intrinsic, and I'll need to do it without starving in the process and somehow still feed the boys.

"Are you chewing?" Marcia looks up from her notes to ask, her eyes bright behind the lenses. She holds herself with such fine posture, she even seems to make the couch look less worn out.

"Like Oreo the cow."

"Who's that?"

"Just an old friend."

She has good enough sense to laugh. "What does that mean?"

"It means I don't want to admit to more laziness."

"You have to chew thoroughly. At least fifty chews per bite; really, one hundred would be better. It's essential to your intestinal health. Chewing your food helps alkalize your blood more than anything else. Your saliva is alkaline, and when you chew well, you're making an alkaline solution that absorbs into the bloodstream in the process of digestion. Healthy food tastes better, the more you chew. Whole grains and vegetables taste sweeter with chewing. It's the processed foods that taste lousy the longer they're in your mouth." Marcia is very good at this. If I didn't have to give up éclairs, I'd really be interested in what she has to say.

"I'm not sure my teeth have that many chews in them." I hear clipped talk by the elevator. It's Monday, laundry day for housekeepers. We're out of clean clothes, and I'll have to wait until after lunch for the machines. That's going to jam me for school pickup.

"Lauren and I had a chewing contest last night at dinner. Two hundred. Three hundred. On one bite, she got up to three hundred and fifty."

"Did she even remember what she put in her mouth?" I ask.

"Adzuki beans and kombu." Marcia chews on. "On the pressed

salad, she had a chew of three hundred. Remember not to com-
bine chews. If it was cooked separately, chew it separately."

Marcia delivers the mastication report joyfully, as if we're
talking about running away to Tahiti instead of chewing on
steamed kombu. She's happy about all this, she's a happy person. She truly enjoys the macrobiotic experience and how it has
empowered her to build a healthy and happy self and family. I
admire her conviction.

To me, though, the reality feels like deprivation. Giving up
cheese is depressing. She's worked with hundreds of patients, so
the despondence on my stubbly face reads familiar.

"Don't think of it as deprivation," she says, and gently slides
my status report into the binder's front pocket. "You're giving
yourself life."

"I do think of it as sacrifice." Despite my agitation, I'm
snared by Marcia's peace. The light filtered by the cotton drapes
gleams on her. "Like obeying kosher laws. Rather than sacrifice, it's supposed to be an expression of devotion to a caring
God, but if that were the case, God wouldn't have made bacon
so damn tasty. You know the joke. I understand that practicing
macrobiotics is an expression of devotion to health, but I could
make the same crack about losing Gouda." I've been thinking
of the kosherism because, strangely, pickles and sauerkraut
are bridges to both diets. They're recommended with meals for
digestion. I could keep metal dishes of half-sours and kraut on
the dining table, like at Katz's.

"There are new flavors and new skills," Marcia consoles. "At
first you don't feel confident, but you will."

The new mechanics of eating are as onerous as the food:

Chew till your jaw locks; eat a cooked grain and vegetable dish with each meal; eat brown rice daily; eat millet almost daily; have miso soup one to two meals a day; sprinkle digestive enzymes with each meal; don't mix mouthfuls; eat sitting down without reading or doing other things; drink beverages separately from the meal; don't eat or drink anything chilled; wait thirty minutes after a meal before having dessert or fruit; eat moderate portions at all meals; eat meals at the same intervals every day; stop eating three hours before bedtime. The list goes on for two pages in the binder. I feel like I did when Nurse Patty laid out the TPN ingredients and the syringes and the pump and coached me through the eighteen-hour daily regimen. The information drowned me. What was previously easy and intuitive was replaced by a technical manual of complicated procedures. And the payoff was lousy. Macrobiotics is similarly labor-intensive for a relatively small output, like the ratio for making aluminum foil. The macro cooking requires more time for soaking grains and beans overnight, cooking everything from scratch, not using the microwave, and more. The time necessary for me to mend on the macrobiotic plan is impossible to find in my day. Most mornings, I finish my breakfast standing while I'm serving the boys Susan's whole grain waffles.

"You have to work through the transition period," Marcia says, and adjusts a fish earring. Right ear; very yin. "Later, when things are going well, you can have 'free food.' Occasional treats that are off the list. A square of chocolate, a piece of cheese."

Going off the grid permanently is becoming an immediate option in my mind. Is it even possible to eat *a* piece of cheese? Like one potato chip. Is it even legal? I'm un-American again.

"I'm sure you get people who want to give up," I say. "What do you do?"

Marcia smiles through my defeat. "Some people get so frightened by the change that they say, 'I'd rather die than switch to this diet and give up the food I love.' And some do." Steel behind the smile.

Marcia believes that macrobiotics is the essential ingredient for creating a new identity—the method to harmonize the body and mind with the natural world as our ancestors understood, many have practiced, and many more are coming to understand again. It's a past I don't know. Adopting the diet will be my first major step toward a personal transformation. Whatever other serious changes I need to make in my life will follow.

A new identity doesn't sound entirely bad. I suppose anything would be better than the invalid Valerie pitied.

We'll see. Macrobiotics demands an absolute commitment, and I've been trying to moderate my impulse for absolutism. After Dr. Rothschild told me, "You can't have certainty. That's your lot," I rolled it around in my head and have been looking at it from the other side of personal history: the Drinking *Cure*; the extremes between nothing by mouth and you are what you crave; gorging on Thanksgiving Day or starving in the hospital; even the opposites of careerism and unemployment— consciously or not, I've been an all-or-nothing person. Susan has told me so for years. Look where it's gotten me. The highs are gluttonously high, the lows are lifelessly low, almost bipolar. The uncertainty of illness, the uncertainty of life, messes with absolutes, it messes with blueprints, it messes with doctrines. "They say they'd rather die. And some do." Macrobiotics, as it's spelled out, is a neat practice. If I make macrobiotics messy, will it work?

Marcia hands me back the binder.

It's not fair of me to knock macrobiotics before I've really tried it—I do believe in the principles of nutrition. But in order to help me the way Marcia believes it can, macrobiotics requires an all-in approach. *He who is not with me is against me.* The thick manual in my lap prescribes total devotion to the one way, and I've never been good at following someone else's rules.

Marcia leaves the apartment. I sit on the couch turning pages, clueless about how to make lunch.

At dinnertime, Susan and I try a few of the binder's recipes. I pull out three hole-punched pages and stick them on the refrigerator door. She's having a go at blanched vegetable salad with a sweet-and-sour miso dressing. We stand back to back in our small kitchen. Susan trims a bag of snow peas, and I chop burdock, attempting a technique any Boy Scout whittling a stick for a merit badge would recognize. My badge is in question. I'm struggling to cut the burdock in long diagonal slices and maximize the surface area per slice, increasing the nutrients per hundred-chew bite. I can't replicate the sure cuts Marcia demonstrated in her kitchen during our cooking class over the weekend. The nest of botched splinters on my cutting board would be great for beavers.

"Ace, I can't get the cuts right on this bark. You want to give it a shot?" I ask, hoping Susan will take over.

"Sorry, Ace, I'm dealing with this dressing. Do we have barley malt syrup? Marcia made those long slices look so easy. We'll have to get the kind of knife she used. Just do the best you can." Susan stands over me on the stepladder, searching the cabinet for barley malt syrup, but I don't remember buying it. She swings out the tall door, I duck, and my knife slips off the knobby stick. Unless things are running smoothly, two cooks working in our galley kitchen is a mash-up.

"'The best I can' is going to put splinters in our teeth. It's the damn knife's fault. Dumb-ass knife. Maybe you could agree to a cease-fire with the knife-sharpener guy, and we could get this fixed. I saw him this afternoon parked on the block."

"No. I'm still angry about the Global knife. Besides, from what I saw at Marcia's, we're going to need new knives." Susan has stepped down to the stovetop and lowers the flame under a hot pan.

"Then we'll have to gnaw at this whole thing with our back teeth. It works for woodland creatures."

The cooked dressing recipe has Susan frustrated. The miso is scorching. She mixes in more paste with a wooden spoon. "Aaarrgh, it's getting late, and I don't want to have to start over. The kids need to eat, and they're grabbing granola bars. I've never spent so much time having to think about cooking."

"I know. Me, too."

"Ha!" she bursts out, and rattles the sizzling pan. There's a sticky clump at the end of the spoon. "That's a laugh."

"Oh, stop it, Ace. I *am* reading and thinking about the cooking. I'm just inept at it." I steady the knife on the resistant bark and apply pressure on the end of the stick like it's a compress.

Susan turns down the flame again, and I hear the sketchy burner flicker off.

"Cooking macrobiotic goes against my instincts," she says,

shifting the pan, her voice and movements tense. The stovetop gas flame won't catch, and she strikes a kitchen match. "I have to abandon my techniques and strategies and pay too much attention to rules. It's like raising a baby in a Skinner box. I just want to pick up the baby and feed it and hold it, even if it's not the right schedule; I know that's the right thing to do. With this I don't know the right way to cook. It's not just eating vegetarian. I have to pay attention to what's yin and what's yang and have enough of each at every meal, and have the pickles and the tea and soup. I like healthy food and learning to cook more grains and greens. I just want to keep doing what I know how to do, and not be a slave to this type of meal preparation." The burner clicks four times before taking the match's flame. "It would also be nice if my husband tried cooking even one macrobiotic dish, since we are doing this for him!"

"I made the brown rice for breakfast this morning." The burdock is a bungle on the cutting board.

"Brown rice doesn't count. You always made that. I mean something new. Every night I'm soaking grains and chopping vegetables, and that just gets us through dinner. Then I have to think about chopping enough so we have vegetables for breakfast. Have you even made the miso soup Marcia says you should be eating?"

"I need to shop for the type of miso she recommended. It has to be the longer-term miso. I've had a busy week."

Susan stops rereading the dressing's recipe and flings open the refrigerator, pulling a sealed miso package from the door. "Here it is."

What can I say?

The truth is, Susan is cooking the lion's share of the new food. Over our years of living together, I've done a decent job of erasing the traditional gender-based division of labor. I clean the house. I do the laundry. I shop for groceries. I prepare meals. I may not have the body of a domestic goddess, but I've got the sponges. Macrobiotics, though, is challenging my limited cook's skill and reducing me to a worthless man eater. I'm unsure of the terms and the steps I hung on the refrigerator tonight. Every meal, it's like having to learn to foxtrot an hour before the wedding. I'm intimidated by the binder and the cookbooks and the twelve brands of tofu in the organic section of the supermarket and am relying on Susan's greater facility in order to get food on the table. Macrobiotics is making me a spectator in my own kitchen.

Sitting at the dinner table by the stained wall, I say, "The food's good," and the lie fails to convince the cook. Our phony burritos of black beans and brown rice wrapped in corn tortillas taste like pasteboard. The burdock is worse than wood, and Susan is disgusted by her scorched miso dressing. I'm watching the clock for thirty minutes to pass so I can wash away the flavor of the forest with a glass of water. Living large.

Tonight, of all nights, the boys are sweeping each other's plates. Teddy eats Finny's broccoli, and Finny eats Teddy's chicken breast. They've got their own yin and yang and seem perfectly happy. For once, I don't want them to finish their meals. I stare in starved silence at the real food on their plates. As deciduous as my dinner was, I ate all of it, and I know there's nothing left around the stove but a knot of uncut burdock.

"What's burning?" Susan jumps up from her chair and races

into the kitchen. I did smell something noxious but was too transfixed by the grill marks on Teddy's chicken breast to move. "Ace!"
Susan yells from the other room. "You didn't turn off the millet!"

"What?"

"I asked you to turn off the millet when we served dinner,
but you didn't. It's burnt. The pot is burnt. Everything's ruined."

At the kitchen stove, I push a wooden serving fork on the
crunchy millet, showing the pot's charred black bottom. Millet
cooks faster than brown rice, I see. I scrape out burnt grains
into the trash can and start scrubbing the pot in the sink.

"Okay," I say. "I'll take care of the mess." I raise the kitchen
window, grab a broomstick, and prop the back door for a cross
breeze to clear the smoke. A current of night air chills the room.

"Now we don't have millet for breakfast." Susan is loud in
the small space and glares at me cleaning the pot. It feels like
time is running out on the night.

"There's more in the cabinet. We'll make another batch."
The cooked ash coating the pot isn't coming off, even with steel
wool. I'm soaking and scrubbing and burning my hands in hot
water, and I'm not making a difference.

"I don't want to make more millet," Susan objects. "I made
dinner, and it was bad. I made millet, and it's ruined. Why
couldn't you just turn off the stove when I asked you?"

"I didn't hear you." The broom slides out from its propped
hold and smacks the floor. The wind slams the service door shut.

"This is for *your* health, and you're not doing anything.
You're not even listening. Is the macro diet real or some kind
of a stunt?" As if I needed confirmation of Susan's frustration,
she's landed on the kind of brutal truths that her anger always

manages to crystallize. She hates the anger, she hates the yelling, supposedly, but she has a remarkable capacity to think clearly at a high volume. It's ludicrous to yell back.

Susan slices the boys a restricted blueberry pie on the counter behind me, and I keep at the pot, going over the scorched metal again and again. Little ends of choked millet float around my raw fingers in dirty water. Under the sponge, the pot is still black. It is ruined. I borrowed it from my parents' kitchen twenty-five years ago, when I lived off-campus for the first time and had nothing. The Phillips-head holding the handle to the body has worn out its groove, and I have to tighten it after every shuffle around the stove, but the pot is the perfect size and weight, and we use it for cooking everything from rice to greens to hard-boiled eggs. I fill it with soap and water and set it aside on the counter by the open window.

"Susan," I call.

"What?"

"Could you come here?" The boys have finished dessert, and I've gulped my allotted large glass of water. It doesn't wash the sawdust taste out of my mouth. I'm at the sink, rinsing the dinner plates and loading them into the dishwasher.

"What, Ace?" Susan stands in the doorway a few feet from me. She's wearing her black pants and blouse from work. Stuck on the cycle.

"I want to talk to you for a second."

"What is it? I have to get the boys in the shower, and I want to go to bed. I'm exhausted." Teddy and Finny run in the living room, throwing a football. They dive on the couch and tussle over the ball. Susan's bag gets kicked off the coffee table.

Schoolwork spills on the floor. "Boys! That's enough. Finn, take off your clothes and get in the shower."

"Why do I have to go first? I always have to go first. I want to take a bath," he whines.

"There's no time. Just do what I say." Susan stretches the words for emphasis. The boys gripe and throw their clothes on the cluttered floor. Finny mouths off at Teddy and stomps out of the room. I hear the shower water run. "Yes?" she says to me.

"I'll make this fast. I'm sorry about the millet. You're right, I didn't listen to you. This is hard. There's so much I don't know how to do. It makes perfect sense when Marcia's here, and then after she leaves, I can't figure anything out. I'm not good with the binder. Blame it on my mother—she never taught me how to follow a recipe. Blame it on me. Change is hard, and my limitations make it harder, I know."

"I know it's hard. It's hard for me, too," she says and massages her temples, pushing the skin in circles. "But if you're going to quit, then let's stop the charade. I don't want to do this alone."

Teddy jumps back on the couch, disregarding his pile of clothes and toys in front of him. We need to keep him moving or the night will be impossible. He has to be pushed along.

"I do want to try and make this work," I say, shutting off the water. I let the dishes sit, and I face her. "Risking my health isn't fair to anyone. The diet's not working now, but I don't want to quit. I'll just need you to help me for a little while. I'll pick it up."

"Then you'll need to stay together with me on this. I'm figuring it out, too." Susan rolls her shoulders back, and her spine pops two, three times. She stretches her neck and closes her eyes, decompressing in our moment together before resuming shower patrol.

What more could two people want from each other?

"I will."

"Mom," Finn calls from the shower. "Can you bring me a washcloth?"

I finish loading the dishes and help Teddy collect his things.

Marcia first talked to me about macrobiotics the same week I had the CT enterography exam at Dr. Kaplan's and met with Dr. Abrams to discuss the results. The pain in my lower right gut felt foreboding, and I couldn't put off the test any longer. There weren't enough fried eggs on the sandwich at the Third Avenue diner to fill all my holes.

We're in Dr. Abrams's boxy office after a courtesy poke on the exam table. He's looking at the murky CT images on his computer screen and summarizes Kaplan's diagnostic narrative while he scans: "It's a little worse than the enterography last April. There's intermittent dilation, with more thickening. An area of dilated bowel between two strictures. There's a stricture that's narrowing that can build up gas and fluid and cause inflammation and pain."

I finish pulling on my jeans and sweater slowly, to stretch the conversation time before he's on to the next patient. The waiting room is crowded this morning. It's just after Thanksgiving.

"How would you rank 'a little worse' in terms of the usual trend of deterioration? Is the pain I've got a warning sign of another rupture?"

Dr. Abrams digests the report's findings and swivels in his galley chair to face me across the desk. I know what he's going to say. His eyebrows shrug in weary conflict and betray the tan poker mask. "It's all very unfortunate, because the biggest mistake was that you got reconnected in the surgery and kept in bad bowel. Seeing the disease on the X-ray, I'm tempted to have it removed surgically. The last thing I want to do at this point is subject you to more surgery, but that may have to happen, and I'll call Dr. Eberhardt today and let you know what he says. Antibiotics could address the presence of more bacteria."

He makes this last statement in a general way, tilting back in the chair, and it sounds like the short preface to a revised textbook, a breezy update from the previous edition and lightly read. Coming down flat again, he presses both palms against the sides of his oblong head, rubbing the genie's lamp, then returns his attention to me. "My first way of looking at this is, yes, it is a little worse than last spring, and we should treat the problem. However, that's always what stumps us. I don't want to put you back on Remicade; that may have caused the scarring that led to the perforation in the first place. We've tried every combination of antibiotics. Remind me, have we tried Mexaltrexate?"

I've taken so many meds that their convoluted brand names blend into more gibberish—Pentazonesulfaxiafinentrobolica-deuselesscrap—but I do recall this one. We were renting a beach house, and my gas attacks were polluting the island. Gary called in the prescription to the drugstore in the village, an authentic old-time pharmacy shaded by a striped awning and running a lunch counter next to the pills. Teddy was barely four, Finny was an infant, and I spun them on the counter stools and shared a strawberry milk shake while waiting for the drug.

"Yes, we did a few years ago for bad distention and gas, but I can't remember if there were adverse effects. I do know I stopped taking it after two months. I think there was no change."

I've got all my clothes on. His desk phone is blinking both lines. I come clean fast. I tell him what Marcia Berry said about adopting a macrobiotic diet. Gary and I have discussed dietary therapy before. He has recommended probiotics and medium-chain triglycerides like palm oil and coconut oil, and he's well informed about food and its relationship to the gut. He's read the macrobiotic book that Marcia has given me and refers to it, explaining the basic science. However, our food-therapy conversations always conclude with clinical reservation, so I speak preemptively.

"Right, the Remicade was supposed to help, and it may have caused the problem. And my concern about taking an antibiotic is that it will work against what I want to achieve with a macrobiotic diet and more probiotics." The pain isn't terrible, it's just been present, and new, for about three months, and I worry what it means about the progression of illness. The traditional course of meds and food and exercise hasn't prevented this. Shouldn't I move on to something else?

"Macrobiotics is a healthy diet," he tells me, glancing back at the X-ray on the screen, "so there's no reason to oppose it. The question is, can you maintain weight based on the caloric intake, and will the increase in fiber irritate the bowel?" Dr. Abrams pauses before flat-lining his concluding inflection. "Unfortunately, no clinical evidence exists to support any positive findings from taking this approach."

Bingo.

We're at the conversation ender again, and I relace my Eskimo boots, plagued by the same uncertain choice. "Okay. I'm not sure what's the right thing to do. I'd like to start with the diet and see if I get any better or any worse. I'll let you know. Thanks very much, Dr. Abrams."

I've been a patient for almost thirty years, and the chasm between Eastern and Western medicine hasn't closed much in that time. It's tempting to say "Eastern medicine good; Western bad," or that complaining to your doctor is like complaining to the weatherman. What does he really know? What complicates the cutting aphorisms is that the Western doctors who treat me know a lot. They're exceptionally bright and often tremendously dedicated to patients, as their care for me has shown over many, many crises and conversations. They've been top students and tireless practitioners. They are impressive people working in the most vital field. They've kept me alive.

However, I've come to believe they're often in the wrong camp, fighting for the wrong cause, one they may not entirely believe in. The medical equivalent of Robert E. Lee leading the charge to preserve the Confederacy.

Western medicine has become a practice of medicating the symptom rather than addressing the problem. It's an approach that, at best, masks the root cause of illness. That's inverted wag-the-dog logic for a profession that once defined itself by "an ounce of prevention," but not surprising in a country that serves deep-fried chicken parts in school cafeterias and then spends billions to medicate kids freighted with obesity and diabetes. After-the-fact intervention is the way of the land.

Big Pharma is the engine driving the symptom practice. Autoimmune diseases such as mine are catnip to pharmaceutical companies. They apply the razor-blade marketing model to illness. Grossly lucrative, it prevails one prescription pad at a time. The motivation behind the drips, the injections, and the pills is a corruption of true healthcare. It's why I'm suspicious of getting stuck with more infusions or chewing more antibiotics, anti-inflammatories, anticoagulants, or antidepressants like breath mints—tablets that also address the symptom.

Anti, anti, anti, anti. "No clinical evidence exists to support any positive findings from taking this approach." Here, I'm often at odds with the doctors who treat me, and now I'm at a crossroads. Ancient Dr. Goldstein predicted there would be a cure discovered for my illness in twenty years that have long since passed. Why are so many gifted doctors addicted to treating the symptom? Why does the medical community reflexively shrug under the yoke of "no clinical evidence exists" unless the clinical evidence shows 3 percent efficacy for Pentazonesulfaxiafinentrobolicadeuselesscrap in a controlled trial? How different would treatment be if the collective research dollars and the doctors' candlepower were invested in the science of understanding and treating the cause organically? What if it turned out that Eastern practices, diet and homeopathic healing, were the best medicine?

Someone said the same thing to me once, years before Marcia handed me the binder.

My parents had a houseguest one winter break, a Chinese professor of literature named Zhou. Joe, as he asked us to call him, had been allowed to leave China and was trying to rebuild his shattered life in the West. During the Cultural Revolution, he'd been imprisoned for ten years in a labor camp. Now he worked in a laundry with his wife to pay their daughter's graduate school tuition in Colorado. My father gave Joe a sort of academic platform as a guest lecturer, some clothes, a wood tennis racquet, and food. He was a gracious man and took an interest in me because I was a student around his daughter's age. He was also keenly interested in my health. I was sick that winter.

"You belly feel pain?" he asked me one night after a casserole dinner I skirted around.

We stood in the family room by the antique coal stove transplanted from Maine, a forged exception in the sixties tract house. I held the cast-iron door open with an oven mitt and dumped in a shovelful on the fire. "Lately."

"Why you take pills?" Joe winged his arms and opened his palms to me, as if to say, "You stupid."

"My doctor thinks they will help." A knuckle of coal cracked and exploded inside the black stove's potbelly.

"You doctor think pills help. Pills no help. You drink this." He reached a bony hand inside his hand-me-down wool blazer and showed me an envelope holding loose stalks that looked like tiny tree twigs. They had an acrid scent, like he'd found them in the dirt. Joe put his hand on my belly and rubbed a gentle circle. "Tea make your belly better. This Xianzhi from Wuyuan. Green twig tea. You drink three times day every day. You no take pills. You feel better."

I didn't trust Joe. For one thing, he was as skinny as me and half a head shorter. I saw the dandruff sprinkled on his worn clothes, smelled the scent of his occasional bathing, and didn't believe in Chinese quackery. My Western doctor knew more than he did.

On the other hand, the guy had figured out how to survive Mao's prison camp. That should have trumped my cultural prejudices and doubts. In the end, Zhou went back to China, and I stayed with the pills. "The West too much about money," he said. "This not Chinese way."

The trouble for Western patients is that there's no money for the pharmaceutical companies in organic healing and, thus, no financial incentive for our healthcare industry. Big Pharma can patent Pentazonesulfaxiafinentrobolicadeuselesscrap, but they can't patent twigs, and selling twigs won't pay for offices and salaries and fellowships and notepads. Twenty pills a day, thirty, that's good for business. Face it: If food heals me, I won't be a paying customer at the pharmacy or at Dr. Abrams's office. It's a crooked system and a national tragedy driving the population prematurely into the grave.

My method has to change. The Western path encourages my continued decline. There are alternatives besides macrobiotics, some of which I've tried. I hoped for good results from acupuncture and Chinese herbs, but after almost a year, I stayed sick and the blood clots came. I've been on regimens of homeopathic and probiotic supplements. Friends have counseled me about nutritional approaches like the blood-type diet. All the different ways have persuasive logic and true believers, and I have no authority to decide which could be best other than my own gut's reaction.

I'll try food.

The quality and availability of macrobiotic food is light-years from when I was in school, where the dingy co-op in the student union basement sold shriveled green oranges and was run by a Deadhead named Shoshanna with hairy pits and grimy nails. I make extensive shopping lists, much of which I buy in my supermarket's plentiful organic section. I decide among the twelve brands of tofu.

Every day, though, when I get home from dropping off the boys at school, I'm starving. I've eaten a full macro breakfast, and by nine o'clock I'm on my second round of carrots and hummus, but it's never enough. I steam a sourdough slice and spread sardine paste, but that doesn't fill me up. I swing the kitchen cabinet doors, lurking about the shelves for what I want. I want a bagel and cream cheese. I want a banana and Nutella. Crackers and peanut butter. Strawberry ice cream. A chocolate éclair. I can't get fully satisfied on the grains and vegetables.

The hunger makes me think of the restricted food I still crave.

Before starting the macrobiotic diet, I embarked on a farewell eating tour, a series of Last Suppers, going through the stash in the refrigerator and cupboard: The last time I'll eat shepherd's pie. The last breaded pork cutlets and mashed potatoes. The last penne and turkey sausage. The last seared tuna. The last hunk of chocolate cake. The last dried apricot. It's all wonderful, heavenly. It tastes real, like food is supposed to taste, and I can feel the hand of God, and I eat second and third portions, and the meals fill me up, and I'm not hungry. Susan regards me cautiously. She's happy to eat the favorites, too, but the familiar food carries the flavor of danger and harm.

I don't know. The self-imposed NPO doesn't seem right. There's something wrong about canceling out this food, dropping cravings that have been with me since childhood, denying adult cravings, erasing my cultural heritage, leaving those parts of me to memory. My appetite is fighting for my Food-Self.

On a chilly Saturday afternoon, I pick up Finn at his friend Max's house. They're hiding under the kitchen banquette, horsing around with a flashlight. Finn is coming up with nonsense to stall ending the playdate while I search for his sneakers and gloves in the ransacked room by the ground-level entry. He invited himself over after their morning basketball game, and I've got to get him home and changed for a birthday party. Max has a large family, and they're all scattered in the brownstone. It's a house that runs on the voltage of unsupervised chaos. Finn enjoys the atmosphere. There's always a party.

Someone has cooked spaghetti and meatballs for lunch, and the unmistakable aroma fills the large kitchen's air. I can't stay here, and I'm trying to move Finn out, but he's having none of my imperatives. He and Max giggle up the stairs, waving the flashlight. I'm alone in the room.

The boys' lunch bowls are still on the table. Finn has done a good job cleaning his, but Max's bowl is nearly full of red-sauced pasta. A dish of freshly grated Parmesan butts against the untouched bowl. The temptation is sweaty. I ate a lunch of brown rice, broccoli, shoyu pickles, and carrot soup, and I'm empty. I know the pasta would make me happy. My mouth hangs slack over the floating school of tomato chunks chopped in the sauce. The taste is almost with me.

I've been disciplined the past weeks, keeping to the diet despite the relentless hunger and cravings that aren't going quietly. Despite what Marcia predicted, my body's not adjusting.

Footsteps track on the floor above, and I stand frozen at the banquette's bench seat. If I start on the bowl, I know I won't be able to stop. I'll dump my head into the metal tub of spaghetti on the stovetop and roll it like a meatball. The macro regimen will be toast, and I'll move on to the goodies in the double-wide refrigerator. I can imagine the glass shelves full of real food. I've seen it before. Max's family shops like I do but for more eaters. I know they would let me stuff myself. They'd encourage it. This hunger strike I'm on is not normal. A whiff of steam rises from the pasta.

"Come on, Finn," I call from the bottom of the staircase. "We've got to go."

After we run up the avenue home to change, I drop Finn at the birthday party and ask Susan to pick him up when the cake is served. I don't want to stand beside the other parents empty-handed and fight against the temptation of a square of spongy, frosted birthday cake. It's like the crosshairs of Little League snack time. The macrobiotic binder says otherwise, but I feel as though my balance is off. All of this refusing and shutting down and contracting leans too heavily yang to be correct. How can I go to a party and not eat the cake? How can I walk in the city shunning the restaurants and think I'm maintaining a balanced self *and* harmony with my surroundings? In harmony with what—isolation? I'm a dieter. This must be how my mother feels.

How can I survive my supermarket? Supermarkets have no equal when it comes to harvesting the abundance, the thrill, the pleasure of food, and the volume of living to eat. Not all super-markets, of course. Not the lousy one where my mother shopped when I was a kid and the meat sloshed in the package. Not Nat's little sidewalk market in Coney Island. My neighborhood super-market, however, rains a delirium of food in its cramped aisles. It's a sight I craved in my hospital bed. A week after running from Max's spaghetti bowl, I'm fulfilling my family's shopping list and ignoring entire shelves of old friends. Yuri, the Russian writer who cried when I showed him the cereal display in an American supermarket years ago, who knew starvation, would send me to the gulag for blinding myself to the bounty in this store.

Tell me what you crave, and I will tell you what you are.

I see Eduardo the cheese monger from the shoulders up, standing behind the open counter display, and I roll in my cart, wedging it between walls of rounds and slabs and cubes. For months, I've been ashamed to confess to him that I'm off the stuff. I've either gassed some lie, saying I bought cheese on his break, or swallowed a few inane words about the weather or the pathetic Knicks, or skipped the cheese department entirely and flapped a lame wave in passing on my way to the tofu. The diet has choked the social act of shopping.

The market's selection of cheese is mind-boggling. There are varieties from every conceivable farm and cellar. Even in my cheesy years, when I gorged on three servings a day, I barely made a bite in the hundreds of kinds that plug the alcove space in yellow, white, orange, brown, and blue.

"I don't care what they say, I won't live in a world without cheese," I sing to the monger, baring my soul in song.

"Hello, my friend. I no see you in a long time. You feeling better?" Eduardo is a little coy at seeing me. I have broken a trust. The white smock puffs over his stocky body like a cloud. He's wearing a store cap with a straight brim that chops his forehead and flattens his round face. My favorite poster hangs on the tile wall beside him, above a goat-cheese pyramid. It's a large picture of a cow standing sturdily in a Vermont field. Some joker took a snapshot of Eduardo's grinning mug and pasted it over the cow's head.

"I'm good. I see you're smiling on the poster, so the world as we know it still exists. I have news for you. Pitchers and catchers report to spring training Monday. You ready?" I'm standing at the rear of the cart, gripping the handle, a few feet off the counter.

"That, I know, yes. Yankee staff deep, and Posada, he still strong."

"If the middle relief holds up, I see another Series."

"That be so nice." Another monger, half Eduardo's width in a droopy smock, checks in and motions to the congested shelf between cheese and coffee. It's setup time at this hour. "So, tell me how come I no see you?" Eduardo asks me.

Enough lies, I decide. "I've been on a diet, a macrobiotic diet, and there's no cheese allowed. No dairy, no meat, no bread. I haven't eaten cheese since before Christmas." Telling my cheese monger that cheese is bad for me—the ultimate betrayal. I resettle the heavy sauerkraut bottle in the front of the cart.

Eduardo smiles, and a knowing spread splits his face, showing a brown front tooth in the line of yellow. "This crazy."

"Guilty as charged," I say, and laugh.

"Last time I see you, you tense." To illustrate the point, Eduardo sets down the black-handled knife on the counter board pushing into his belly and raises both shoulders to his ears. He's succinct. "Now you look more calm," he concludes, relaxing his shoulders. "You was sick. How you feeling?"

"I'm calm because I've finally decided to buy cheese. I'm not cutting myself off today."

Eduardo wipes the sharp knife on a dish towel, then paper-wraps a triangle of Irish Cashel Blue and places it on the countertop. I can smell it. Very sharp. My mother likes the cheese, and I bring hunks of it to Maine.

"You got to know yourself," he says. "The doctor, he say he

know what best, but it just his advice, you know? You wife, she could give you all the medicine and the best food, but you got to do what right for you."

"How do you know what that is?" I step around the cart and stand close by the cheese at the counter's edge, by the hand-lettered DON'T TOUCH sign. A loud squeal revs from the neighboring coffee grinder, and the other monger leaves. I can talk to Eduardo directly. "I thought I was doing that, but it didn't work." I don't sound like I'm here to talk baseball.

"I'm a diabetic. The doctor tell me what he want me to do. 'Cut out, cut out, cut out.' But I say 'moderation.'" Eduardo's chunky eyeglasses are reflecting images of the cubed cheddar displays in their lenses, a cheese vision. "Instead of four piece of bread, I eat two. Instead of half a pound of meat, I take half that. You got to *live*."

"That's what I'm trying to figure out," I say, nodding.

Eduardo's counsel makes enormous sense. The guy's world is cheese, I think, and this corner of the store smells sharp and alive. It's like the apricots in the paper bag: How can something so good be bad for you? Macrobiotics has me living in a Schoolmarm State. Don't eat this. Don't drink that. Like repression is the key to good health. The essence of craving is first dismissed, and then missed. Nonsense. My Food-Self has been buried under Eduardo's counter, and before that, in the guts of a mechanical pump. I've been on the dark side of the road. I know we eliminate cravings at our peril.

"Let me have that Irish Blue you cut."

I cab the groceries home, and the driver helps me unload the trunk, carrying bags to my building's front steps. Most drivers don't bother getting out of the seat, but he's been a pleasantly engaging man on the short ride from the supermarket. He's West African and opinionated, and we agree entirely on the news-radio story about Wall Street thieves. When he stands and grabs half the eight bags, I see that he's taller and fitter than I guessed from the gray head on the driver's headrest. The river wind blows the shopping bags when we set them on the steps. My fingers are freezing.

"You eat watermelon?" The driver points to a container of chopped pieces sitting at the top of a bag he carried.

"My kids love it, and I thought I'd surprise them with a treat in the middle of winter. They'll go through it by breakfast."

"If you have cancer, if you have something else, you drink watermelon and papaya juice three times a day." He speaks in a strong voice that's undaunted on the blustery corner.

"What happens?"

"You cut a piece of watermelon, you put it in the juicer. Skin, seeds, everything. You do the same thing with the papaya, skin, you put it all in and blend it to juice. Three times a day. It heal you." The driver prescribes his remedy with a friendly urgency. His large hands are strong. His dark skin is unlined. He could be anywhere from thirty to seventy years old.

"Do you drink the watermelon papaya?" I ask, firming my leg against a rattling bag.

"Of course I do," he answers brightly. "I'm a homeopath."

Lugging the groceries into the lobby elevator, I wonder what it was that got the driver on my case. He saw the watermelon in the bag, sure, but why would he jump to talk about disease? Is there something he saw in me that registered as sick? The community food bank is following me offline. Everybody's got a cure. The question is, which one? Papaya isn't on my diet.

CHAPTER 11

It has been snowing all day, and Ellen is concentrating at the wheel of her father's minivan, trying to steady this tub on a sloppy upland road. The parkway is narrowed to one slippery lane, and we're in a slow line of cars behind a flashing plow, hoping to get home before the worst of the weather.

Today the boys skied on a mountain an hour from the house in Millbrook with Ellen and Matt's sons, Sam, who's Teddy's classmate, and Harry, who's thirteen and taller than I am. Actually, Harry didn't ski. He's afflicted by an ordinary case of adolescent mopes and idled in the lodge on a laptop most of the day.

February thirteenth. It's impossible not to pay attention to the date, the anniversary of my gut's explosion. I'd prefer to sleepwalk through it, and Susan has been conspicuously quiet on the subject. I'm happy to be away in the country.

For Ellen, the calendar has a different meaning. Her mother died a year ago of a cerebral hemorrhage, around the time of our canceled trip, in a hospital room just five doors from my own. Ellen's parents bought and decorated the farmhouse, and it's emotional for her to be here this week. Dotty's pictures and possessions and her hand are everywhere in the tasteful rooms. Dotty was a Mainer by birth, and there are Maine pictures and objects that are familiar to me, like reminders of my own parents' house.

Ellen's dad is generous with his country home, though he's not around this weekend. It feels odd to be here without the usual hosts, displaced, like we've broken in to get out of the cold.

Matt is also not with us on the school winter break. His father is dying in the city. He's been on dialysis for years but, eerily, was struck by a cerebral hemorrhage, too, earlier this week and is in the hospital. We've all got reason to dread this day. It helps to be together. The kids take our mind off the troubles.

Matt calls on Ellen's cell, and I take the phone in the passenger seat so she can drive. He sounds composed and hopeful, as he always does, his voice still a college jazz station DJ's. "There may have been movement in his eyes when he saw us this afternoon. It's been four days, so we're at a crucial time. That would be good news."

I report the upbeat prognosis to Ellen, and her response is muted. The details are too close to her mother's case. She keeps both gloved hands on the wheel.

The four boys are silent in the rear seats with Susan. The sky bled quickly to dark when we left the mountain, and they're zonked out after downhilling all day in whipping snow. For much of the afternoon, I got showered on, leaning against a split-rail fence to watch the end of their runs. The severe weather didn't stop them from having a great day. Sam is a second child like

Finn, intuitive in his body, and he motivates Teddy to be fearless. The snow is heavy and wet, and the hatchback ahead of us
fishtails up an incline.

In my honor, Ellen proposed that we cook a macrobiotic
dinner for the seven of us. We shopped at a supermarket after
skiing. We'll cheat with chicken, since the boys won't go for a
plate of cooked tempeh, but we bought broccoli, ingredients for
a pressed salad, parsnips, carrots and turnips to roast, olive oil,
sea salt, soy sauce, ginger, garlic, and wine. Susan has brought
up lentils and brown rice that she made in the city. They're
packed in the cooler with Eduardo's blue cheese. The four boys
got loud in the store, choosing a dessert away from us.

More than a foot of snow has fallen on Ellen's unplowed
driveway, and we turn carefully off the county road to the house.
Beneath the drifts, the drive is unpaved dirt and rocks that wind
a quarter mile through a comb of woods at a steep pitch. I'm
prepared to park at the bottom and walk the groceries up the
hill, but Ellen's making gradual progress in the Honda Odyssey
better suited for an outlet-mall parking lot. We climb slowly, and
our jostle over the covered rocks wakes the boys. The snow surprises them. "Why didn't somebody plow?" Harry groans. Ellen
laughs at the city kid, and he's not amused. The front property's
small pond is blanketed smooth, and the beached paddleboat is
a white sugar lump against a drooping fir tree.

A deer, startled by the van's headlight beam, shoots across
the untracked snow in front of us. "Shit, hang on!" Ellen brakes
short, and the animal vanishes into the trees. "That was close."

The sudden stop stalls our grinding momentum on an uphill
stretch. The minivan's wheels spin out and whir on the packed

snow like mixers in a bowl. We slide sideways off the navigated center path and sink back on the driveway. Ellen shifts to park. The wipers are smearing snow into a skin of ice on the windshield. There's about two hundred feet left to get to the house.

"We've just got the last hill. What do you guys say? Push? Harry? Sam?" Ellen floats the request to the boys settled in the dark.

Multiple whines and a grumpy official statement from Harry, who speaks for the group. "Just leave it here."

"I don't know, sweetie. We're close to the edge of the drop," Ellen says, looking out her window. She smoothes brown curls off her forehead and turns to the rear seats. "It might not be safe to leave it."

"Mom, it's fine." Louder now.

There's a perverse pleasure in seeing someone else fight a familiar battle, and Susan and I share a couple's glance over the seat, but what's a houseguest for? Ellen schlepped us to skiing and is going to eat tempeh instead of real food. I unbuckle and open the passenger door. The interior dome light annoys the cranky boys.

"Come on, you bums," I challenge them. "There's a carload of testosterone in this beast. What are you, men or wimps?"

"Be quiet. We're tired," Harry complains.

"Let's go." I step down into the deep snow and get behind the van. We are indeed just a few inches from the S-curve's edge. "Men, get out on my side of the van."

"Why?" They back up Harry's defiant lead.

"Out the other side is going to send you straight down the slope."

Yells ricochet inside the van around Harry's swat, and the passenger door slides open. The boys spill out. I put Harry and Sam in the back with me against the closed hatch. Teddy and Finn are on the passenger side at the mirror. We carefully rock the van in its skid trap and start to push.

Ellen has it in first, and the slogged radials catch intermittently for small jogs, then lose their grip. Our shoulders brace against the van's snub rear, and my rubber boot soles slip in the treaded snow. I hadn't considered the possibility of the van skidding back and crushing all of us down the rocky drop. I plant in my footsteps for traction. The falling flakes are wonderfully cold on my face. The exhaust of our breath heaves into the black air. We're sliding back.

"Teddy, Finny, come here," I call. "We need more push."

All five of us corral across the bumper and shove hard. I see through the rear window that Susan has gotten out of the car with the heavy bags. From this position, it feels like we're trying to lift a tank. Ellen shifts again from park to first, and I hear the pleading tire spins. My left boot slides on the edge of the driveway, inching toward the slope. Teddy has his back up to the door.

Suddenly, the van jolts in a great spasm. It has footing. We're getting somewhere.

"Push, guys, we've got movement." The van is heavy on my shoulder, and the tires don't engage strongly enough with the icy ground to jump forward by much, but our pushing steadies the tub up the incline until it comes to rest against a snowbank near the side of the house where the driveway levels off. Ellen turns off the engine.

"What a mule team!" I hoot and applaud us. "Triumph!"

Ellen presses the minivan's horn in victory toots that echo off the white trees.

The workout energized the boys. They throw snowballs and run off to the powdered backyard. Susan and I carry the groceries in the house and unpack quickly. We're all hungry.

It's our first time cooking tempeh, and Ellen is adventurous to experiment with us. We have three pots heating on the stove, and everyone has a different station of food prep. Susan and Ellen are at the tiled wall counter, seasoning the chicken and chopping salad. I'm dicing carrots and parsnips at the small wooden table in the kitchen's center. Dotty chose aesthetics over function, and we keep running into one another around the impossibly cute schoolhouse table.

Finn comes in from the snow first, and I help him in the mudroom out of his soaked clothes and into sweats and slippers. He joins us in the kitchen, and Ellen puts him to work setting the table in the dining room. Ellen was one of the lead organizers of the online food bank, the community service that kept Susan and the kids fed when I was nothing by mouth, and her inspired resourcefulness is again welcome. After our long day, we get this oddball four-course meal for seven on the table in thirty minutes. I help Finn set the heavy dishes, serving bowls, and glassware that are shelved in an antique sideboard. We finish the place settings and pour water all around.

The dinner is good. I think the tempeh is quite tasty. It has enough bite to feel close to real food in my mouth, and I clean through the no-thank-you helpings left on the boys' plates. Susan's lentils are delicious, and we empty the bowl. I cheat on the chicken but stop at a few forkfuls, containing my corruption of the diet. The chicken is very good. Ginger and garlic.

There are two sides to the menu, always facing off. With the pressure between them, it's a challenge to stick to the macrobiotic.

Ellen raises her glass at the head of the table. She clears her throat like a lawn mower to get the boys' attention, then lets go of a sweet giggle. "Harry, Sam, honored guests. I'd like to make a toast. First, to the cooks, for making this fabulous dinner. I love eating healthy. I'm now a fan of tempeh, and the lentils are so good that I want the recipe. To us, the cooks. And to my mother, Dotty Dubin, who I wish were here to tell us how she definitely would *not* eat this fabulous dinner." Ellen grinds the word "not" like a wrong-answer buzzer. She's taken off her glasses for the toast, and I can see her eyes twinkling at the jab. "And to Jon, for living to eat it. I'm so glad you're here."

I'm moved by the toast, and by everything that's happened. "Ellen, thank you. I am happy to be alive and eating our food." I get up from the table to clink my glass to hers and kiss Susan, who's smiling.

The day is almost over, and the totality of the anniversary is starting to sink in. I've survived one year. As my brother-in-law told me on the phone in the hospital, not all that long ago I probably would have died. The trauma was explosive and nearly deadly. But it also brought about change, much of it necessary and looking better as I heal.

My health has improved in the past few months. I'm not where I was before the emergency, I can't gain back the weight, but I'm stable and active. The macrobiotics may be helping. I generally feel good after eating and have even fashioned a miso-soup recipe that I make every day: a tablespoon of miso, cubed tofu, chopped scallions, and wakame flakes. It tastes fresh and salty, and I look forward to it. Teddy runs from the room when he smells the miso. It's putrid to him.

Susan and I have come through it all together. The pain of illness and the pleasure of recovery were more courses in the meal of our marriage. We still love each other and have learned that we have to be each other's cheerleader. I think we root for each other's success more than we ever did. There's faith for our future. We will find a special-occasion replacement for Chanterelle.

I've stopped taking pills for now. Too many years of too many empty capsules down my gullet. I see Dr. Abrams and manage my health with checkups, diet, supplements, and exercise.

And I've stopped sending résumés down a black hole. They were just more empty capsules. After a career in the wilderness, I've written some magazine stories and am writing a book. As Mark said to me, "You almost had to die to get published." Working with what I have is more satisfying than working against it.

Change is inevitable. It requires commitment and sacrifice and sometimes comes at a cost. It's also the only certainty in our uncertain lives. I'm excited to accept the new reality.

After the main courses, I dish out shelled toasted chestnuts from a vacuum package. Astonishingly, chestnuts are approved on the macro diet. They're rich in healthy oils, calcium, and vitamins. These chestnuts are softer and tastier than Sid's. There's no coughed-up spider fur in my mouth, and I have to force myself to quit eating them at Marcia's one-quarter-cup recommended limit. I do miss the smell of the roasting pans and cutting Xs in the shells. *That's something.* Just like at Sid and Marly's, the boys won't eat the nuts, and they ask for the dessert they picked at the supermarket. They've done a good job on a healthy dinner, so sure.

Susan and I get up and clear the dinner plates. I rinse at the sink and load the dishwasher. Even with the chestnuts, I'm still hungry and nibble at the bottom vegetable scraps in the serving dishes I'm washing. Susan figures out the space-age tea kettle and starts a pot of twig tea. Zhou would be pleased. He's still alive in Beijing. *Drink tea every day.* We hear the boys chomping through dessert in the other room.

Finn struts down the steps into the kitchen. He's holding one of the fancy-scrolled dessert plates out from his body in both hands, impersonating a waiter, to make a formal presentation. Chocolate lines his lips, evidence of the boys' chosen sweet, a craving spinning his head since the moment they agreed at the supermarket case. He's laid a single, unbitten, perfect éclair across the elegant plate.

Finn's face lifts, excited and proud. He planned this and carried it off despite the older boys' claims on the pastry. He presents the éclair to me and flourishes it like treasure. It's vanilla-cream-filled.

"There were five in the box," he says. "I saved one for you."

ACKNOWLEDGMENTS

Family, friends, neighbors, doctors, nurses, and strangers are the soul of this story. Your support, care, wisdom, compassion, and love guided the journey. I'm grateful we made it.

The story would not have been told without the work of four people, each responsible for opening a door: My friend and *Esquire* editor Mark Warren, who saw a man at the bottom and offered a way up; my dear friend and agent Mitchell Waters, who believed in the potential of this book from the start and shepherded it to completion; Patrick Price, who first championed its publication; and my editor Tricia Boczkowski, whose dedication, encouragement, skill, and vision elevated the book from beginning to end. And to Kate Dresser, who helped keep the operation running.

Thank you all.

I happily acknowledge the prescient words of John Berryman, which came to mean more than I ever imagined: "The artist is extremely lucky who is presented with the worst possible ordeal which will not actually kill him. At that point, he's in business."